Evaluating public management reforms

Books are to be returned on or before
the last date below.

D0416597

MANAGING THE PUBLIC SERVICES

Series editor: Alan Lawton, Professor of Organisational Ethics, Teeside Business School, University of Teeside.

Current titles in the series:

£3.04

Evaluating public management reforms
Principles and practice

George A. Boyne
Catherine Farrell
Jennifer Law
Martin Powell
Richard M. Walker

MULTIDISCIPLINARY LIBRARY
PRINCE PHILIP LIBRARY

SUP.	REC'D.
CLASS	

Open University Press
Buckingham · Philadelphia

Open University Press
Celtic Court
22 Ballmoor
Buckingham
MK18 1XW

email: enquiries@openup.co.uk
world wide web: www.openup.co.uk

and
325 Chestnut Street
Philadelphia, PA 19106, USA

First Published 2003

Copyright © The authors 2003

All rights reserved. Except for the quotation of short passages for the purpose
of criticism and review, no part of this publication may be reproduced, stored
in a retrieval system, or transmitted, in any form or by any means, electronic,
mechanical, photocopying, recording or otherwise, without the prior written
permission of the publisher or a licence from the Copyright Licensing Agency
Limited. Details of such licences (for reprographic reproduction) may be obtained
from the Copyright Licensing Agency Ltd of 90 Tottenham Court Road,
London, W1P 0LP.

A catalogue record of this book is available from the British Library

ISBN 0 335 20246 2 (pb)   0 335 20247 0 (hb)

Library of Congress Cataloging-in-Publication Data
Evaluating public management reforms / George A. Boyne . . . [et al.].
        p.   cm. – (Managing the public services)
    Includes bibliographical references and index.
    ISBN 0-335-20247-0 – ISBN 0-335-20246-2 (pbk.)
        1. Organizational change–Great Britain–Evaluation.   2. Administrative
agencies–Great Britain–Management–Evaluation.   3. Civil service reform–Great
Britain–Evaluation.   4. Health care reform–Great Britain–Evaluation.
5. Housing policy–Great Britain–Evaluation.   6. Educational change–Great
Britain–Evaluation.   I. Boyne, George A.   II. Series.
    IN329.O73 E93 2003
    352.3′67′0941–dc21
                                                                    2002072271

Typeset by Graphicraft Limited, Hong Kong
Printed in Great Britain by Biddles Limited, Guildford and Kings Lynn

Contents

Series editor's preface

Managing the public services is, increasingly, a complex activity where a range of different types of organization are involved in the delivery of public services. Public services managers have had to develop new skills and adopt new perspectives as the boundaries between public, private and voluntary sector organizations become blurred. The management task becomes one of managing ambiguity in an ever-changing world. At the same time, however, there is a certain timeliness to any debate concerning the management of public policies and managers will need to acknowledge the continuing relevance of traditions and the enduring nature of the themes of accountability, responsibility, acting in the public interest, integrity, probity and responding to citizens, clients and customers.

This series addresses key issues in managing public services and contributes to the debates concerning the appropriate role for managers in the public services located within a contested governance arena. Through the use of original research, case studies and commentaries on theoretical models, the books in the series will be of relevance to practitioners and to academics and their students. An underlying theme of the series is the inescapable intertwining of theory and practice such that theory will be tested out in practice and practice will be grounded in theory. Theoretical concepts and models need to be made relevant for the practitioner but at the same time good practice will need to be analysed, tested against theoretical models and disseminated. In this way the series will fulfil its commitments to both an academic and a practitioner audience.

Alan Lawton

Preface

This book has developed as a result of a series of working relationships in South Wales that stretch back to the 1980s. Boyne and Powell worked together at the (then) Polytechnic of Wales in the academic year 1986–87. Boyne, Farrell and Law were at the Polytechnic of Wales/University of Glamorgan from 1989 to 1995, and Farrell and Law have continued to work together at that institution. Boyne and Walker have collaborated on a variety of projects at Cardiff University since 1995.

Our individual and joint thoughts on public management reform have been combined to produce this book. Although the book is a 'team effort' the primary responsibilities were as follows: Boyne (Chapters 1, 2, 3 and 7), Farrell and Law (Chapter 6), Powell (Chapter 4) and Walker (Chapter 5). We take collective responsibility for the strengths of the book, and for any weaknesses.

We are grateful to the series editor, Alan Lawton (another former colleague at the Polytechnic of Wales), for his advice on earlier drafts. We are also grateful to Alan for his patience in waiting for a book that, like most public management reforms, took much longer than expected to come to fruition.

one

Introduction

On the morning of 8 June 2001, only hours after the UK Labour Party's second successive election victory, Tony Blair announced that he had received a 'mandate for reform' and 'an instruction to improve public services'. He is not alone in his concern for reform and improvement. Even the Conservative Party has recently been converted to the priority of public service improvement rather than tax cuts. Politicians and voters frequently believe that public management needs to be reformed, and that this is both possible and likely to be beneficial. In the last twenty years, such beliefs appear to have become stronger. Governments in numerous countries have embarked upon reform programmes that are intended to make public sector organizations perform better. According to Pollitt and Bouckaert (2000: 1), 'the period since 1980 has witnessed a pandemic of public management reforms which has swept across the OECD world'. Wright (1997: 8) also argues that 'public sector reform is in fashion, and no self-respecting government can afford to ignore it'. However, if reforms themselves have reached pandemic proportions, the same cannot be said of the *evaluation* of reforms, either by academics or government agencies (Pollitt 1995; Broadbent and Laughlin 1997c).

Although the number of books on reform has grown in recent years, there has been little focus on the impact of new arrangements for public service provision. For example, Zifack (1994: 138) presents a diagram that summarizes his model of administrative reform. The elements of the model are: environment, content, strategy, dynamics, and outcome. All of these are then discussed in the text, with the exception of outcome. Similarly, Pettigrew *et al.* (1992: 267) concentrate on 'why, how and when change occurs' in the UK health sector, but pay very little attention to the impact of change. Although Lane (1997: 1) argues correctly that 'it is time to make an assessment of the outcomes of the public sector reform drive', the contributors to his edited book largely ignore this injunction. The authors of the chapters in Kickert's (1997) and Olsen and Peters's (1998) edited collections on public management reform also mainly analyse causes rather than effects. This emphasis on explanation rather than evaluation persists in Pollitt and Bouckaert's (2000) comparison of reforms in ten countries. They argue that

> there is a paradox at the heart of the international movement in favour of performance-oriented management reform. The reformers insist that public sector organisations must reorient and reorganise themselves in order to focus more vigorously on their results . . . Yet this philosophy has clearly not been applied (by governments) to many of the reforms. (2000: 131)

This same point could be made about Pollitt and Bouckaert themselves: only one of the eight chapters in their book is concerned with 'results'. The absence of evaluation has not prevented conclusions from being drawn on the impact of reform. For example, Leemans (1976: 6) claims that unsuccessful reforms 'are far in the majority', but provides no evidence to substantiate this. Similarly, Caiden (1988: 344) asserts that 'no matter what might be done, administrative problems persisted; reorganizations had little impact on costs, efficiency or control'.

In short, the academic community has not taken seriously the need to evaluate public management reforms. Most work in this field has analysed the economic, political and administrative antecedents of reform. By contrast, the consequences of reform for the performance of public organizations have been neglected. Our aim in this book is to begin to remedy this gap in the academic literature, by providing an evaluation of some of the key reforms associated with new public management in the UK. These are the introduction of markets and competition in the public sector, the use of indicators of organizational performance, and changes in the size of agencies that provide public services. We explore each of these reforms in the context of three major traditional elements of the UK welfare state: health, education and housing. The focus on the UK provides a major advantage for a book on the evaluation of public management reforms: many of the initiatives that we analyse were tried in the UK first, especially under the Thatcher governments in the 1980s, and were later adopted elsewhere (Peters and Savoie 1998). If these reforms have led to an improvement in performance, then there may be a better opportunity for detecting this in the UK than in other countries, simply because they have been in place for a longer period.

In this introductory chapter we proceed to discuss the meaning of the term 'reform', justify our theory-driven approach to the evaluation of public management reforms, and summarize the contents of the main chapters of the book.

What is reform?

We define a public management reform as a *deliberate change in the arrangements for the design and delivery of public services*. For example, reform may alter the internal characteristics of organizations (e.g. the number of layers in a hierarchy, the division of responsibilities between them) or the features of a whole set of organisations (e.g. a shift from a two-tier system of local government to a single-tier system, the creation of new relationships between service delivery agencies). The term 'reorganization' is often used to refer to such structural changes. Our definition of reform is broader because it also covers other aspects of organizations that provide public services. For example, reforms of processes include changes in systems of budgeting, in the recruitment of public officials, and in the management of information.

An important element of our definition is that reform is *deliberate*. In other words, reform is not accidental, nor does it consist of changes in structures or processes that are unintended. A reform implies some element of planning: the pattern of reform reflects a design, however loose or vague, that has been developed by policy-makers. As Leemans (1976: 6) puts it, reform is 'a consciously induced and directed change in the machinery of government'. Similarly, Dror (1976: 129) emphasizes that reform is a 'directive and conscious activity, rather than a post-factum classification of administrative change phenomena'. Thus reform must be distinguished from mere change which may be a spontaneous response by public officials to new circumstances. In this sense, reform cannot be 'bottom-up': it inevitably involves an element of 'top-down' imposition by senior players in the policy process. Caiden (1982: 85) argues that 'the whole essence of reform is getting someone to do something they would not otherwise do by themselves of their own accord'. This implies that reform is bound to encounter resistance. After all, if the organizations that are to be altered were already adopting the desired structures or processes, then reform would be unnecessary.

Our interpretation of reform includes innovations in public management – that is, ways of working or providing services that are new to a specific agency or to the public sector as a whole. However, reforms need not be innovations in this sense. They may be attempts to implement a structure or process that existed previously but was subsequently replaced or simply decayed over time. Indeed, many reforms appear to be replicas of their predecessors. For example, the current Best Value regime for UK local authorities has strong echoes of the corporate management systems that flourished briefly in the 1970s (Boyne 1999). Furthermore, reforms often seek to return to a past position that is subsequently believed to have been falsely rejected. The 'unitary' local authorities that were created in England and Wales in the 1990s re-established a system of local government that had been abolished a quarter of a century earlier when county boroughs were replaced by counties and districts. The movement of reform appears to swing like a pendulum: from large organizations to small organizations, from collaboration to competition in service provision, and from a dearth of performance indicators to a deluge. Such swings may be especially likely when reforms result in the loss of long-serving members of staff, thereby weakening the 'institutional memory' of public organizations (Brunsson 1989). They may also occur when one party replaces another in government, and reintroduces a policy that was scrapped by its predecessors. In other words, political as well as organizational amnesia can turn the revolving door of public management reform.

The content of a reform must also be distinguished, both conceptually and empirically, from its anticipated and actual consequences. Caiden (1991: 1) argues that administrative reform can be defined as 'the induced systematic *improvement* of public sector organisational performance' (emphasis added). This confuses the act of reform with its possible effects: an 'induced change' that results in a deterioration rather than an improvement in performance is still a reform. Furthermore, although new ways of working may be intended to improve organizational performance, they may equally be designed to serve the self-interests of politicians or officials. As Pollitt and Bouckaert (2000: 18) argue, 'simply announcing, discussing, and beginning to implement reforms may bring benefits to some politicians and public servants, even if later, more "substantive" effects are elusive or counter-productive'. We make no assumptions about the link between motives and outcomes. It is worth emphasizing that policies framed with 'good' intentions may have 'bad' results; similarly, bad intentions may have good results that were never foreseen. For example, the Thatcher governments in the 1980s sought unprecedented controls over local authority expend-iture. This policy was widely condemned as centralist, unjust and an affront to local democracy. Yet the unintended result was a closer match between local service needs and local spending; that is, an improvement in territor-ial justice occurred, which is generally viewed as a positive attribute of a system of local government finance (Boyne *et al.* 2001).

Theory-driven evaluation of reforms

Public management reforms can be assessed on the basis of a variety of criteria. For example, did the reforms have the impact envisaged by their supporters, or have the adverse consequences predicted by their opponents? Were the formal purposes, as contained in government documents or ministerial speeches, actually achieved? Were informal aims, perhaps part of some 'hidden agenda' of policy-makers, realized in practice? In addition to the intended effects, were any unintended side-effects produced by the reforms? Taking all resources expended and positive and negative consequences into account, did the benefits of reform outweigh the costs?

These are all important questions. If they were all answered, then a comprehensive assessment of the impact of reform would be provided. However, such information is not, in itself, enough to evaluate public management reforms. It is necessary for policy-makers and academics not only to know *whether* a reform worked but also *why*. For this reason, an analysis that seeks simply to catalogue and weigh costs and benefits is a weak basis for drawing lessons for practice or research. According to Chen (1990: 18), traditional evaluation research has been

> characterized by a primary focus on the overall relationship between the inputs and outputs of a programme without concern for the transformation process in the middle. Such simple input/output or black box evaluation may provide a gross assessment of whether or not a programme works but fail to identify the underlying causal mechanisms that generate the treatment effects, thus failing to pinpoint the deficiencies of the programme for future improvement or development. A black box evaluation is usually not sensitive to the political and organizational context of inputs and outputs.

In order to promote both organizational learning and academic knowledge, evaluation must be *theory-driven*, which means that it is based on assumptions and arguments concerning the relationship between a reform and its effects. Chen (1990) argues that only this style of evaluation can allow general conclusions to be drawn from specific reforms; that is, conclusions on whether deliberate changes to structures or processes are likely to succeed or fail. If a theory is correct, then policies that flow from it will probably produce positive consequences; otherwise, the effects are likely to be at best neutral and at worst negative. Thus evaluation requires not only precise measurement and methodological rigour, but also theoretical depth.

Now, accepting the need for theory-driven evaluation does not help to determine *which* theory is to be used to predict the impact of a reform. Furthermore, public policy-making is a messy and complex procedure. The interplay of competing participants and ideologies implies that many theories contribute to the shape of reforms. The task therefore becomes the identification of the *dominant* theoretical perspective that lies behind a reform programme.

The major theoretical basis of the reforms associated with new public management, in the UK and elsewhere, is *public choice* (Aucoin 1990; Self 1993; Stretton and Orchard 1994; Zifack 1994; Udehn 1996). Indeed, seldom has an abstract theory of bureaucracy had such a powerful influence on public management reforms. Ingraham (1997) recounts that Niskanen's (1971) *Bureaucracy and Representative Government*, the key text in the public choice corpus, was required reading for members of

Margaret Thatcher's first Cabinet. The extent of their understanding of its economic arguments and mathematical formulae has not been recorded. Although not perhaps so prominent on the Blair reading list, public choice ideas are still a strong influence on New Labour policies, for example those concerning the responsiveness of services to customers rather than staff. The *Modernising Government* White Paper states that Labour aims to 'deliver public services to meet the needs of citizens, not the convenience of service providers' (Cabinet Office 1999: 7). Similarly, Labour's 2001 manifesto for a second term in office made plain its commitment to the use of performance indicators in the public sector, and to markets and competition as methods for improving public services.

Public choice theory and public management reforms

Public choice theory assumes that bureaucrats are motivated primarily by self-interest rather than the public interest. Moreover, this problem is exacerbated by the absence of appropriate organizational structures and processes in the public sector. Three specific characteristics of public bureaucracies are believed to lead to a lack of efficiency and effectiveness: the monopolistic structure of public service markets; the absence of valid indicators of organizational performance; and the large size of many government agencies.

Monopoly in public service markets

Public choice arguments on the costs of monopoly draw directly on neo-classical economics (Jackson 1982; McMaster and Sawkins 1996). The neo-classical view of the 'welfare loss' associated with monopoly is in turn reflected strongly in the 'structure–conduct–performance' paradigm of industrial economics (Shepherd 1990). This paradigm suggests that a competitive market structure has a positive influence on the conduct of the owners and managers of private firms, which leads to high levels of industrial performance. Similarly, public choice theory suggests that if appropriate market structures are created in the public sector, then the behaviour of bureaucrats will be steered towards the general welfare of society rather than their own selfish objectives. As McKean (1965: 500) argues, 'if well designed, the invisible hand can go a long way toward turning private "vice" into public virtue in government as well as in the private sector'.

Public choice theorists assume that public organizations have been unduly protected from the pressures of competition. Public agencies have traditionally had a large share of the national UK market in services such as health, education and the provision of rented housing. In addition, in particular localities, the public had little option but to use the services offered by monopolistic public suppliers. The small private sectors in health and education provided an 'exit' option for dissatisfied wealthy customers. The bulk of the population, however, were forced to exercise 'voice' if services were unsatisfactory, or simply to express a passive 'loyalty' to the products of the local bureaucracy.

Public monopoly is assumed to lead to poor performance because officials have little incentive to keep their costs down or to find innovative methods of service delivery. Whereas in the private sector the rewards of managers and the very survival of firms are linked to profitability, such pressures are absent in the conventional public organization. Officials seldom reap the benefits or bear the costs of changes in efficiency. Furthermore, financial resources are provided not by customers, but by a 'political sponsor' who allocates funds to public agencies. Therefore, to the extent that bureaucrats are responsive to external pressures, they are more likely to pay attention to the desires of politicians than to the needs of the public. However, according to public choice theory, politicians are also motivated by self-interest (as reflected in votes and power) rather than public welfare (Downs 1957).

Information on organizational performance

Even if public agencies are monopolists, bureaucratic behaviour need have no adverse consequences if it can be easily monitored and controlled. Close scrutiny and effective management could, in principle, lead to organizational activities that promote the public interest. The problem, according to public choice theory, is that there are no unambiguous indicators of performance in the public sector, so it is difficult to evaluate or influence the behaviour of agencies or individuals. Niskanen (1971) notes that bureaucrats and their political sponsors who allocate public funds are in a position of 'bilateral monopoly', which would appear to bestow equal power on each side. However, officials are more powerful than politicians because of the difficulty of measuring service outputs and costs. Niskanen argues that only the bureaucrats know the true cost of delivering the level of output desired by their political sponsor. It is, therefore, easy for officials to persuade politicians to allocate more money than is really required for service provision. By contrast, bureaucrats are able to make an accurate guess about the maximum funds that politicians are prepared to provide for a given level of service activities.

Taken together, the selfishness and monopoly power of public officials result in a number of negative effects on the production of public services. Tullock (1965: 193) goes so far as to claim that many public agencies serve no useful function: 'much of modern bureaucracy is simply a mistake. . . . Over time, the vested interests of the bureaucrats themselves become more and more important in justifying the organization'. Somewhat less sweepingly, Downs (1967) argues that the principal problem of bureaucracy is excessive growth. Although all organizations have inherent tendencies towards expansion, this phenomenon is especially pronounced in the public sector where the 'ability to obtain income in a market cannot serve as an objective guide to the desirability of extending, maintaining or contracting the level of expenditures it undertakes . . . the inability of bureaus to rely on markets as objective indicators of output value affects their entire operation' (1967: 30).

Organizational size

Public choice theorists argue that the adverse effects of monopolistic market structures and opaque standards of performance are compounded by the large size of many bureaucracies. Tullock (1965: 51) claims that problems of co-ordination and control grow disproportionately with organizational size, and that increases in scale eventually reduce performance: 'It seems clear that the declining "marginal efficiency" associated with increasing size would guarantee that a point would be attained at which further gains from expansion would be less than the added cost'. This suggests that the attainment of organizational objectives is maximized at some point, but then begins to decline. At the extreme, Tullock (1965: 187) asserts, performance will fall to zero at very large scales of operation: 'Efforts to set up administrative structures to perform sizeable tasks will always fail. An administrative structure may be set up; and it may accomplish something, but it will not perform the task for which it is designed'.

Downs (1967: 160) criticizes large public bureaucracies on the grounds that they do not respond to new circumstances and are slow to deliver services:

> The increasing size of the bureau leads to a gradual ossification of operations . . . the bureau becomes a gigantic machine that slowly and inflexibly grinds along in the direction in which it was initially aimed. It still produces outputs, perhaps in truly impressive quantity and quality. But the speed and flexibility of its operation steadily diminish.

This argument does not imply that very large organizations fail completely. However, agencies that operate at a small scale are more likely to recognize new service needs and produce services quickly. Niskanen (1971) also argues that the greater the scale of operations, the greater the degree of monopoly power. He claims that big bureaucracies are especially able to extract revenue from their political sponsors, provide low-quality services at high cost, and evade attempts to monitor their performance.

Public choice prescriptions

Public choice remedies for the problems of bureaucracy follow directly from the diagnoses outlined above. First, the structure of public service markets should be more competitive. This implies rivalry between public organizations, and between public and private providers. The latter form of competition is advocated by Niskanen (1968: 305), who argues that

> the type of goods and services now provided by bureaus could be financed through government . . . but the provision of these services would be contracted to private, profit-seeking economic institutions. The bureaucracy, as such, would disappear, except for the review and contracting agencies.

A second public choice prescription is to force public agencies to produce more information on their performance. This would shift the balance of power from bureaucrats to politicians, pressure groups and the public at large. Downs (1967) recognizes that the creation of special monitoring agencies may generate a new bureaucracy and eventually become counter-productive. At the limit, the benefit of additional performance measures may be less than the cost of generating the data. However, the public choice view of the traditional public sector bureaucracy is that this point is far from being reached. The final reform which is recommended by public choice theorists is to break large agencies into smaller units. This implies separating 'conglomerate' departments into 'single-function' organiza-tions, so that performance becomes more visible; and disaggregating big bureaucracies into smaller, free-standing 'firms' which can then compete with each other for a share of the public service market.

Public choice and theory-driven evaluation

Public choice meets the main conditions for a theory-driven evaluation of public management reforms. Chen (1990: 40) argues that this style of evaluation should be based on 'a specification of what must be done to achieve the desired goals, what other important impacts may also be anticipated, and how these goals and impacts would be generated'. Public choice writers provide clear statements on the 'desired goals' (efficiency and responsiveness), 'what must be done' (more competition and perform-ance information, and smaller organizations) and 'how these goals and impacts would be generated' (changes in the behaviour of bureaucrats and consumers). Public choice theorists, by contrast, have little to say on 'other important impacts', and largely ignore *negative* impacts because they focus on the beneficial effects of the reforms that they advocate. Critics of this theoretical perspective have been quick to fill this gap, and have drawn attention to the adverse effects of public choice reforms on the *equity* of public service provision. This issue is explored further in Chapter 2 where criteria for assessing the impact of public management reforms are discussed.

Chen (1990) adds one further major element to his definition of theory-driven evaluation that is cited in the preceding paragraph. This is the identification of variables that may modify the relationship between a reform and its consequences. Such variables include the 'contextual and intervening factors that hinder or facilitate programme processes and outcomes' (1990: 45). In other words, the impact of a reform may depend upon two characteristics of the target organizations: their environmental circumstances (e.g. whether they already operate in a market that is partly competitive, in which case further competition may have only a small effect on performance); and their internal characteristics (e.g. whether they are highly professionalized, in which case implementation may be thwarted by strong resistance).

This emphasis on the potential importance of the external and internal context of reform has recently been repeated by Pawson and Tilley (1997). Their model of 'realistic evaluation' is based on the formula 'context + mechanism = outcomes'. In this formula 'mechanism' can be interpreted as a public management reform, and 'context' as the circumstances that are favourable or unfavourable to its success.

Both Chen (1990) and Pawson and Tilley (1997) effectively reject 'universalistic' theories of the link between reforms and outcomes. Such theories postulate that there is 'one right way' to achieve good performance, regardless of the environmental and organizational context. By contrast, 'contingency' theories assume that the same organizational strategy may succeed or fail in different contexts (Child 1974; Greenwood and Hinings 1976). Thus a theory-driven evaluation of public choice reforms should incorporate such contingency effects: in other words, the circumstances that are conducive to success or failure need to be identified.

This raises an immediate problem which is, nevertheless, an opportunity for theoretical development. The problem is that public choice is a universalistic rather than a contingency theory. Its advocates assume that public choice prescriptions are valid for all organizations at all times: for example, competition is always better than monopoly, and a reduction in organizational scale will always lead to improvements in performance. A theory-driven or realistic evaluation of public choice reforms may therefore appear to be impossible. We reject this view because we do not believe that public choice theory's claim to universal validity deserves to be taken seriously. No other theoretical perspective on the management of the public sector, or for that matter the private sector, has yet achieved this universalistic status. Furthermore, policy-makers or managers who are asked the question 'will reform A, B or C work?' are most likely to answer 'it all depends on circumstances X, Y and Z'. On an entirely inductive basis, then, it is implausible to assume that public choice theory constitutes the first universal truth in the study of organizational performance.

For these reasons we proceed with a theory-driven evaluation despite the universalistic content of public choice propositions. This is where the problem of universalism becomes an opportunity. By evaluating public choice reforms in this way, we may be able to develop the theory itself by identifying the environmental and organizational contexts that modify its validity. In particular, the comparison of the three service contexts of health, education and housing will enable the contingency effects of public choice theory to be explored. This approach could take some of the heat out of the intense academic debate between public choice theorists and their critics, which has become polarized into opposing camps who believe that reforms such as marketization are bound to succeed or doomed to fail (Boyne 1998a). Our theory-driven evaluation has the potential to reveal whether public choice should properly be viewed as a contingency theory rather than a universalistic theory. This would not only add significantly to the theoretical sophistication of the public choice perspective, but also provide better insights for practitioners on the conditions for successful public management reforms.

Structure of the book

Public choice theory makes a number of prescriptions for the reform of the public sector, and predicts that favourable outcomes will ensue if these prescriptions are followed. The principal reforms are more competition, more performance information, and smaller organizations. The main outcomes that are hypothesized are higher efficiency and stronger responsiveness to public demands.

In principle, then, the effects of reforms that are inspired by public choice ideas are easy to evaluate. All that has to be done is to observe whether the reforms lead to the predicted outcomes. However, the practice of evaluation is much more complicated. In this book we explore the practical problems of evaluation, and illustrate the difficulty of drawing conclusions in the presence of these problems. We argue that good evidence on aspects of performance such as efficiency and responsiveness is generally thin; and that even where such evidence is available, it is difficult to attribute changes in performance to specific reforms. Nevertheless, the broad effects of public choice policies can be discerned, even if their shape is cloudy and shifting rather than clear and stable.

In Chapters 2 and 3 we develop a framework for the evaluation of public management reforms. This consists of four main elements. First, we identify criteria for evaluating impact, and analyse the problems of operationalizing these criteria. A second issue is whether the reforms that are actually adopted are accurate reflections of the theoretical principles. Third, are the reforms put into practice? Even if the reforms are theoretically appropriate, there may be a substantial gap between the policy that is formulated and the policy that is implemented. Finally, are the effects of reform consistent with theoretical expectations? This last question raises a host of methodological issues concerning the establishment of cause and effect. We show that the severity of this 'attribution problem' varies with the way that a reform is designed and put into practice.

In Chapters 4–6 we apply this framework to public management reforms in health, education and housing in the UK. Each chapter follows a common format. First, to what extent have changes occurred in the extent of competition, the number and quality of performance indicators, and the size of service delivery organizations? In other words, has reform actually occurred, and is it in the direction prescribed by public choice theory? How different are the 'pre-reform' and 'post-reform' structures and processes? Second, what have the consequences been for efficiency, responsiveness and equity? How have these variables changed? Are the changes in the direction predicted by public choice theory? To what extent can better or worse performance be attributed to changes in market structure, performance reporting or organizational size?

In Chapter 7, general conclusions are drawn from the analysis of reforms in health, education and housing. What are the problems of establishing the extent and impact of public management reforms, and what are the prospects for solving these problems? Have the reforms been a success or a failure, and is public choice theory a suitable basis for redesigning the public sector? Under what circumstances are public choice prescriptions likely to succeed or fail?

In a sense, this book is a series of case studies on three levels. First, it is a case study of a particular theoretical perspective on the need for public management reform. An investigation of alternative theoretical perspectives might yield different evidence and conclusions. Second, it contains case studies of three specific types of reform. Again, different reforms might produce different signals about success or failure. Third, there are three case studies of parts of the public sector in the UK. It is conceivable that marketization, performance indicators and changes in organizational scale have had different consequences in other areas of service provision and in other countries. For all these reasons, our conclusions cannot be sweeping or comprehensive. Nevertheless, our evaluative framework does provide a firm basis for judging whether the reforms have worked as expected, and for assessing the potential impact of such reforms in the future.

two

Criteria of evaluation

The current Labour government in the UK claims to be open-minded about methods of providing public services. Traditional dogma has, so we are told, given way to the 'modern' maxim that 'what counts is what works' (Davies *et al.* 2000; Newman 2001). But does this mantra, in itself, provide a clear basis for judging different approaches to the management of public services, or is it all style and no substance? An answer to the apparently simple question whether a reform has worked turns out to be very complex. This question comprises numerous sub-questions, all of which raise thorny conceptual and empirical issues. For example, what criteria should be used to evaluate reforms? What information is required to apply these criteria? What counts as 'good evidence' on the impact of a reform? What methods can be used to disentangle the separate impact of a reform from other influences on its intended consequences?

In this chapter and the next we develop a set of principles for evaluating the consequences of public management reforms. In the present chapter we identify criteria for evaluating reforms. Here we explore the meaning of public choice theorists' preferred measures of policy impact: efficiency and responsiveness. We also analyse different interpretations of the 'missing' criterion identified by critics of public choice theory: the equity or fairness of public service provision.

In Chapter 3 we consider fundamental questions that are seldom given much attention in the literature on public management reforms. Did reform actually take place? How different were the arrangements for public services before and after the supposed reform? Even if radical reforms were adopted, to what extent were they actually implemented? If only minor changes occur in the design of public services, and if even these are implemented only in part, then there is little reason to expect significant shifts in efficiency, responsiveness and equity. Politicians and their officials may have an interest in 'talking up' the scale of a reform, and in emphasizing that their policies differ substantially from those of their predecessors. It is important to be sceptical about such claims, and to assess carefully whether public management reforms have really occurred.

Later on in Chapter 3 we identify the problems of establishing whether organizational performance in the public sector has improved or deteriorated, and whether this is the result of reforms. Have movements in efficiency, responsiveness and equity been positive or negative? This raises issues about the existence of a baseline for monitoring such movements (progress is difficult to judge if there is little information on the 'pre-reform' level of performance), and the availability of information on the 'post-reform' trajectory of change. We also analyse questions of cause and effect, or 'attribution'. Put simply, is it possible to establish 'beyond reasonable doubt' that any observed changes in performance can be attributed to reform rather than other variables (e.g. changes in social and economic conditions, or changes in other aspects of government policy)? It is possible that efficiency and responsiveness have improved in spite of, rather than because of, the reforms imposed on public sector organizations. Throughout Chapter 3 we deal with such issues at a fairly broad level, in order to clarify the general principles that we are proposing for the evaluation of reforms. More specific and detailed questions will be addressed in Chapters 4–6 when the evaluative principles are applied to the reform of health, housing and education.

Criteria for assessing the impact of public management reforms

Evaluation research is bedevilled by a lack of agreed criteria for judging policy consequences (Hogwood and Gunn 1984; Pollitt 1995). This reflects wider problems in the evaluation of organizational performance (Hall 1996). There are many dimensions of success or failure, and many different stakeholder groups who place different weights on these dimensions (Connolly et al. 1980). For example, service users may pay most attention to service quality and quantity; staff in public organizations may be more concerned with how a service is provided (including their own working conditions) than with what is provided; and taxpayers are likely to place as much emphasis on cost as on effectiveness.

A variety of methods for establishing evaluative criteria have been proposed. One is to assess reforms against the goals of policy-makers, as expressed in legislation, government documents and other pronouncements (such as speeches by government ministers). However, these can be vague and conflicting, and may reveal only the official objectives of public management reforms. For example, the stated intention of compulsory competitive tendering (CCT) in UK local government in the 1980s was to improve the efficiency of local service provision, but it has been argued that the unstated intentions were to break the power of local government trades unions and cut the size of the public sector workforce (Cutler and Waine 1997). Another approach is for evaluators to use their own criteria to judge the success or failure of public management reforms. In the specific context of our analysis, the implication is that the five authors of this book should develop their own list of evaluative criteria. This method, too, is problematic: it could be idiosyncratic and subjective, and would encounter all the problems of multiple dimensions of performance and multiple perceptions of their relative importance.

A third approach to the development of evaluative criteria deals directly with the latter set of problems. This 'multiple constituency' method consists of three steps: identifying all of the relevant stakeholders who are affected by a public management reform; eliciting their evaluative criteria and the relative importance that they attach to these; and attaching weights to the preferences of each stakeholder group. These steps are all very difficult and likely to be politically controversial. Which stakeholders should be included? Do they have clear preferences, and can they rank them in order of importance? What weights should be attached to the views of the various stakeholders? One approach to this last question is to use their relative power to alter the behaviour of organizations that provide public services, but how is power to be measured, and by whom?

In sum, all of these approaches to the identification of evaluative criteria pose as many problems as they solve, and are impractical in various ways. Moreover, for the purposes of the analysis in this book, they tend to miss the point of evaluation. This is because we are undertaking a *theory-driven* evaluation. Therefore, the relevant criteria are those stipulated by the theoretical perspective that is adopted, which in this case is public choice theory. The key writers in this tradition have consistently advocated two principal performance improvements that are expected to follow from the reforms which they advocate: efficiency and responsiveness (Boyne 1998a; Mueller 1989). These criteria, which are explained in more detail below, provide the basis for an 'intrinsic' evaluation of public choice reforms. In other words, improvements in efficiency and responsiveness are the appropriate criteria for judging public choice theory on its own terms, because they have been selected by the advocates of this approach to the design and delivery of public services.

Nevertheless, an intrinsic evaluation of public management reforms is too narrow. An exclusive focus on intended outcomes effectively loads the evaluative dice in favour of the theoretical perspective that has been selected. A theory can appear to be an appropriate prescription for change because it only considers a restricted range of (supposedly) positive outcomes. What about the unintended consequences of reform that are overlooked by public choice theorists? An answer to this question requires a broadening of focus to 'extrinsic' as well as intrinsic evaluative criteria. Yet, this wider perspective must not become a *loss* of focus: in principle, a long 'shopping list' of extrinsic criteria could be added to the intrinsic criteria of efficiency and responsiveness. In order to retain the emphasis on theory-driven evaluation, and to make the task manageable, it is essential to consider only those unintended outcomes which themselves have a strong theoretical basis. The most sustained and coherent critique of public choice reforms is that they have an adverse effect on the equity of public service provision (e.g. Self 1993; Udehn 1996). We have, therefore, added this extrinsic evaluative criterion to the two intrinsic criteria of efficiency and responsiveness, and now proceed to consider each of these yardsticks for the assessment of public management reform.

Efficiency

The idea that public services can be produced more efficiently has been widespread since the expansion of the modern state in the early twentieth century (Downs and Larkey 1986). The distinctive twist added by public choice theory is that public organizations are *inherently* and *massively* inefficient. The root problem is regarded as the monopoly power of public officials. Niskanen (1971) argues that the cost of services in a monopolistic public market is up to *twice* as high as in a competitive market. The trio of public choice reforms (more competition, smaller organizations, more performance information) is intended to reduce if not remove the supposed existence of this chronic waste.

But what is the meaning of 'efficiency', and how can it be measured? Economists usually distinguish between two concepts of efficiency (Jackson 1982). Technical efficiency is the ratio of service 'inputs' (e.g. spending) to 'outputs', which are the goods or services actually produced by an organization (e.g. new houses built, teaching provided in schools, operations performed in hospitals). Allocative efficiency is the match between such outputs and the preferences of the public (e.g. whether the houses built meet the needs of families who lack suitable accommodation, whether the teaching reflects the demands of parents and pupils, whether priority is given to operations for the most urgent medical complaints). This second definition of efficiency overlaps closely with the concept of responsiveness as used by public choice theorists. The concept of efficiency will, therefore, be interpreted in this book in its technical sense. Moreover, this is the meaning of the term that has become familiar to policy-makers and managers through debates on the 'three Es' of economy, efficiency and effectiveness (Tomkins 1987).

Measures of technical efficiency usually focus on 'unit costs', which can be interpreted simply as the financial resources required to produce a 'unit' of service provision. If public choice theorists are correct, and if the reforms which they advocate were adopted and implemented, then unit costs should fall over time. In other words, there should be a significant difference between the unit costs of public services in the pre-reform and post-reform periods. This check on whether public choice reforms have worked sounds straightforward in principle, but is rather more complicated in practice. Here we focus simply on the *measurement* of unit costs – other problems, such as attribution, are discussed in Chapter 3.

First, which costs are to be included in the calculation? One option is to focus only on the direct expenditure of the organizations which provide a service that has been reformed. However, this may neglect the indirect costs of reform that are borne by other agencies. For example, the introduction of CCT in UK local government in the 1980s was associated with lower spending on services such as refuse collection that were 'contracted out' to private firms (Boyne 1998a). Yet these expenditure savings were largely achieved by redundancies amongst former local authority employees. This had direct consequences for the social security budget (through payments to the unemployed). It may also have put pressure on the budgets of the National Health Service and local social services departments (which tend to deal with problems that are partly associated with lack of income). Thus lower spending in one part of the public sector can lead to higher spending elsewhere. A comprehensive assessment of reform should attempt to take direct and indirect costs into account. More mundanely, but equally importantly, it is necessary to measure both revenue and capital costs (because an apparent saving on staff may be accompanied by the need to purchase new equipment), and to ensure that inflation is taken into account so that costs are judged on a truly comparable basis before and after reform. Not adjusting for inflation could result in a reform being judged a failure (absolute spending has risen) when it has been a success (real spending has fallen).

Second, what counts as a 'unit' of service provision? At face value, this refers to the *quantity* of the outputs of a public organization (for example, number of dwellings made fit, number of music lessons for school pupils, number of patients treated by general practitioners). However, judgements about the consequences of reform also need to consider *quality*, which refers to the standard of service provided (Walsh 1991; Reeves and Bednar 1994). Relevant questions for the services cited above would include: what facilities (e.g. double glazing, central heating) the newly renovated dwellings had; what range of music was taught, and on how many instruments; and whether patients were treated with appropriate respect and courtesy by their doctors. All these issues imply that the definition of efficiency that was given above needs to be reformulated more precisely. In particular, measures of efficiency should capture the 'cost per unit *of constant quality*'. Efficiency, in other words, comprises not two but three variables:

Table 2.1 Combinations of service cost, quantity and quality that are consistent with higher efficiency

	Cost	Quantity	Quality
1	Lower	Higher	Higher
2	Lower	No change	No change
3	Lower	No change	Higher
4	Lower	Higher	No change
5	No change	No change	Higher
6	No change	Higher	No change
7	Higher	No change	% increase higher than the % increase in cost
8	Higher	% increase higher than the % increase in cost	No change
9	Higher	% increase higher than the % increase in cost	% increase higher than the % increase in cost

cost, quantity of output, and quality of output. Movements in all three need to be included in an evaluation of public management reforms. Otherwise, an improvement in efficiency may be missed (even if costs and quantity have stayed the same, quality may have improved); or an apparently successful outcome may turn out to be an illusion (costs have fallen, quantity has remained constant, but quality has fallen by even more than costs).

The separation of efficiency into its three components reveals that a variety of reform outcomes are consistent with public choice theory. The most clear-cut support for public choice reforms would be a combination of lower cost, higher service quantity and higher service quality. However, eight other outcomes also support public choice arguments to a greater or lesser extent (see Table 2.1). Similarly, the clearest contradiction of public choice claims would be a combination of higher cost and a lower quantity and quality of service outputs. Yet nine other outcomes are also inconsistent with higher efficiency (see Table 2.2). Note that the apparently 'neutral' outcome of no change in all three variables does not support public choice predictions on the impact of reform.

In sum, higher spending does not necessarily indicate lower efficiency, and lower spending does not automatically entail higher efficiency. Rather, judgements about the impact of public management reforms on efficiency must be based on information concerning the cost, quantity and quality of services. Moreover, at least nine possible combinations of these variables are consistent with improvements in efficiency, and at least ten combinations are consistent with a deterioration in efficiency. Thus careful tracking of relative movements in cost, quantity and quality is required in order to

Table 2.2 Combinations of service cost, quantity and quality that are inconsistent with higher efficiency

	Cost	Quantity	Quality
1	Higher	Lower	Lower
2	Higher	No change	No change
3	Higher	Lower	No change
4	Higher	No change	Lower
5	No change	No change	No change
6	No change	No change	Lower
7	No change	Lower	No change
8	Lower	No change	% decrease greater than the % decrease in cost
9	Lower	% decrease greater than the % decrease in cost	No change
10	Lower	% decrease greater than the % decrease in cost	% decrease greater than the % decrease in cost

measure whether a public management reform has been successful on this evaluative criterion.

Responsiveness

State intervention in areas such as education, health and housing was, in part, intended to deal with the failure of private markets to provide such services (Fraser 1984). In other words, the economic system, left to its own devices, was not believed to be able to meet public needs and demands. Public provision was deemed necessary because 'market failure' led to an insufficient quantity of services (e.g. too few schools to meet the educational needs of the economy) or to a politically unacceptable distribution of services (e.g. mansions for the rich and hovels for the poor). In short, the growth of the welfare state was intended to remedy a lack of *responsiveness* in private systems of service production and allocation.

Public choice theorists stand this conventional logic on its head. Instead of market failure, they emphasize 'government failure' (Wolf 1988). Responsiveness to public preferences is argued to be at least as weak in public as in private organizations. Government failure results from a combination of the problems of bureaucracy that were outlined in Chapter 1: monopoly power, absence of performance information, and excessive size. According to public choice theorists, bureaucrats look inwards towards their own interests rather than outwards towards the interests of the public. They are, therefore, either unaware of the needs of their supposed clients and customers, or pay too little attention to them.

In order to judge whether public management reforms have led to more or less responsiveness, it is necessary to address two main questions. First, *in what respects* should public services be responsive? High responsiveness implies that members of the public are happy with public services – but happy with which aspects of them? It would, in principle, be possible to take 'consumer satisfaction' as a proxy for responsiveness – but satisfaction with what? Second, *to whom* should public officials be responsive when making decisions about the design and delivery of services? The public can be divided into a variety of 'stakeholders'. Should all of these potential stakeholders be given equal weight?

The activities and achievements of public organizations can be divided into a variety of categories (Boyne and Law 1991; Boyne 1997a). These typically fall into three broad headings: *inputs* to services (such as expenditure, staffing and equipment); *outputs* of services (such as quantity and quality, which in turn can be divided into the speed and accessibility of service delivery); and *outcomes* which relate to whether formal objectives are achieved (e.g. whether school pupils pass exams, whether houses are renovated) and whether any positive or negative side-effects occur (e.g. job creation as a result of house renovation programmes). Public organizations can also be judged on their *probity* (e.g. whether money is spent for legitimate purposes, whether any of it has been diverted for fraudulent use by politicians and officials). Furthermore, some of the activities and achievements can be combined to form important performance ratios (e.g. *efficiency* is the ratio of outputs to inputs, and *cost-effectiveness* is the ratio of outcomes to inputs, otherwise known as 'value for money').

Public choice theorists have emphasized responsiveness to public demands concerning a restricted subset of these dimensions of organizational performance. In particular, they have focused narrowly on expenditure inputs and technical efficiency. Their obsession with these financial aspects of responsiveness is based on their belief that the public sector is bloated, spendthrift and profligate in its use of resources. Perhaps they assume that if these problems are solved then responsiveness on the remaining dimensions of performance will also improve. However, this line of argument is, at best, implicit in public choice thinking. A more plausible interpretation is that wider aspects of responsiveness have simply been ignored by public choice theorists. Even if citizens are happy with expenditure and efficiency, this does not guarantee that their preferences are fully reflected in all aspects of public services. It is, therefore, important to expand the intrinsic evaluative criterion of responsiveness to include not only expenditure and efficiency but also outputs, outcomes, probity and cost-effectiveness.

Another problem with public choice theory is that it is unclear to whom bureaucrats should be responsive. Whose demands are to be reflected in the pattern of public services? Are all demands to be treated equally and met in full? Classical public choice arguments on bureaucracy make little reference to these issues (e.g. Tullock 1965; Downs 1967; Niskanen 1971). Nor has more contemporary work in the field addressed such questions (see recent volumes of the 'house journal' of the movement, *Public Choice*). Improvements in responsiveness are regarded as urgent, but the intended beneficiaries of this improvement in performance are shadowy figures.

An alternative strand in public choice theory sheds some light on this issue. This is the literature on the behaviour of political parties rather than bureaucrats. According to Downs (1957), the ideal political system would be like a highly competitive economic market. In a contest between two major political parties, each 'firm' would seek to maximize its share of the vote by appealing to the 'median voter' in the middle of the ideological range. Thus, in a hypothetical electorate with 99 voters, a government should try to match its policies with the preferences of voter number 50 in the distribution (an equal number of 49 voters are to the left and right of this position). Any other position can be defeated by an opposition party that successfully targets the median voter.

If this argument is carried over to the behaviour of public officials who design and deliver services, then their objective should also be responsiveness to the median voter. However, this is unsatisfactory for a number of reasons. First, it implies that public services are delivered in an undifferentiated and 'Fordist' manner: anyone can have any service that he or she wants, provided that it is the service demanded by the median voter. Even perfect responsiveness to the demands of the median voter would leave most people to the left and right of this position deeply unsatisfied with public services. Second, the 'party competition' view of responsiveness focuses exclusively on the electorate, but this is a subgroup of the adult population (indeed, only around 60 per cent of the *registered* electorate actually voted in the 2001 general election in the UK). Thus the median voter and the median citizen may differ significantly in their preferences. Third, the Downs (1957) model of responsive parties deals with policy on a single dimension, usually taxation or expenditure (see Hoffman 1977; Boyne 1987). However, as noted above, responsiveness can vary over numerous dimensions that also include service outputs and outcomes. The distribution of voter preferences may differ between these, so that there are as many 'median voters' as there are dimensions of responsiveness (Mueller 1989). In short, if the public choice answer to the question 'responsiveness to whom' is 'responsiveness to the median voter', then this is an impractical and inappropriate basis for evaluating public management reforms.

An alternative approach is to divide the public into a variety of stakeholder groups, and to judge the level of responsiveness to their diverse preferences (Boschken 1994). These groups include direct service users and their representatives (e.g. parents of pupils at school, carers for senile relatives who require medical treatment), members of the public who use services indirectly (e.g. employers who recruit school leavers to their workforce), and taxpayers (who may pay for services that they do not use because they opt for private provision of education, health and housing). These different constituencies are likely to have different interests and demands (Fountain 2001).

A final major stakeholder group needs to be taken into consideration: the staff who provide public services. Even if the public choice assumption of bureaucratic selfishness is rejected, the view that service users and service providers have different interests remains plausible (Wilson 1993). Different segments of staff are in turn likely to have conflicting interests (Dunleavy 1991). However, for the purposes of exposition, they will be treated here as homogeneous. Public choice theorists argue that bureaucrats place too much weight on their own interests, but presumably would accept that some attention has to be paid to staff preferences in the design and delivery of services. Otherwise, the public sector workforce could be completely demotivated and demoralized. This may not be a recipe for successful reform – high organizational performance seems unlikely to follow from low individual performance. Thus the extent to which services are matched with staff preferences is relevant to an assessment of responsiveness.

It is possible to evaluate the impact of public management reforms on responsiveness by constructing a matrix that combines stakeholder groups with dimensions of organizational activities and achievements. Figure 2.1

Stakeholder groups

Organizational activities and achievements	Direct service users	Indirect service users	Taxpayers	Staff
Expenditure				
Outputs				
Outcomes				
Efficiency				
Cost-effectiveness				
Probity				

Figure 2.1 Matrix for evaluating the impact of public management reforms on service responsiveness

shows a simplified version of this matrix (with only four groups and only six dimensions of service provision). Even this 'checklist' of 24 boxes, however, represents a formidable evaluative challenge: first, because of the range of information required to fill the matrix; and second, because a clear conclusion of success would require higher responsiveness in all 24 boxes, and an unreserved judgement of failure would be possible only if responsiveness were lower in all of the boxes. Anything in between these extreme (and perhaps equally unlikely) outcomes is ambiguous. A clear picture can only be produced if weights are attached to the service elements on the vertical axis, and if weights are attached to the preferences of the different stakeholder groups on the horizontal axis. Such weights could then be entered in a formula which produces a 'magic number' that reveals how responsiveness has been affected by a public management reform. However, this would be not so much a mathematical as a political process, because the weights would be deeply controversial and contentious. Nevertheless, an important first step is to begin to put numbers in the boxes and thereby provide an 'evidence base' for policy debates.

Equity

Critics of public choice reforms have questioned whether the intrinsic evaluative criteria of efficiency and responsiveness have been met (see Self 1993; Boyne 1998a). However, their major objection to public choice propositions has focused on the extrinsic criterion of equity. Even if reforms such as more competition do lead to higher efficiency and responsiveness, they argue, these positive outcomes are outweighed by greater unfairness in the provision of public services. This is a particularly sore point because, as noted above, a major rationale for state provision of services is that private markets allocate resources inequitably. Public organizations are expected to redress the imbalance that would otherwise occur in the distribution of services such as health, housing and education. If public choice reforms undermine the achievement of equity, then this can be regarded as a fundamental flaw in their design.

Products in private markets are generally allocated on the basis of ability to pay: people with higher incomes can obtain, for example, better cars, bigger houses, and more exotic holidays. For many goods and services, this is widely regarded as fair. In other words, the criterion of equity is 'you get what you pay for'. However, in some aspects of life this criterion is regarded as politically unacceptable, and so the state intervenes to supplement or supplant the market mechanism. When this happens an alternative criterion of equity is required (Blanchard 1986). After all, if the state also allocated resources on the basis of ability to pay there would be little point in providing public services. The standard of fairness that is normally used in the public sector is 'need' (Doyal and Gough 1991). Thus the most important criterion of equity for judging public management reforms is not 'do people get what they pay for?' but 'do they get what they need?'

An evaluation of equity requires answers to two questions that have been debated widely in the social policy literature. First, which aspects of public services are to be provided equitably? For example, should equity be judged against the expenditure inputs offered to different groups, or against service outputs? Second, what are the relevant groups in society who are to be treated equitably? If different segments of the population have different needs, then equity requires that services should be allocated in proportion to these needs.

Le Grand (1982) has developed a widely cited conceptual framework that seeks to answer the first of these questions – see also Powell (1995) for a critique of the framework. Le Grand argues that the fairness of public services can be judged in the following five ways:

1 *Spending.* Criticisms are frequently voiced that the distribution of public expenditure between different people and geographical areas is unfair (Boyne and Powell 1991). A problem with spending measures is that efficiency varies across public organizations, so equity in spending may not lead to equity in outputs. Furthermore, spending may vary across areas because of differences in labour costs (for example, public sector salaries are higher in London than in the North of England). Thus spending is a weak criterion of equity.

2 *Use.* Different groups may use the same service to varying degrees through choice. Thus perfect equity in use could only be achieved by enforcing consumption in proportion to need. This infringement of individual liberty is likely, in a democratic society, to be regarded as too high a price for the achievement of equity in use. Yet, equal use for equal need remains a reasonable objective, even if it can never be perfectly attained. Thus if public choice reforms lead to less equitable use, they can be viewed as unsuccessful.

3 *Access.* This is partly a question of the physical proximity of services (e.g. how far patients have to travel to a hospital) and partly a question of 'opening hours' (e.g. whether outpatient clinics are held at convenient times). Le Grand (1982: 15) argues that 'the requirement that all individuals should have equal access to a service can most easily be interpreted as implying that the costs to all individuals of using that service (per unit) should be equal'. Again, fair access is not much help in achieving equity for service users if the distribution of output quantity and quality is unfair (hospitals that are equally spread in relation to population and 'open all hours' may meet the standard of fair access, but still provide services that do not reflect different needs in different locations).

Nevertheless, if a public management reform leads to less equitable access then this can be regarded as a negative result.

4 *Outcome*. This is analogous in some ways to the concept of effectiveness that was discussed earlier in this chapter. Le Grand (1982: 15) argues that 'precisely what is meant by outcome will vary from service to service. For health care it could be an individual's state of health; for education, the bundle of skills with which an individual emerges from the education system, . . . for housing the conditions of individuals' dwellings.' Thus outcomes in this sense refer to whether various 'end states' (e.g. better health) have been achieved. Average improvements across the population as a whole are probably consistent with more responsiveness (people want to be more healthy), but do not logically entail more equity. Rather it is the distribution of service outcomes that counts. The success of a health reform on this criterion can be assessed by whether the distributions of morbidity and mortality become more equal. This does, of course, open up the perverse possibility that success would be achieved if otherwise healthy people became more ill and died earlier. Greater equity, in other words, can imply the redistribution of death as much as the promotion of health.

5 *Final income*. This refers to the combined value of all material resources at the disposal of different groups in society. According to Le Grand (1982: 14), this criterion of equity implies that 'services should be allocated in such a way as to favour the poor, so that their "final incomes" (roughly private money income plus the value of any public subsidy received in cash or kind) are brought more into line with those of the rich'. Thus any public management reform that results in a lower share of services for poor households can be categorized as a failure on this criterion of equity. This, again, could lead to the apparently perverse outcome that economic decline accompanied by redistribution to the poor would count as success. However, for people who regard the 'final income' criterion as paramount, this is presumably a price worth paying.

In sum, four of Le Grand's (1982) criteria of equity seem relevant to the evaluation of public management reforms: use, access, outcomes and final incomes. Public choice reforms are widely believed to have negative consequences for these variables (Cutler and Waine 1997). For example, more competition between service providers is claimed to lead to the neglect of 'difficult' but especially needy patients and pupils; performance indicators for schools and the 'league tables' associated with them are believed to have created an increase in the exclusion of disruptive pupils (and thereby less equity in service use); and smaller organizations supposedly find it more difficult to switch resources between prosperous and needy clients. To some extent, such arguments may be based on an inappropriate point of comparison: the post-reform level of equity is not compared with the

Illustrative population characteristics

Criterion of equity	Income	Age	Sex	Race
Use				
Access				
Outcome				
Final income				

Figure 2.2 Matrix for evaluating the impact of public management reforms on the equity of service provision

pre-reform level, but with an 'ideal state' that never existed. This issue will be explored further in Chapters 4–6.

The second major question concerning an evaluation of equity can be dealt with more briefly: which groups in society should be included in the analysis? Le Grand (1982) notes that the major focus of studies of equity has been on social class, usually defined in relation to income. However, this a somewhat anachronistic agenda. Debates about equity in contemporary society have expanded to include issues concerning age, gender, race, language, sexual orientation and the 'differently abled'. If Le Grand's (1982) four criteria of equity are combined with a list of different population groups, then a matrix such as that shown in Figure 2.2 can be constructed. This can then be used to establish whether public management reforms have led to a growth or decline in the equity of public service provision. As with the evaluation of responsiveness on the basis of the matrix in Figure 2.1, the only unambiguous evidence of success would be greater equity in all of the boxes in Figure 2.2. Similarly, an unconditional conclusion of failure would only be justified by a decline in equity in every box in the matrix. In between these extremes, judgements about equity can only be made if weights are attached to the different criteria and population groups.

Conclusion

Public choice reforms can be evaluated on the basis of changes in efficiency, responsiveness and equity. In principle, a theory-driven evaluation can offer crisp and clear criteria for assessing the impact of reforms. However, we have shown that in practice this procedure quickly becomes complex and contestable. Each of the criteria consists of numerous sub-criteria that are either not defined within public choice theory or not given relative weights. Only a handful of the many potential outcomes of public choice reforms can be unambiguously deemed a 'success' or 'failure'. Furthermore, even if precise judgements can be made on efficiency, responsiveness or equity, no theoretical guidance exists (in the public choice literature or elsewhere) for determining the relative importance of these three policy objectives. For example, are improvements in efficiency and responsiveness more valuable than a deterioration in equity? Is a decline in efficiency worth trading off for increases in responsiveness and equity? Thus even a theory-driven evaluation leads to loose ends, because it encounters political rather than technical questions.

three

Methods of evaluation

Our aim in this book is to evaluate the consequences of public management reforms. The principal question concerns the impact of reform. We have already shown in Chapter 2 that it is first necessary to establish by what criteria reform should be evaluated. In this chapter we first consider another logically prior question: whether reform did actually occur. We then turn to an analysis of the problems of measuring the impact of reform.

The extent of public management reform: myths and measures

To some extent the contemporary notion of 'continuous reform' is a myth propagated by governmental spin doctors. The language of reform implies dynamism and determination on a variety of fronts by political leaders. Organizations that have been subjected to reform also complain loudly about the disadvantages of 'constant revolution'. Some academics, too, contribute to the impression of widespread upheaval through apocalyptic commentaries on ostensibly radical policies. For example, the 'death of the welfare state' has been announced many times since the 1970s. By contrast, careful measurement of whether reform is real rather than rhetorical is rare.

The extent of public management reform can be assessed in four ways. These involve comparisons of the 'policy as adopted' and 'policy in action' before and after reform (see Figure 3.1). The policy as adopted concerns the formal arrangements for service design and delivery, as reflected in legislation, statutory guidance, circulars or other documents issued by central government. The policy in action refers to the behaviour of service delivery organizations in practice. The potential for an 'implementation gap' between

Old regime

		Policy as adopted	Policy in action
New regime	Policy as adopted	**I** Extent of change in principle	**II** Extent to which new policy formalizes old practice
	Policy in action	**III** Extent to which practice continues to reflect old policy	**IV** Extent of change in practice

Figure 3.1 Four comparisons of the extent of public management reform

policy and action has been widely discussed (e.g. Barrett and Fudge 1981; Marsh and Rhodes 1992). Implementation problems can arise for a variety of technical and political reasons, such as a failure to communicate the policy clearly or a lack of control by central government over local organizations (Boyne 1993).

The literature on public management reform often focuses on comparisons of policies as adopted in 'old' and 'new' regimes (cell I in Figure 3.1). This may be the easiest way to assess whether reform has occurred, because conclusions can be based largely on the analysis of documents. No fieldwork or measurement of the behaviour of service delivery organizations is required, which may explain why this research method is frequently employed. However, this form of comparison can be highly misleading. Neither the old nor the new policy as adopted may bear much resemblance to the policy in action. In other words, substantial changes in policy principles can coexist with trivial changes in management practice. Now, a formal announcement of a new policy direction is clearly an inherent part of reform as a 'top-down' process. There is also an argument that symbolic statements of intent are in themselves important (Edelman 1964). Nevertheless, the *impact* of reform may be weakly correlated with the extent of change in formal policy. Unless policy in action is different after a reform, the consequences for efficiency, responsiveness and equity are likely to be minor. Thus the identification of whether the policy as adopted has altered significantly is only a starting point in the measurement of reform.

Further information on the extent of public management reforms is provided by the types of comparison in cells II and III of Figure 3.1. Each of these forms of comparison goes beyond policy pronouncements by measuring some aspects of policy in action. The assessment of reform in cell II focuses on whether a new policy merely formalizes pre-existing practice. If reform follows this pattern, simply 'catching up' with what is already happening on the ground, then there are unlikely to be significant shifts in organizational outcomes such as efficiency. The analysis in cell III also compares policy and practice, but this time the old policy as adopted and the new policy in action. It is possible that even when formal policies are changed, the behaviour of service delivery organizations continues to reflect the old policy, for example because of bureaucratic resistance. Indeed, this is precisely what public choice theory would predict: public officials will attempt to block policies that are intended to undermine their power. In this case, again, a radical new policy is likely to produce few tangible results, except frustration for the reformers and displaced effort on resistance by the bureaucracy (Downs 1967).

The final method for assessing the extent of public management reform is a comparison of the old and new policy in action (cell IV in Figure 3.1). This involves a comparison of how services are designed and delivered in practice, both in the old and new regimes. This is methodologically challenging for two reasons. First, it requires the measurement of changes in organizational behaviour rather than the measurement of policy pronouncements. Second, instead of assessing the content of a single set of documents, it is necessary to track the behaviour of a variety of organizations. There may be as many versions of the policy in action as there are agencies that deliver services (e.g. almost 400 local authorities are responsible for implementing housing reforms in England and Wales). The correspondence between the policy as adopted and the policy in action is likely to vary substantially across such service delivery organizations. Moreover, the difference between the policies in action in the old and new regimes is also likely to vary. Although this approach to the measurement of reform is complex, it is more accurate than the alternatives. The extent of change in the policy in action is the most meaningful answer to the question whether a public management reform has occurred.

In sum, the extent of public management reform can be assessed in two stages:

1 Whether a new policy has been adopted. As discussed in Chapter 1, in the absence of a deliberate shift in direction there may be 'change' but not reform.
2 The size of the gap between the policy in action in the old and new regimes. Significant shifts in efficiency, responsiveness and equity are unlikely to occur if reforms are initiated but not implemented.

We now consider how the three public choice reforms that are the focus of this book can be defined and measured. How is it possible to tell whether a public management reform has made a difference to competition, performance indicators, and organizational size, and whether any change is in the direction prescribed by public choice theory?

More competition

The concept of competition can be defined as a contest between rival producers for a share of a market. This definition is derived from the model of 'perfect competition' in neo-classical economics (Reekie 1979; Clarke 1985). In this idealized view of competition, consumers have a free choice between a large number of alternative suppliers of goods and services, each of which has a small share of the market. Firms are able easily to leave a market in pursuit of higher profits elsewhere, and to enter a new market (there are no monopolists or cartels that can prevent the latter strategy). Private companies can also become bankrupt and cease to exist because they are inefficient and/or unresponsive to consumer demands.

This abstract model of perfect competition has few parallels in real economic markets – neither producer nor consumer choice is so unrestricted in practice (e.g. some private industries are dominated by a handful of suppliers). Furthermore, even when 'quasi-markets' have been introduced in the public sector they have been heavily regulated by central government (Le Grand and Bartlett 1993; Bartlett *et al.* 1998). Unlike private markets, money seldom changes hands between producers and consumers; markets are highly segmented because of the territorial boundaries of local authorities and health authorities (only a minority of consumers cross these geographical boundaries to receive services, and these trips are usually to gain access to specialized services such as complex operations in hospital); within each geographically segmented market the public sector remains a monopolist (public schools and hospitals have a market share of over 90 per cent in the education and health markets in the UK); and direct consumer choice does not always exist (e.g. patients do not choose hospital services directly, but are referred to them by general practitioners).

Nevertheless, the model of perfect competition does provide some general guidelines for establishing whether a public management reform entails more competition in service provision. In particular, a reform is likely to reflect public choice prescriptions concerning competition and consumer choice if the following conditions are met:

1 The number of separate service producers is higher after the reform.
2 The division of market share between producers is more equal because the dominant position of major suppliers has been weakened.
3 Consumers have more choice between public suppliers of services (e.g. between schools, landlords, and general practitioners).
4 Consumers have more choice between public and private suppliers (e.g. between state and private schools, between local authority and private landlords).
5 Consumers have more direct choice (i.e. less use of 'third-party' intermediaries who make choices on their behalf).

6 There is more exit from a market (because 'failing' public organizations are shut down).

7 There is more entry into a market (because entry barriers are lower – e.g., regulations may be eased so as to help private firms to provide publicly funded services such as health and education).

All of these conditions refer to the formal *structure* of a market. At the extreme, such changes may be enforced by central government through legislation (e.g. by compelling local education authorities to allow parents to choose between schools). In this way, the implementation gap between a policy as adopted and the policy in action may be bridged. However, there are further conditions for extra competition that are less amenable to direction by central government. These concern the attitudes and behaviour of producers and consumers. Thus our final two criteria for assessing whether a public management reform has resulted in more competition are:

8 Producers actively strive to defeat their rivals, and to expand their revenues and share of the market.

9 Consumers exercise their market power by switching between suppliers (or threatening to do so), and thereby pressurize service providers into paying more attention to their demands.

More information on performance

Economic markets require information in order to function efficiently by matching producer supply with consumer demand. Prospective purchasers of goods and services want information about price and quality, so that they can offer cash to the companies that best meet their preferences. Private firms also desire information about their own performance and that of their rivals. This can help them to judge whether their competitive strategies have been successful.

Thus, to some extent, information on performance is a corollary of the injection of more competition into public services. If parents are to choose accurately between schools, tenants between landlords, and patients between hospitals, then they all need to make informed decisions about the relative performance of different service providers. Managers also need to know whether their organizations are improving, deteriorating or staying the same. Otherwise they could lose business in the public sector marketplace, and their jobs might be at risk.

These arguments imply that the collation and publication of performance indicators (PIs) can considerably improve the operation of market mechanisms for public services. In effect, PIs enhance consumer power by enabling them to choose an 'exit' option if performance is unsatisfactory. According to public choice theorists, PIs make visible and clear the previously hidden and opaque activities of public bureaucracies. The monopoly position of public service providers is thereby greatly eroded because their customers have the information necessary to switch between suppliers. In this way, good performers are rewarded with revenue and market growth, whereas poor performers are punished through loss of income and status.

PIs may bring benefits even in the absence of a competitive market for public services. Taxpayers, consumers and voters may wish to influence the behaviour of public organizations through 'voice' as well as exit (Hirschman 1970). Although voice is a minor theme in the public choice literature on bureaucracy, it is an important element in public choice arguments on the broader operation of political systems (Mueller 1989). Voice mechanisms include voting, pressure group activities, or simply seeking individual redress for unsatisfactory decisions. Thus, regardless of whether more competition occurs, more PIs can be expected to have an influence on efficiency, responsiveness and equity.

How can the extent to which a reform results in more PIs be assessed? An answer to this question must cover not only the quantity but also the quality of PIs. Put differently, what does a PI that is consistent with public choice prescriptions look like? What is a 'good' PI from this perspective? As noted in the discussion of the evaluative criterion of responsiveness in Chapter 2, public choice theory places special emphasis on expenditure and efficiency. However, it also emphasizes the importance of meeting public preferences, and these are likely to cover other elements of performance, such as output quantity and quality, effectiveness and probity. Thus 'more PIs' implies extra information on all of these aspects of organizational performance. In addition, public choice theory highlights the role of consumer choice between providers. Such information should, therefore, be made available on a comparative basis. Furthermore, consumers and the political masters of public bureaucracies need to be able to see whether service standards are rising or falling over time, so historical comparisons are important.

In sum, a public management reform can be judged as producing more performance information if the matrix shown in Figure 3.2 becomes more complete. The higher the number of PIs in each of these boxes, the greater the consistency between a reform and public choice prescriptions. However, ticks in all of these boxes might only reflect the policy as adopted. For the policy in action to reflect public choice theory at least three further conditions must also be met. First, local organizations must comply with the requirement to collect and disseminate the PIs. Second, they must produce *accurate* PIs: performance can hardly be expected to improve if false or distorted data are provided to consumers. However, public choice arguments imply that precisely this perverse outcome will occur, because bureaucrats will seek to present a rosy picture of their achievements. And third, assuming that PIs are roughly accurate, they must actually be used by the public to make decisions on exit or voice. Again, there is little reason to expect

Number of PIs that show:

Dimensions of organizations and achievements	Current performance	Past performance	Performance of other organizations
Expenditure			
Outputs			
Outcomes			
Efficiency			
Cost-effectiveness			
Probity			

Figure 3.2 Matrix for assessing the quantity and quality of performance information

efficiency, responsiveness or equity to change if PIs are simply ignored by their intended beneficiaries.

Smaller organizations

Size is widely regarded as an important aspect of organizational structure, not only by public choice theorists but also by researchers working with other perspectives on organizational behaviour and management (Dawson 1996; Hall 1996). Policy-makers, too, seem to be convinced that size matters: many reform programmes have sought to create larger or smaller organizations. Perhaps this is because size is one of the few variables that can be manipulated directly by reformers. Whereas changes in organizational processes and managerial attitudes may occur slowly and be resisted, changes in size can be mandated and implemented quickly. For example, the size of central government departments is frequently altered immediately after a general election or Cabinet reshuffle in the UK.

During the 1960s and 1970s the idea that 'big is beautiful' held sway. In central government, separate administrative units were merged into giant departments such as the Department of Health and Social Security (DHSS) and the Department of the Environment (Pollitt 1984). In local government, reorganizations in London in 1965 and the rest of the UK in the 1970s created some of the largest local councils in the world (see Norton 1994). These reforms cut the number of separate local authorities by 69 per cent in England, 73 per cent in Wales, 80 per cent in Scotland and 64 per cent in Northern Ireland (Boyne 1996b).

The fashion for big bureaucracies drew upon ideas concerning economies of scale and service co-ordination. Large units were expected to provide services more efficiently because the employment of specialist staff and equipment would be more feasible at higher levels of output. Also, bigger organizations would find it easier to distribute services across different client groups and thereby ensure reliability and equity of provision. In local government, in particular, it was also expected that larger authorities would attract politicians and officials of higher calibre (see Dearlove 1979). Big organizations were viewed as consistent with policies that stressed planning rather than markets, co-ordination rather than competition, and professional service in the public interest rather than bureaucratic manoeuvring for private gain.

By contrast, in the 1980s and 1990s one of the main thrusts behind Conservative policies towards the public sector was 'an antipathy to large bureaucracies and the structured planning of services' (Taylor-Gooby and Lawson 1993: 1). Many parts of central government departments were divided into 'Next Steps' agencies. As Gray and Jenkins (1993: 16) argue,

> a fundamental tenet of the Next Steps philosophy . . . is that agencies will be better able to serve their clients or customers. This assumption is based on the argument that smaller, more clearly identifiable organizational units will attract a more motivated and committed staff who will take a greater interest in the recipients of their services.

There has also been a move against large organizations in local government. The biggest local authorities in England, the Greater London Council and the six metropolitan counties, were abolished in 1986 and many of their powers transferred to smaller councils. Similarly, most of the large Scottish regional councils and Welsh county councils were abolished in 1996 and replaced by almost three times as many 'unitary' authorities (Boyne 1997b). Parallel reforms in rural England led to the transfer of the powers of large county councils to smaller unitary councils (Boyne and Cole 1996).

There are specific public choice arguments in favour of small local government units. Tiebout (1956) argues that a highly fragmented local government system provides a 'market-type' solution to the problem of matching local services and taxes to local preferences. A fragmented structure provides households and businesses with information on the performance of neighbouring councils, thereby increasing the competitive pressure on decision-makers. In order to attract and retain mobile residents, small units of local government must ensure value for money in service provision, otherwise their customers will vote with their feet. By contrast, if a single local council covers a large geographical area, policy-makers need have little fear that residents will relocate in response to poor performance. Niskanen (1971: 155) also argues that a highly fragmented local government system can contain or even eliminate the monopoly power of service providers:

> Competition among local governments . . . assures that the combination of services will be responsive to the preferences of residents and that the services will be supplied at near the minimum cost, regardless of the political structure of the local government and even, as is usually the case, if the services are supplied by each local government through monopoly bureaus.

Some limited defence of the benefits of large organizations in the face of this public choice onslaught has been provided. For example, in an admitted 'polemic' in favour of bureaucracy, Goodsell (1994: 150) claims that when public sector organizations grow 'they do not necessarily outpace the tasks they are assigned, and they do not necessarily deteriorate in quality'. Also, Rhodes (1994: 147) is critical of the recent disaggregation of the structure of the public sector: 'Fragmentation leads to functional and jurisdictional overlap, otherwise known as duplication and waste'. Where Rhodes sees co-ordination, public choice theorists see collusion; and where he sees duplication, they see competition.

In order to determine whether a reform is in the direction favoured by public choice arguments, it is necessary to measure organizational size. Three main indicators of the size of public bureaucracies have conventionally been used. First, debates on structure of local government have focused on *population* size. A change in the average number of inhabitants of local jurisdictions is an inescapable consequence of a reform that raises or cuts the number of authorities. However, it is doubtful whether this is a good measure of the size of local organizations themselves. Population is effectively a reflection of the size of the market for a service, rather than the size of the organization that provides the service. Furthermore, even when the total population served by a council or health authority changes, the size of the 'front-line' delivery agencies (schools, hospitals) may remain the same (Boyne 1995).

A second and more direct approach to establishing whether organizations have grown or shrunk is to focus on service *inputs* (e.g. expenditure, staffing). These measures closely reflect public choice arguments that public bureaucracies overspend and are over-staffed, and should therefore be reorganized into smaller units. They are, therefore, especially relevant to an analysis of the extent of public choice reforms.

The third measure of size is the level of *output* of an organization (Boyne 1996a). This is closely linked to arguments concerning economies and diseconomies of scale. Economic theory suggests that bigger organizations are more efficient because they can spread their fixed costs (e.g.

equipment, specialized staff) across higher and higher levels of production. Public choice theorists either ignore this argument or claim that government bureaucracies are so big that diseconomies of scale have set in. If variables such as efficiency are related to the level of service production, then it is important to measure the size of organizations though not only their inputs but also their outputs (e.g. number of hospital operations, quantity of houses built, number of hours of teaching in schools). It has also been suggested that size should be measured through service outcomes or effectiveness (Milleti *et al.* 1980). However, this confuses the concepts of organizational size and organizational achievements. We therefore reject this approach.

All of these arguments on size assume that the *disaggregation* of large organizations will lead to better performance, partly because the smaller units will compete with each other for resources and rewards. However, disaggregation in itself is insufficient to produce this outcome. A reform may create more agencies that are responsible for providing services, but fail to liberate them to respond to public preferences. Thus, from a public choice perspective disaggregation must be accompanied by *decentralization* of power in order to achieve more efficiency and responsiveness (Boyne 1998a). In other words, for disaggregation to work, power must be spread out from central government to local agencies (Pollitt *et al.* 1998). If small organizations are forced to follow the same strategies as their large predecessors, there is little reason to expect a change in performance. There may appear to be an inconsistency here: public choice theorists wish to reduce the power of bureaucrats, but are proposing a reform that gives them more autonomy. However, this is simply resolved: the purpose of decentralization is to allow smaller organizations to compete more effectively. The intention is to constrain local bureaucrats to respond to market pressures, rather than giving them autonomy to pursue their own interests. Thus it should be consumers rather than producers who are empowered by this form of decentralization.

In sum, in order to judge whether a reform is consistent with public choice arguments on organizational size it is first necessary to gauge whether the average level of service inputs and outputs has declined. Following this, it is also important to assess whether the new smaller organizations are more or less autonomous than the big bureaucracies that they replaced. For example, do they have the power to set budgets, hire and fire staff, and select the range of services that they wish to offer? Only if disaggregation is accompanied by decentralization can a reform be considered consistent with public choice prescriptions.

Summary

A crucial step in a theory-driven evaluation is to establish whether reform has occurred in the 'desired' direction. In the case of public choice theory this means measuring whether market structures and the behaviour of consumers and producers became more competitive, whether more indicators of relevant dimensions of organizational performance were not only made available but also used by managers and consumers, and whether service delivery organizations became smaller and more autonomous. If all of these conditions are in place, then a 'full' public choice reform programme has been adopted, and a substantial improvement in performance would be predicted by its supporters. We now turn to consider the problems of establishing a clear link between such reforms and subsequent changes in efficiency, responsiveness and equity.

Does reform matter? Problems of measuring impact

The following basic information is required in order to assess the impact of a public choice reform:

(a) measures of efficiency, responsiveness and equity, both before and after the introduction of a reform;
(b) measures of competition, performance indicators and organizational size, both before and after a reform;
(c) evidence on the empirical relationship between movements in the reform variables and movements in the performance variables.

Such information would allow the direction of changes in organizational performance and public management reforms to be checked against each other. Clearly, from a public choice perspective, it is expected that the greater the extent of the three reforms the greater the improvement in performance. In other words, public choice theory predicts that reform and service standards are positively correlated.

This hypothetical relationship is illustrated in Figure 3.3(a). The vertical axis shows performance, and the horizontal axis measures time. Around half-way through the time period (say, 20 years), a reform is introduced. This is shown by a dotted circle to illustrate that the *exact* time when a new regime comes into force may be unclear (e.g. because of an implementation delay between the policy as adopted and the policy in action). The solid line shows the trend in performance both before and after reform, and the dotted vertical line shows the point at which reform begins to 'bite'. In this example, reform has the predicted effect: performance shifts sharply upwards when the new arrangements for service delivery are in place.

This is, of course, only one possible outcome. Figure 3.3(b) also shows an improvement in performance, but only after a substantial delay. Even after the policy in action has changed, it may take time to work. For example, efficiency may initially dip because of the disruption caused by shifting from one regime to another. There is little prior theory or evidence

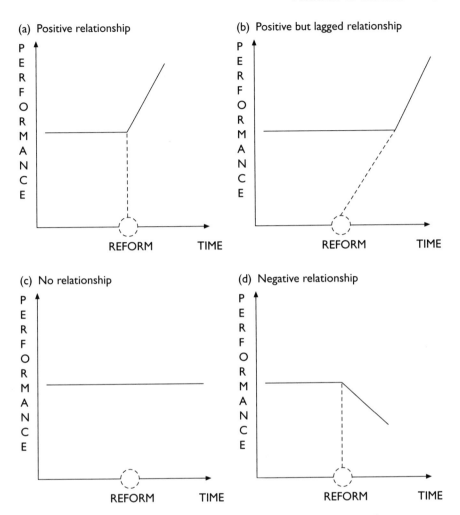

Figure 3.3 Potential relationships between reform and organizational performance

to guide the analysis of such 'lagged effects' of public management reforms. This problem highlights the importance of having data on organizational performance that covers a long time period. Otherwise, the potentially positive consequences of a reform may be missed by an evaluation that ends prematurely. Figures 3.3(c) and 3.3(d) show outcomes that are inconsistent with public choice theory. In the former case, performance turns neither up nor down after reform is introduced (and thus no 'bite point' is included in the diagram). In the latter case, performance deteriorates in the post-reform period. This pattern flatly contradicts public choice theory, but is exactly what its critics argue has happened to service equity as a result of more competition, more performance indicators and smaller organisational size.

Figure 3.3 paints a deceptively clear picture of the potential consequences of reform. It implies that the task of evaluation simply involves tracking the explanatory variable (reform) and the dependent variable (performance) over a suitable time period. Determining the result is then much like reading a thermometer to see if the condition of the patient has improved or worsened. In the remainder of this chapter we first discuss two types of problems that greatly complicate this apparently simple procedure: the absence of data on changes in policies and performance; and the presence of other variables, in addition to public management reforms, that influence performance. We then proceed to examine the extent to which different evaluative methods can alleviate these problems.

Absence of data

Missing data

Even if reforms and their hypothetical consequences can be defined clearly, the data to measure them may be unavailable. Six concepts must be operationalized for a comprehensive assessment of the impact of public choice reforms: competition; performance indicators; organizational size; efficiency; responsiveness; and equity. Furthermore, as discussed earlier in this chapter, each of these concepts consists of a number of sub-dimensions (e.g. efficiency comprises the cost, quantity and quality of services). Gaps in the data set will impair an evaluation of the impact of reform, and may seriously constrain the conclusions that can be drawn on the validity of public choice propositions.

Missing the target

Although data may be available for all of the core concepts, the information collected by government agencies or constructed by academic researchers may be inaccurate. In other words, the data may miss part or all of the conceptual target that they were intended to hit. For example, measures of reform may be derived from descriptions of policies as adopted but not policies in action; or measures of competition may be based on the structure of a market but omit behaviour in the market. Detailed issues concerning the operationalization of the six key public choice concepts will be discussed in later chapters in the specific context of health, housing and education reforms. The important point to note here is that the less accurate the data, the greater the risk involved in trusting the evidence in an evaluative study. Strong conclusions cannot be based on weak data.

Consequences of reform

Reform	Efficiency	Responsiveness	Equity
Competition			
Performance indicators			
Organizational size			

Figure 3.4 Matrix of evidence on the connections between reforms and their consequences

Missing connections

Even if data are complete and accurate, they may not have been brought together in a way that allows public choice propositions to be tested. For example, data on equity may be available in one academic study, and data on competition may exist in another. Furthermore, the two data sets may refer to different time periods, services or organizations. In order to assess the effects of public management reforms, it is necessary for such data sets to be *connected* and for the relevant variables to be correlated with each other. Only then will it be possible to establish whether the links predicted by public choice (or any other) theory are actually present. The full set of connections for a comprehensive assessment of public management reforms is shown in Figure 3.4. Any empty cells in this matrix represent crucial gaps in the body of evidence.

Missing organizations

The purpose of a theory-driven evaluation of public management reforms is to establish the *general validity* of a set of propositions concerning service design and delivery. Does competition generate more efficiency in schools? Do more performance indicators lead to greater customer responsiveness by hospitals? Is smaller organizational size associated with less equitable behaviour by public landlords? Empirical studies will inevitably be restricted to a particular set of organizations at a particular time, and a given national and policy context. Nevertheless, answers to such questions should have a reasonable chance of being valid for other schools, other hospitals, and other providers of public rented housing operating within the same broad conditions. This is essentially an issue about 'external validity' which refers to whether the results obtained in a study can be generalized to other organizations (Rossi and Freeman 1996). The bigger and more representative the sample, the greater the confidence that general conclusions can be drawn from the evidence. At the other end of the scale of plausibility and reliability is evidence from a case study of one organization, which may be wildly unrepresentative of other service providers. This is not to dismiss such evidence completely. Results from a set of case studies that point broadly in the same direction may offer a convincing narrative about the impact of reform. Yet, a handful of case studies is no substitute for a large and representative sample of organizations that have been subject to public management reforms (Boyne 2001). Most importantly, qualitative case studies cannot provide precise or rigorous estimates of the net effect of reform by setting aside other influences on performance. As Pollitt (1995: 140) argues, 'case studies alone will not provide a synoptic picture of the extent of reform and neither are they a particularly convincing way of measuring the transitional and continuing costs and benefits of reform'.

Presence of other variables

For the purposes of the discussion in this section we assume that the four data problems listed above have all been solved. It is also assumed that sufficient data points are available before and after reform to prevent erroneous inferences that may arise because of statistical artefacts in the data (e.g. problems of maturation and regression to the mean – see Cook and Campbell 1979). The major remaining difficulty in conducting an evaluation is to separate the impact of reform from other potential influences on efficiency, responsiveness and equity. If the impact of other variables is not considered then the consequences of reform may be underestimated or overestimated. In other words the 'gross' impact of reform must be distinguished from its 'net' impact (Rossi and Freeman 1996). For example, performance may have deteriorated over time, but still be higher than it would otherwise have been in the absence of extra competition. In this case, even though the superficial evidence suggests that the impact of reform has been negative, its net impact is actually positive. In Figure 3.5(a) the extent of the positive contribution to performance is shown by the gap between the gross and net effects. Similarly, performance may be substantially higher after a reform, but simply continue on an upward trajectory that was present even before the arrangements for service provision were altered. In this case, even though the performance trend is consistent with a positive effect of reform, its actual effect may be neutral (see Figure 3.5(b)). Even worse, the net effect may be negative because performance would have improved further in the absence of reform (see Figure 3.5(c)).

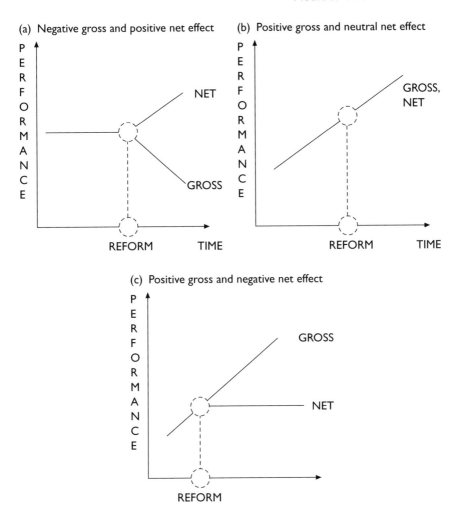

Figure 3.5 Gross and net effects of reform

Which other variables should be taken into account in separating the gross and net influences of reform on organizational performance? In principle, the number of other influences on performance is huge, if not infinite. Each of these potential influences is a 'rival hypothesis' that may explain why performance has changed, and render the argument that reform has succeeded or failed invalid. However, as Campbell (1969: 411) argues, 'the mere possibility of some alternative explanation is not enough – it is only the *plausible* rival hypotheses that are invalidating' (emphasis in original). Therefore, we now proceed to identify two other categories of variable that are most likely to cloud the relationship between public choice reforms and their anticipated consequences.

Socio-economic context

A reform may appear to succeed or fail because changes in the external environment of the organizations that provide services have occurred. These could include:

(a) changes in economic prosperity – for example, health outcomes may become more positive because incomes have risen, and the educational achievements of school pupils may improve because standards of nutrition are better. More direct movements in the economic fortunes of organizations may also occur. For example, the introduction of compulsory competitive tendering in UK local government in the 1980s coincided with a period of fiscal stress. Thus local authority services may have become more efficient because of financial constraints rather than competitive pressures (Boyne 1998a).

(b) cultural change – public demands concerning service standards may shift during a period of reform. Indeed, the announcement of reform may in itself raise expectations concerning the performance of public organizations. Also, attitudes towards public services may be conditioned by customers' experience of improvements in product quality in the private sector. Such cultural changes may make it more difficult to achieve high responsiveness in the public sector, and thereby cloud any positive impact of public management reforms.

(c) technological advances – this type of change in the socio-economic context may lead to higher efficiency and responsiveness in public services, regardless of the effect of reform on the unit cost of service provision. For example, new drugs could improve the quality of health care, the introduction of computers could lead to better educational outcomes, and more sophisticated materials and methods of building may result in better housing.

Other policy changes

Public choice reforms were not introduced into a political system where everything else was standing still. Other policies were also changing at the same time. As Hogwood and Gunn (1984: 226) argue, 'big problems tend to have a lot of solutions thrown at them'. Most importantly, a whole 'new public management' reform programme was set in motion in the 1980s and 1990s, some of which was inspired by ideas that were not directly derived from public choice theory. For example, officials in public organizations were encouraged to emulate the supposedly successful management techniques of their private sector counterparts (Boyne 2002). Any apparent changes in performance may be attributable to this wider reform agenda. This is an especially tricky problem because a variety of new policies were sometimes introduced either simultaneously or in quick succession. Such 'rapid fire reform' is likely to blur the effects of any single initiative. Indeed, public choice reforms themselves pose this problem because they consist of the three closely linked elements of competition, performance indicators and organizational size. Thus it may be difficult to disentangle the separate effects of each element, let alone to isolate their collective impact from that of other policy changes.

Methods of evaluation: experiments and quasi-experiments

An evaluation methodology should strive to eliminate contaminating influences from the relationship between reform and its predicted consequences. Rossi and Freeman (1996: 230) argue that 'the problem of establishing a programme's impact is identical to the problem of establishing that the programme is a cause of some specified effect'. They also recognize that causality cannot be established with certainty, but only with varying degrees of plausibility. The extent of this plausibility depends partly on the way that a reform is designed, and partly on the way that evidence is gathered and analysed. In this section we examine two types of reform and the methodologies that can be used to evaluate them.

Reforms as experiments

If a reform were purely experimental it would involve the following procedures:

(a) random assignment of the organizations to be reformed to a 'control group' and 'treatment' group;
(b) introduction of the reform only in the treatment group;
(c) no other post-reform differences between the control and treatment groups;
(d) comparison, after a suitable period, of performance in the treatment and control groups.

This type of reform would avoid many of the evaluative problems discussed above because all extraneous factors are effectively held constant through the random assignment of organizations to the two groups. They are identical in the pre-reform period, and new arrangements for service provision are the only significant difference between them in the post-reform period. It can, therefore, be concluded with some safety that any improvement or deterioration in performance is attributable to reform.

In practice, reforms are never truly experimental for political as much as technical reasons (Campbell 1969). For example, if a government really had discovered a means to improve public sector efficiency then it would be squandering votes by withholding this from a control group of organizations. Randomized experimental reforms also pose technical problems: it may be impossible to construct two sub-samples of organizations that are 'alike in all relevant respects'. Indeed, there may be little theory or evidence to identify such 'relevant respects' in the first place.

A loose approximation to an experimental reform is the 'piloting' of an initiative on a subset of organizations before it is introduced across the board. Labour governments in the UK since 1997 have been fond of such piloting because it fits in with their proclaimed commitment to pragmatism and evidence-based policy-making. A major example of this approach was the 'Best Value' pilot programme in England from 1998 to 2000. This was not, however, an experiment. The pilots were largely self-selecting and were not a random sample of local authorities. Moreover, non-pilots quickly began to adopt Best Value processes in anticipation that legislation would follow (which it did, long before results from the non-experimental pilots were known – see Boyne 1999).

Although reforms are not like laboratory tests, the experimental method remains an important baseline for establishing cause and effect. Theory-based evaluations, as much as traditional 'black box' evaluations, need to tease out the separate impact of reform. The greater the distance from this baseline, the deeper the mud in which evidence of success or failure is embedded.

Reforms as quasi-experiments

Almost all public management reforms are effectively quasi-experiments because there is no 'control group' except organizations themselves at previous points in time. For example, in the UK in the 1980s, national legislation sought to apply competition to all hospitals, and performance indicators to all schools and housing authorities. However, even when the policy as adopted is uniform across all organizations, the policy in action is likely to vary widely. In other words, *implementation failure facilitates evaluation*. Problems of implementation introduce unintended variations into the extent of reform, which can then be tested against variations in organizational performance. If public choice theory is correct, then those organizations that most closely follow its prescriptions should show the biggest net gains in performance. By contrast, organizations that have the biggest implementation gaps may stand still or deteriorate.

A variety of methods can shed light on whether such quasi-experimental reforms have been successful. They are, in ascending order of sophistication and rigour:

1 A comparison of performance *levels* after reform in 'strong' and 'weak' implementation groups. This method is problematic because it fails to control for the pre-reform position of organizations. It is possible that high performers are most likely to adopt new arrangements for service

delivery. Thus the pattern of cause and effect may actually be the opposite of that predicted by public choice theory: high performance leads to the implementation of reform, rather than vice versa.

2   A comparison of performance *changes* after reform in strong and weak implementation groups. This alleviates the difficulties associated with the previous method, because the measurement of reform is temporally as well as logically prior to the measurement of performance. It is, therefore, possible to conclude with greater confidence that the sequence of cause and effect runs from reform to performance. However, the evidence would still be clouded by a failure to take account of the performance trajectory prior to reform.

3   A comparison of performance *changes, before and after reform,* in strong and weak implementation groups. This method solves the 'trajectory' problem in the previous method. It also effectively combines the strengths of longitudinal (across time) and cross-sectional (between organizations) methods of evaluation (Rossi and Freeman 1996). Furthermore, it is possible to introduce a variety of statistical controls for socio-economic circumstances and policy context, so as to separate the impact of reform from other variables (Hutton and Smith 2000).

In sum, evaluation methods must usually be quasi-experimental because this is the form taken by new arrangements for public service provision. Evidence on the impact of public management reforms is more credible when it is based on a large sample of organizations, compares performance before and after reform, and takes account of the influence of other socio-economic and policy variables. Reforms do not enter a world in which 'all other things are equal'. Nevertheless, it is possible through quasi-experimental methods to simulate such a world, not through the *random assignment of organizations* but through the *systematic analysis of data* on reforms and their consequences. Evaluations which follow this approach can provide compelling evidence on whether public management reforms have worked. Whether such evidence exists in practice will be explored in Chapters 4–6.

Conclusion

In this chapter we have set out principles for the evaluation of public management reforms, and begun to explore some of the problems of applying these principles. It should already be clear that definitive judgements on efficiency, responsiveness and equity are likely to be very difficult. Yet it must also be emphasized that the success or failure of reforms cannot be assessed unless conceptual criteria and empirical evidence are in place. Debates on the impact of reforms in the absence of such criteria and evidence are simply intellectual tennis without a net. Our task in subsequent chapters is to make the best of a bad job, by judging the results of matches that have been played with nets that are frequently too low and full of holes.

Each of the chapters on public management reforms in health, housing and education tackles the following questions in the same sequence. First, have the reforms advocated by public choice theorists actually occurred – were the relevant policies adopted, and were they implemented as intended? Second, what evidence is there that efficiency, responsiveness and equity are different in the periods before and after reform? Third, to what extent are the observed outcomes attributable to the reforms inspired by public choice theory? And finally, in the light of the answers to the first three questions, has the impact of public choice reforms been positive or negative?

four

Health care reforms

Introduction

The public choice means of competition, performance information and organizational size, the 'internal' ends of efficiency and responsiveness and the 'external' end of equity that were discussed in Chapter 1 feature significantly in recent health policy. In general terms, both Conservative and New Labour governments have favoured performance information, efficiency and responsiveness. The Conservatives emphasized competition. Although against competition, New Labour stresses incentives and consumerism. It also claims that, in contrast to the Conservatives, it stresses an equitable National Health Service. However, there has been little *explicit* discussion of public choice theory in the literature on the NHS reforms. For example, there is no entry for it in the index to West (1997); Paton (1998); Ranade (1998); Ham (1999a); P. Smith (2000) and Klein (2001). The exception is the index of Scarpaci (1989), which lists a relative torrent of three pages that contain the term 'public choice theory'. Nevertheless, Dowling (2000: 15) claims that 'in many ways the reforms have their origin in public choice theory'.

Moreover, many of the criteria that are used to examine health care are similar to our public choice theory triad. Equity has long been a major criterion of evaluation for the NHS (Powell 1997). More recently, the quasi-market approach has outlined a set of criteria such as efficiency, equity, quality, choice, responsiveness and accountability (Le Grand and Bartlett 1993; Robinson and Le Grand 1993; Le Grand *et al.* 1998). Similarly, Ham and Woolley (1996) examine equity, efficiency and responsiveness. New (1999) discusses the 'NHS values' of health, universality, equity, choice (including responsiveness), democracy, respect for human dignity, public service, and efficiency. Scott (2001) examines efficiency, cost-containment, equity and choice. More importantly, Harrison and Dixon (2000: 212) point out that recent editions of the NHS Executive's annual *Priorities and Planning Guidance* set out three broad criteria of equity, efficiency and responsiveness. However, as they suggest, there is not only a lack of more precise definitions in these broad 'first-order' principles but also disagreement about the mechanisms to achieve them and the trade-offs between them (see Chapter 2; cf. New 1999; Scott 2001). These criteria are broadly in line with those used in other countries (Saltman and Figueras 1997; World Health Organization 2000).

This chapter analyses the impact of the NHS reforms of the Conservative government of 1979–97 and the New Labour government from 1997 to date. More specifically, it focuses largely on reforms in England, and discusses the period to the end of the first term of the Labour government in May 2001. It examines the extent to which the means of competition, performance information and organizational size are associated with ends of efficiency, responsiveness and equity. The next section gives a brief and selective history of recent NHS reforms, with particular stress on the ends and means highlighted above. This is followed by a closer examination of the extent to which the means of greater competition, more performance information and smaller organizational units occurred. The changes in the ends of the 'internal' criteria of efficiency and responsiveness and the 'external' criterion of equity (see Chapter 2) are then analysed. The next section draws these discussions together, discussing the impact that public choice prescriptions had on our selected ends.

Health reforms and public choice theory

This section gives a brief overview of the main policies that are related to public choice theory. It is therefore a selective history, emphasizing developments that are relevant to the mechanisms of competition, performance information and organizational size, and objectives of efficiency, responsiveness and equity. More detailed treatments of these themes will be given in the relevant sections below. Wider accounts of the NHS are available in sources such as Powell (1997, 1999, 2000); West (1997); Ham (1999a, 1999b); Griffith (2000); Iliffe and Munro (2000); P. Smith (2000) and Klein (2001).

The 1979 Conservative manifesto stated: 'We will simplify and decentralise the service and cut back bureaucracy'. It also promised to end 'Labour's vendetta against the private health sector'. Decisions should be taken 'as near to the point of delivery of services as is possible'. The decentralization promise was delivered in the 1980 Health Act that created smaller Health Authorities (HAs). Private medicine was promoted, and lubricated with tax relief. Efficiency rose to the top of the NHS agenda in the 1980s (Powell 1997; Klein 2001). The search for efficiency was also associated with the appointment of Sir Derek Rayner from Marks & Spencer as the Prime Minister's 'efficiency adviser'. He introduced 'Rayner scrutinies' in areas such as the ambulance service (Harrison *et al.* 1990: 131–2). District Health Authorities (DHAs) were required to find annual 'efficiency savings' from 1984.

Roy Griffiths, the Managing Director of Sainsbury's, was invited to cast his business eye over the NHS. He produced a 25-page letter to the Secretary of State that produced 'the most important single change to the NHS since 1948' (Timmins 1996: 409). He contrasted the NHS with private business and found it wanting. 'Businessmen have a keen sense of how well they are looking after their customers. Whether the NHS is meeting the needs of the patient, and the community, and can prove that it is doing so, is open to question' (DHSS 1983b: 10). The solution was to introduce general managers, the equivalent of the private sector's managing director, at all levels of the NHS. This dovetailed with the increasing emphasis on performance measurement. Griffiths recognized that general managers needed information on how well their organization was performing, and this was to be found in the newly introduced package of performance indicators (PIs). Greater competition was introduced for general practice, optical and dental services.

However, for most commentators all these measures are largely a prelude to the main feature of the introduction of internal or quasi-markets, which Klein (2001: Ch. 6) terms the 'politics of the big bang'. Holliday (1995: 59) argues that

> where the Griffiths reforms had sought to turn the NHS into an efficient but still unified business, the internal market reforms seek to split the NHS into efficient and competitive units. Efficiency thus remains a central objective, but it will now be generated not by an efficient monolith, but by the most efficient units in an internal market.

Two Department of Health (DH) White Papers, *Working for Patients* (DH 1989a) and *Caring for People* (DH 1989b), on acute health care and social care respectively, formed the basis of the National Health and Community Care Act of 1990, which was implemented in 1991. The main change was to create an internal or quasi market by separating the NHS into 'purchasers' and 'providers' (Le Grand and Bartlett 1993).

The Labour manifesto of 1997 contained a commitment to 'abolish the internal market'. The White Paper, *The New NHS* (DH 1997: 2) claimed that this represented a turning point for the NHS, replacing the internal market with integrated care, combining efficiency and quality with a belief in fairness and partnership. However, there would be no return to old centralized command and control, nor to the divisive internal market of the 1990s. The document proposeed a 'third way', a 'new model for a new century' that goes with the grain of staff efforts moving from outright competition towards a more collaborative approach. It outlined six key principles: a national service, but with local responsibility; partnership; efficiency; excellence; and rebuilding public confidence. The approach stressed evolution rather than revolution, building on what has worked, but discarding what has failed. It introduced a series of new national initiatives. The National Institute for Clinical Excellence (NICE) sets standards and will slowly move towards a national menu of NHS treatments. National service frameworks set out good practice in particular areas and for particular groups. The Commission for Health Improvement (CHI) is regarded as an inspectorate that enforces national standards. However, in addition to these proposals for a 'one-nation NHS', it is also argued that local doctors and nurses who best understand patients' needs will shape local services – precisely the argument that justified general practitioner fundholding (GPFH). The new local commissioning agencies are the new primary care groups (PCGs) covering an average of about 100,000 population that could evolve over time into free-standing primary care trusts (PCTs). This essentially universalized GPFH, with the hope that the larger PCGs/PCTs would produce the benefits of GPFH without its disadvantages.

The *NHS Plan* (DH 2000) claims – as did the *Working for Patients* (DH 1989a) – to be the most fundamental and far-reaching reform of the NHS since 1948. It promises more resources, but expects reform in return. The main problem is that the NHS is a '1940s system operating in a 21st century world' (DH 2000: 26). The document outlines a series of underlying problems: a lack of national standards; demarcations between staff; a lack of clear incentives; barriers between services; a lack of support and intervention; over-centralization; and disempowered patients. The Plan represents a 'fundamental package of reforms to address the systematic weaknesses inherent in the NHS since its creation in 1948'. It emphasizes two major themes of consumerism and devolution. Finally, the document proposes for the first time national targets for reducing health inequalities. While the 1997 White Paper is inconsistent with public choice theory in its rejection of competition, there are some signs of its revival in the more recent document, with its stress on incentives for producers, devolution for commissioners and producers and empowerment of consumers.

Table 4.1 examines reforms in terms of policy documents rather than by Acts of legislation as this is the more usual approach in accounts of health policy. It is difficult to summarize the often twisting directions of reforms over more than two decades in a simplistic form. However, in very broad terms, of the 14 policy reforms, seven promoted greater competition, nine provided more performance information and six were associated with smaller organizational units. Only GPFH is consistent with all three

Table 4.1 Health reform and public choice theory

Policy (Act or key document)	Key reforms	More competition?	More information?	Smaller organizations?
Health Act 1980	Reorganization	No	No	Yes
Compulsory Competitive Tendering Circular (DHSS 1983a)	CCT in hotel services	Yes	Partial	Yes
Griffiths Report (DHSS 1983b)	General management	No	Yes	Yes
Promoting Better Health (DH 1987)	General practice,	Yes	Yes	No
	optical services,	Yes	Yes	No
	dental services	Yes	Yes	No
Working for Patients (DH 1989a)	Providers: hospitals	Yes	Yes	No
	Purchasers	Yes	Partial	No
Health Act 1990	GPFH	Yes	Yes	Yes
Patient's Charter (DH 1991)	Consumer standards and rights	Partial	Yes	No
The New NHS (DH 1997)	Providers: hospitals	No	Partial	No
Health Act 1999	PCG/PCTs	No	No	Yes (from HAs)/No (from GPFH)
The NHS Plan (DH 2000)	Providers: hospitals	Partial	Yes	No
	PCG/PCTs	No	Yes	Yes

prescriptions, while a further seven are associated with two. The 1997 general election provides a clear watershed in that Conservative reforms before this date are more associated with public choice prescriptions than Labour reforms after it. Some of New Labour's early reforms are negatively associated with public choice theory in that they advocate less competition and larger organizational units. However, there are some indications that public choice prescriptions may be more important in New Labour's second term.

The extent of public management reforms

As we saw above, there was certainly much activity on the policy front that was linked to the proclaimed ends of efficiency, responsiveness and equity and the means of competition, performance information and organizational size. While few politicians may be familiar with public choice theory, many of its main elements were present in policy discourse. However, there are two main problems to consider. First, the 'implementation gap' (Marsh and Rhodes 1992) is perhaps more marked in the case of health care than for the other policy sectors of education and housing. This is because the main 'street level bureaucrats' (Lipsky 1980) have considerable degrees of professional power (Wilding 1982), with doctors being described as 'dominant interests' (Alford 1975). This may result in a wide gap between 'policy as adopted' and 'policy in action'. Second, a simple word count of terms such as 'efficiency' does not tell us how efficiency is to be achieved, or give an indication of any trade-offs between conflicting aims. In other words, it is necessary to examine the degree of fit between different ends, and between means and ends. This section examines in more detail the means of competition, performance information and organizational size. The following section examines changes in efficiency, responsiveness and equity from the perspectives of policy as adopted and policy in action.

More competition

The Conservatives stressed marketization inside and outside the NHS. The private sector was encouraged in word and deed. Tax relief on medical insurance schemes operated by employers was restored. The numbers of private hospitals, private beds and those with private health insurance increased. Inside the NHS the 'politics of value for money' led to an efficiency drive (Klein 2001: Ch. 5). In 1983 the government required DHAs to put their 'hotel services' – catering, cleaning and laundry – out to tender. This would force the NHS in-house staff to compete with the private sector. The contract would be given to the most efficient operator, offering the best service at the lowest price. At one level the impact was modest, with only 18 per cent of contracts in the first cycle going to private contractors. It is generally considered that the direct financial savings were similarly modest. For example, by 1986 annual savings had reached £86 million. Even this, claimed critics, was achieved only at the cost of lower quality. Similar moves to open up competition took place in optical and dental services. Instead of offering 'NHS frames' to patients with low incomes, they were given vouchers that enabled them to shop around for spectacles.

The themes of choice and competition were also present in the Government's Green and White Papers on primary health care (DH 1986, 1987). The aims included giving patients a wide range of choice; encouraging providers to be responsive to the needs of the public; and providing the taxpayer with value for money. The specific proposals aimed to create more competition in general practice. It was made easier for patients to change their general practitioner, with the hope that patients would keep doctors on their toes by voting with their feet. The share of GPs' income from capitation was increased. This meant that good doctors who attracted and retained more patients on their list would be rewarded with more income for their practices. Finally, more money was linked to greater activity, giving incentives for more night visits and immunizations.

In many ways, the above policies opened the curtain for the main act of the NHS quasi-market. The DHAs were the main purchasers and would buy health care on behalf of their resident population. Hospital and community units became providers, in the form of independent NHS trusts. The two sides were linked together by contracts. Purchasers would shop around in the NHS market in order to get the best deal. For example, they might purchase hip joint operations from one hospital, but cataract operations from another. The 'wild card' of the reforms was the GPFH practices. Initially practices with more than 11,000 patients (subsequently reduced to 9000 and later 7000) could elect to hold their own budgets, purchasing a limited range of services from NHS trusts (Glennerster et al. 1994). In effect, these 'mini-purchasers' bought retail while the DHAs purchased wholesale. A number of other purchasing models below the DHA level such as locality purchasing, multifunds, community fundholding and total purchasing developed (Le Grand et al. 1998; Mays and Dixon 1998; Mays et al. 2001).

Many accounts give major importance to the moves from hierarchy to markets in health care. However, this is too simplistic, as some forms of competition existed before 1991 and many elements of hierarchy lingered after 1991. At best, moves may be seen as being from quasi-hierarchies to quasi-markets (Exworthy et al. 1999). There was always some limited competition between GPs as they were paid on capitation or list size. In secondary care, hospital consultants competed for scarce resources (Klein 2001). In one sense, the private sector 'competed' with the NHS. However, while doctors gained in the form of private fees, and the NHS gained in the form of reduced workload, the major losers were the patients who 'paid twice' (in taxes and private fees) (Calnan et al. 1993; Yates 1995). Moreover, in contrast to some early predictions, many later accounts stress the limited degree of competition that took place (Boyne 1998b; Klein 1998, 2001; Paton 1998, 1999, 2002; Le Grand 1999; Powell 1999, 2000). The market wolf tended to wear sheep's clothing. There was an implementation gap between policy as adopted and policy in action for three main reasons.

First, the Conservatives' stress on market competition declined over time. There was a rapid retreat from market language, and the Conservative government encouraged purchasers to develop longer-term relationships.

'Competition' became 'contestability'; 'purchasing' became 'commissioning' (Klein 1998: 2001). The verdict of Alain Enthoven (1999) – who was often credited or blamed for suggesting the internal market in the 1980s – was that on a scale of 0 to 10, where 0 is a totally centrally planned and managed system and 10 is the relatively free American economy, the internal market scored somewhere between 2 and 3 for a year or so, and then fell back.

Second, the structure or preconditions for a market were not clearly in place. The standard quasi-market accounts (Le Grand and Bartlett 1993; Robinson and Le Grand 1993; Bartlett *et al.* 1998) examine 'indirect evidence' of whether the structural conditions that quasi-markets have to meet if they are to achieve certain goals are present. The most important relate to market structure, information, and transaction costs. Unlike the USA (see Arnould *et al.* 1993), few studies have examined market structure in terms of its degree of potential competitiveness on both the purchaser and provider side. Appleby *et al.* (1993) used the Hirschman–Herfindahl index derived from industrial economics to examine the degree of potential competition between hospitals in the West Midlands. They found that there was a significant degree of monopoly or oligopoly power for about a quarter of the providers, covering nearly 40 per cent of patient episodes. In other words, in one region the majority of the hospitals had the *potential* for competition. There were differences between areas and between services. It is unclear whether GPs were willing to refer or patients were willing to travel to more distant facilities (Le Grand 1993: 254). While the potential for competition clearly existed in some large cities, notably London, where there were many possible competing suppliers within relatively short distances, many areas had *de facto* spatial monopolies. After all, in the previous 40 years the NHS had attempted to build up a network of district general hospitals to serve their local areas. Ironically, the 'excess' capacity in the London hospital service was addressed not through the market, but through the political planning process of the Tomlinson Inquiry (see Powell 1997). Moreover, while in principle, purchasers could contract with distant providers for certain elective services, this is not possible for 'core' services such as 'casualty' or accident and emergency (A&E) services. On the purchasing side, Le Grand (1993: 255) considers that some HAs are close to bilateral monopolies, with a single purchaser and a few large providers. The situation may be becoming even less competitive, with mergers between purchasing authorities being actively encouraged. 'Perhaps the best hope for a competitive market to emerge, particularly with respect to purchasing, lies with the GP fundholding scheme' (1993: 255). Information was seen as a major problem, in that accurate data about costs, prices, and quality was generally lacking. Analysing transaction costs is problematic, but there are some indications that districts may have the advantage over GP fundholders as purchasers, at least in terms of *ex ante* (agreement) costs but perhaps not in terms of *ex post* (monitoring) costs.

Third, market behaviour was limited for both producers and consumers. While the government could take the horses to the trough of competition, they did not force them to drink. It was clear that rather than money following the patients, in practice the patients followed the money, being referred to the hospitals where HA managers had placed their contracts. Unlike education (Chapter 6), individual consumers had very little chance to choose providers as contracts were drawn up by agents of the patients rather than patients themselves. Patients had more information (see below), but few mechanisms to use it: as Klein (2001: 179–81) puts it, the mimic market produced a mimic consumerism. In short, there was at best only a limited development of consumerism (North 1993; Shackley and Ryan 1994).

Le Grand *et al.* (1998: 130; cf. West 1997) consider that the market incentives were too weak and the constraints were too strong. However, GPFH had the strongest incentives and the weakest constraints. For example, there were some incentives for GPFH to make a financial surplus as, in contrast to trusts, they could invest any surplus income in their practice. The main financial incentive for trusts was to break even. Similarly, fund-holding practices were subject to fewer constraints. These 'retail' purchasers could threaten to change suppliers unless they received better service. For the 'wholesale' purchasers of HAs, this tended to be an empty threat. They could not flex their purchasing muscles because it was politically difficult to switch contracts from a local hospital as this might lead to closure. 'It is no coincidence that the area where it has been easiest to detect some significant changes is where the incentives were strongest and the constraints the weakest' (Le Grand *et al.* 1998: 131). Le Grand (1997, 1999) develops a more fundamental explanation for the failure of the internal market to have the impact its proponents hoped for. Those working in the NHS tended to prefer mutual trust rather than adversarial competition. They were 'knights' rather than 'knaves'. As such, financial incentives did not have the desired effect.

New Labour proposed keeping the purchaser–provider split, but abolishing the internal market. It claimed that its policies would 'go with the grain' of clinicians working in (or against?) the internal market, and promote cooperation rather than competition. It tends to reject competition between hospitals as a 'weak lever for improvement, because most areas were only served by one or two local general hospitals' (DH 2000: 56). Similarly, 'by itself, the threat of switching work is often a weak lever to drive improvement in a local NHS trust, as was shown by the failures of the internal market' (2000: 65). Klein (1998: 113–15) points out that while the keywords in the 1991 reforms were choice and competition, for New Labour they were collaboration and cooperation: 'Etzioni has replaced Enthoven'. Certainly, New Labour made some changes to the internal market (Powell 1999, 2000). It stressed longer-term contracts of 3–5 years rather than annual contracting. Instead of the 'purchaser–provider apartheid', NHS trusts would be active participants in the planning process. They would no longer simply be agents, responding to the demands of principals. Many commentators stress moves from adversarial towards relational contracting. However, as suggested above, many of these moves were pushing at an open door. What had occurred was 'marketisation at the margins' (Boyne 1998b), and New Labour reduced and refined rather than abolished the (limited) internal market. Klein (1998: 116) endorses an NHS manager's likening of Labour's decision to abolish the internal market to the fall of the Bastille: by the time the Bastille was stormed, there were only seven prisoners left to be set free, and the destruction of the fortress was important largely for its symbolism.

Although New Labour wishes to reduce competition between providers, it stresses the importance of incentives. According to DH (2000: 28), the NHS has suffered from a lack of clear incentives of the kind that many private sector organizations have to improve performance. Worse still, it is claimed that there have been perverse incentives that have inhibited improvements. The document continues that existing incentives for improved performance by NHS organizations are too narrowly focused on efficiency and squeezing more treatment from the same resources. The incentives have not supported quality, patient responsiveness and partnership with local authorities. The document concludes that the current system penalizes success and rewards failure.

New Labour certainly speaks the language of consumerism (Crinson 1998). For example, DH (2000) argues that it is necessary to develop 'a health service designed around the patient'. It claims that today we live in a consumer age. Services have to be tailor-made not mass-produced, geared to the needs of users not the convenience of producers. It contrasts 24-hour banking with an NHS that bears too many of the hallmarks of the 1940s (2000: 26). Patients are disempowered: the relationship between service and patient is too hierarchical and paternalistic. It reflects the values of 1940s public services (2000: 30). 'For the first time patients will have a real say in the NHS.' However, the details are less than inspiring. Letters about an individual patient's care will be copied to the patient; patients' views on local health services will help decide how much cash they get; patients' advocates will be set up in every hospital; patients' surveys and forums will help services to become more patient-centred. It is noticeable that these are largely indirect rather than direct, reflecting 'voice' rather than 'exit'. Labour generally stresses not economic but political incentives that operate through comparison and benchmarking (see below): the visible political fist rather than the invisible economic hand (cf. Paton 1999). Labour initially focused on sanctions or managerial sticks in the form of top-down regulation and inspection rather than incentives or financial carrots linked to bottom-up consumerism. More recently, the NHS *Plan*

(DH 2000) introduces clearer notions of organizational incentives. More-over, there are some signs of 'green shoots' of direct consumer power. As a result of an EU judgement, patients on long British waiting lists can be treated in a continental European hospital, with the NHS picking up the bill. In March 2001 pilot schemes were set up in three areas that forced hospitals that cancelled an operation on the day of surgery to offer another operation within 28 days, or pay for the patient's treatment at a time and in a hospital of the patient's choice, including private hospitals (DH 2001a). In other words, rather than the early rhetoric of abolishing the internal market, New Labour has more recently extended the 'external market' by increasing the number of NHS patients treated in private hospitals, and introducing an external, international market in exporting NHS patients to continental Europe. In late 2001 the Health Secretary Alan Milburn was 'considering' 'exit' options for patients, while leading health policy analyst Julian Le Grand considers that 'we are beginning to see a revival of the idea of competition', with some return to the competitive pressures of the internal market (BBC, *On the Record*, 2 December 2001: ww.bbc.co.uk/otr/20011202_film_2.html).

To conclude this section by returning to the specifications set out in Chapter 2, competition was limited. There was no significant increase in the number of producers, nor was market share clearly more equal. In principle consumers had more choice, but in practice their direct choices did not significantly increase. The early 1980s saw an increase in private medicine that increased the 'exit' option for some. At the margins, some 'public' NHS patients were treated in private hospitals. However, the main theme of the internal market was weak incentives and strong constraints. As Le Grand (1999: 37) concludes, in one view the British quasi-market in health care neither succeeded nor failed, simply because it was never tried. The government constrained the principal actors in the quasi-market from responding to market signals, while providing them with few true market incentives. As he puts it, in the battle between market competition and central control, control won. The Conservatives failed to translate public choice prescriptions of competition in policy as adopted into effective policy in action. New Labour initially reduced competition in terms of policy as adopted, but it is less clear that this will lead to reduced competition in terms of policy in action in the future.

More information on performance

Recent years have seen a world-wide explosion in the volume of health care performance data published. While this has been particularly pro-nounced in the USA, there has also been a proliferation of various types of PIs in Britain (Carter *et al.* 1992; Goddard *et al.* 1999, 2000). It is import-ant to differentiate the type of and audience for the PIs. The initial set of

NHS PIs was mainly aimed at NHS managers who wished to compare the performance of their organizations with other NHS organizations. Critics pointed out that they suffered from problems of validity and reliability (Powell 1997: 76–7). They were largely concerned with crude and narrow aspects of 'efficiency' such as length of stay in hospital, and tended to be concerned with inputs and throughputs rather than outputs and outcomes. They did not compare like with like, and the data to calculate them was often inaccurate. Harrison *et al.* (1990: 130) claimed that they tended to fall into the economy, efficiency and process categories, while few assessed outcomes. Moreover, only a minority of consultants and even fewer of the Community Health Councils took much notice of them.

The quality of PIs slowly increased. A comparative performance guide (DH 1994) covered targets such as waiting times in outpatient and A&E departments. Stars were given for good performance, with large variations both between and within hospitals (Powell 1997: 84–5). The following year saw the information updated, showing whether a provider's performance had significantly increased or decreased (DH 1995). The PIs for 1995–6 (DH 1996) showed in the main continued improvement in performance (Powell 1997: 85–6).

Some professional initiatives occurred during the same period (Harrison *et al.* 1990: 132–5). The 'Confidential Enquiry into Post-Operative Deaths' (CEPOD) was mounted by the medical profession, and was published in 1987. Participation was voluntary and the survey data were destroyed after analysis. The profession voluntarily monitored its own quality of practice, but information was not made available to government or to patients. Medical audit, later extended to other staff groups under the umbrella term of clinical audit, was made a professional obligation (DH 1989a). This coincided with the rise of 'evidence-based medicine' and the Guidelines movement (Davies and Nutley 2000). Since 1994 the Scottish Executive has published clinical outcome indicators collated by the Clinical Resource and Audit Group (CRAG) for all Scottish NHS acute trusts and health boards. However, data from both a postal questionnaire survey and semi-structured interviews suggest a conclusion compatible with evidence from the USA, which is that the indicators have had little impact on behaviour (Mannion and Goddard 2001). They suggest several possible explanations for this limited impact, such as credibility, timeliness, awareness, training and facilitation, incentives, supplementary information, outcome rather than process indicators, and external accountability.

New Labour criticised the Conservatives' obsession with a narrow dimension of efficiency, arguing that in the internal market, performance was driven by what could readily be measured: the financial bottom line and the numbers of 'finished consultant episodes' (DH 1997: 17). New Labour indicated that it was necessary to change what was measured, how it was measured, and how the information would be used.

DH (1997) outlined a new performance assessment framework (PAF), focusing on six dimensions to capture what really counts. The document claimed that this would indicate a more rounded assessment of NHS performance, representing a huge break with the past. A subsequent document (DH 1999a: 4–5) performed some linguistic gymnastics in discussing the six interdependent dimensions. From an initial view of the diverse communities of the local population under consideration (health improvement), we need to ensure that everyone with health care needs (fair access) receives appropriate and effective health care (effective delivery) offering good value for money for services (efficiency) as sensitive and convenient as possible (user/carer experience) so that good clinical outcomes are achieved (health outcome of NHS care), to maximize the contribution to improved health (back to health improvement). Health improvement consists largely of mortality rates. Fair access consists of a more diverse set concerned with surgery rates, waiting lists, registration with dentists and early detection of cancer. However, these are very limited measures of fair access, comparing performance at the HA level, but with nothing on measures such as social class, gender and race at the intra-authority level (cf. Goddard and Smith 1998). Effective delivery consists of nine indicators, including cancer and surgery rates. Efficiency includes the day case rate, length of stay, generic prescribing and unit costs for maternity and mental health services. User/carer experience includes waiting at A&E, cancelled operations, delayed discharge, outpatient waiting and waiting lists. Health outcomes include avoidable deaths, decayed teeth, infant deaths and cancer survival rates. These measures were presented at the HA rather than trust level. It is stressed that the data set 'very much represents a first step and improvements to the indicator set will be made over time' (DH 1999a: 6).

A document issued at the same time, DH (1999b), focuses on six clinical indicators of: deaths in hospital following surgery; deaths in hospital following a fractured hip; deaths in hospital following a heart attack; readmission to hospital following discharge; returning home following a stroke; and returning home following treatment for a fractured hip. It presents summary data for 1995/96, 1996/97 and 1997/98 for the 100 or so HAs and 389 trusts in England. It also shows graphs for 1997/98, with extremely wide confidence intervals for some indicators. In other words, it is not clear whether much certainty can be placed on apparently wide inequalities of performance. Again, the indicators are a first step and will be improved over time (1999b: 6). However, it presents a fairly limited and partial picture, with a great deal of variation. For example, some hospitals show good performance on one indicator, but bad performance on another.

In September 2001, hospital league tables were issued. They contained nine core targets: waiting times for inpatients; for outpatients; waiting more than 18 months; waiting for breast cancer patients; number of 'trolley-waits' for more than 12 hours; financial performance (keeping within budget);

number of operations cancelled on the day; treatment of staff; and hospital cleanliness. The tenth target, deemed more important than the others, was the outcome of CHI inspections. The tables show 35 'three-star', 103 'two-star', 23 'one-star' and 12 'no-star' hospitals. They do not include clinical outcomes, but 'for the first time hospitals are being ranked on their performance'. With these data, Alan Milburn 'explodes the myth' that money and the level of deprivation in the local community are what make one hospital better than another. He claims that it is about management and organization, pointing out that South Tyneside NHS Trust, which serves one of the poorest areas in the UK, won three stars, while Epsom and St Helier in wealthy Surrey won none.

A new package of performance indicators was issued in February 2002 (www.doh.gov.uk/nhsperformanceindicators/2002). It is claimed that for the first time the new statistics are robust enough to allow year-on-year comparisons for 64 out of the 79 indicators. They show a range of striking improvements (e.g. cancer survival rates) and relatively few declines in performance (e.g. suicide rates). However, it is possible to suggest some interactions in the figures. For example, there were increases in the rate of emergency readmissions to hospital when a general election was looming and hospitals were driving down waiting lists to meet government targets.

New Labour is attempting to blend these diverse elements into its PAF. However, there is a danger that these different elements will be like oil and water, and fail to mix. A PAF for everyone may end up pleasing no one. For example, it is unlikely that providers will see improved performance on all 79 measures. In the absence of clear weighting of the indicators, and bearing in mind possible trade-offs between indicators, it is likely that most managers will focus on the perceived 'bottom line' of financial balance and waiting lists. In other words, a set of performance measures nominally composed of 79 PIs may essentially boil down to a few selected key indicators. Moreover, decision-makers often attempt another synthesis between 'hard' (quantitative) and 'soft' (qualitative) information (Goddard *et al.* 1999). For example, a trust that appears to be doing badly according to the 'hard' data may be viewed more favourably by the regional office or health authority, or vice versa. The problem of focus may be explored briefly using the example of 'quality' (cf. Ferlie and Shortell 2001). New Labour claims that 'The new NHS will have quality at its heart' (DH 1997: 17). However, the issues of who defines quality and how it is ensured are less clear. It argues that quality must include the wider patient experience as well as the narrow clinical result. It sets out three areas for action to drive quality into all parts of the NHS: national standards and guidelines, local measures, and a new organization to adress shortcomings. Throughout the UK, there will be national service frameworks and NICE. Locally, there will be a new system of clinical governance, backed by a new statutory duty for quality in NHS trusts. 'Quality will quite literally be on

Table 4.2 The availability of performance information in health

Dimensions of organizational performance	Current performance	Past performance	Performance of other organizations
Expenditure	Yes	Yes	Yes
Outputs	Yes	Yes	Yes
Outcomes	Yes	Yes	Yes
Efficiency	Yes	Yes	Yes
Cost-effectiveness	No	No	No
Probity	No	No	No

the agenda of every NHS Trust Board' (DH 1997: 47). Finally, CHI will oversee the quality of clinical services at local levels. However, quality may be everyone's concern, but no one's responsibility. There has been a retreat from professional self-regulation, particularly since the 'club' or 'clan' culture that was exposed by the Bristol Royal Infirmary Inquiry. However, it is less clear what will move into this vacuum. Doctors, managers, patients, inspectors and the Secretary of State may have different views about 'quality'. The period of the Bristol scandal was covered by medical audit, the earlier incarnation of clinical governance. Simply placing quality 'on the agenda' of managers and making it a statutory duty will not ensure satisfactory outcomes. Bad practice has escaped the eyes of inspectorates in the past. Finally, there appears to be no clear mechanism by which consumers can contribute towards increasing quality.

In addition to these official sources, there are a number of unofficial sources. For example, the *Sunday Times* 'Good Hospital Guide' (14 and 21 Jan. 2001) was termed by Claire Rayner, President of the Patients' Association, 'the most authoritative and accurate measure of hospital standards'. It contains data on patient mortality, the number of doctors and nurses, the results of the national patient survey on coronary care, inpatient and outpatient waiting times; urgent breast cancer referrals; complaints; and the percentage of hernia repairs carried out as day cases. However, these data are not aggregated into an overall league table.

Certainly, the amount of performance information available to managers, clinicians and consumers has increased significantly in quantity and quality over the last twenty years or so. Table 4.2 indicates the current situation. Nevertheless, the *NHS Plan* (DH 2000: 29) argues that performance has been inhibited by a lack of reliable information for clinicians, managers and patients. It can be argued that the Conservatives tended to concentrate on narrow efficiency concerns. While they made a large amount of information available to consumers, they failed to provide many opportunities to use this information. New Labour has introduced a more rounded performance framework. While efficiency or cost-effectiveness remains important, it has been joined by other dimensions. Labour has also placed greater emphasis on the quality dimension, and has produced outcome or clinical indicators. There has been little concern with probity (but see Audit Commission 1994). Alan Milburn (DH 2001b) claims that patients will have more information, more influence and more power over the services they receive. The balance of power in the NHS will shift decisively in the patient's favour. While it is indisputable that they have more information, the other claims are more problematic. It is likely that the public tend to judge the NHS by the level of input or expenditure and the size of the waiting list. Moreover, performance information remains largely at the aggregate level. Some information is available for hospitals, but is not generally disaggregated to individual surgeons. Patients do not know whether Dr Jekyll or Mr Hyde will be holding the knife. Clinicians have more information, although whether this will lead to improved quality is difficult to say. Arguably the most important stakeholders in performance information are those involved in vertical performance management. They now have a profusion of performance data composed of a torrent of different types of quantitative data, supplemented by inspection data. The problem is that it may be difficult to see what counts. There are so many indicators that it is unlikely that any organization will do well on all of them. Moreover, as old indices are replaced, it is difficult to see a consistent and coherent data set over time. Finally, it is possible that organizations will respond to the PI rather than the problem. For example, the Patient's Charter requirement to be seen by a health professional within specified periods of time led to 'hello nurses' who greeted the patients. Similarly, it has been claimed that clinical priorities have been distorted in an effort to reduce waiting lists and avoid the telephone call from the Secretary of State. For example, ten hip joints or cataract operations reduce the list more than one major, time-consuming, complex and more expensive operation. It seems that more information on performance may be a fairly weak lever to substantially increase levels of performance unless the information is comprehensive, accurate and used effectively by producers and consumers. Despite improvements over time, the extent to which performance data are valid and reliable remains unclear. For example, the National Audit Office (2001) pointed out that there had been 'inappropriate adjustments to NHS waiting lists'. Even if the information is valid and reliable, it is unclear how long it will take before any impacts on performance can be detected.

Smaller organizations

While the Conservatives favoured competition and New Labour stressed cooperation, and both governments have advocated more performance information, views on organizational size are less clear. This lack of clarity is for four main reasons. First, organizational size has rarely featured as a direct variable in debates. Views about organizational size have to be inferred from statements about other dimensions such as devolution, and terms such as devolution may mean very different things with varying implications for organizational size (Saltman and Figueras 1997). Second, this ambiguous policy variable changes over time. While, for example, the Conservatives were broadly in favour of and New Labour broadly against competition, their implicit views on organizational size varied over time. Third, it is important to differentiate purchasers and providers. On the one hand, there are debates about the size of structural entities such as hospitals and organizational units such as trusts. On the other hand, there are largely independent debates about the size of purchasing organizations. Fourth, changes to organizational size may occur through local policy (e.g. mergers) without a clear and explicit central line. In the terms of Chapter 1, variations in organizational size tended to reflect a 'change' rather than a 'reform'.

The Conservatives' early moves were consistent with the public choice prescription of smaller organizational units. They inherited some 90 newly formed area health authorities covering an average population size of about 500,000. The 1982 reorganization created some 200 district health authorities with average population size of around 250,000. These administrative units should be 'the smallest possible geographical areas within which it is possible to carry out integrated planning, provision and development' of health services (in Klein 2001: 104). The then Secretary of State for Social Services, Patrick Jenkin, saw the NHS 'not as a single national organization, but . . . as a series of local services run by local management, responsible to local needs and with a strong involvement from the local community' (in Klein 2001: 106). The policy of contracting out or compulsory competitive tendering forced the 'in-house' hotel services to compete with private contractors. Many critics argued that the result of this would be to shrink the NHS workforce, substituting lower-paid and mainly non-unionized workers.

After the purchase–provider split in 1991, two different sets of arguments relating to optimum size of purchasing and providing units emerged. The picture is confused on the purchasing side. On the one hand, there have been moves towards larger authorities and a stronger line management structure. NHS Regional Health Authorities (some after amalgamation) were transformed into Regional Offices of the NHS Executive. In effect, these outposts of Whitehall fitted into a more centralist chain of command that implemented top-down orders. At the more local level, many DHAs merged to become units similar to the larger units abolished in 1982. In 1996 DHAs and the Family Health Service Authorities combined to become single purchasing authorities. On the other hand, Mays and Dixon (1998: 176–7) examine purchaser plurality, setting out the different models ranging from conventional HA purchasing with a population size of 250,000 or more to community fundholding with less than 6000. They note that each model has a different combination of merits and drawbacks, and that there is rarely or never a single 'optimal' organizational response to complex policy problems. The Conservative government appeared to favour the smaller purchasing organizations, mainly because they were regarded as innovative and responsive to patients. Labour's position is less clear. On the one hand, it wishes to decentralize responsibility for operational management, and states that decisions about how best to use resources for patient care are best made by those who treat patients: 'this principle is at the heart of proposals in this White paper' (DH 1997: 9–12). So far, so Conservative, as this was precisely the argument used to justify GPFH. However, Labour also wishes to end the fragmentation, unfairness, distortion, inefficiency, bureaucracy, instability and secrecy of the internal market. It favours PCGs/PCTs as an intermediate solution between the large HAs and small GPFH. In other words, Labour claims that purchasers can be too large (DHAs) and too small (GPFH). It follows that the 100,000 size of the 500 or so PCGs/PCTs is regarded as optimal, although no evidence is produced for this. Moreover, the population size for the PCGs/PCTs ranges from about 50,000 to over 250,000, meaning that even it it were possible to specify an optimal size, many PCGs/PCTs would vary from this. Mays and Dixon (1998: 198) note that proposals for PCGs/PCTs are also implicitly based on the hope that larger purchasers will incur lower transaction costs. They go on to say that there is a clear trade-off between the desire for patient choice and the desire to minimize 'two-tierism', concluding that the latter is being seen by the government as a higher priority than the former. These moves will reduce the number of commissioning bodies from around 3600 to as few as 500 (DH 1997: 12). However, this figure of 3600 lumps together all purchasers, equating HAs with GPFH. PCGs/PCTs will mean that 'for the first time in the history of the NHS the Government will align clinical and financial responsibility'. That will better attune local services to meet local needs, but within a framework of national standards (DH 1997: 9).

According to the *NHS Plan*, the government by 2004 wants PCGs/PCTs to control 75 per cent of the NHS budget (DH 2000). It is claimed that the relationship between central government and the NHS has veered between command-and-control and market fragmentation, but neither model works. The document continues that the NHS cannot be run from Whitehall, but standards cannot simply be set locally either. It sets out a new model where intervention is in inverse proportion to (centrally defined) 'success'. (2000: 30). It proposes 'maximum devolution, based on the principle of subsidiarity' (2000: 57). This operates within a framework of 'earned autonomy' where organizations are designated red, amber or green. Green organizations will have more freedom than their red counterparts. Just before the general election of 2001, the Health Secretary, Alan Milburn announced that the next stage in the reform of the NHS will see the centre of gravity move from Whitehall to front-line staff (DH 2001b). This will involve a number of major structural changes. By 2004 two-thirds of the 99 HAs will have merged, devolving many of their responsibilities to PCTs. There will be around 30 new 'strategic health authorities' each covering about 1.5 million people. This devolution will give those responsible for providing local services the freedom to shape them in the way that they see fit, within a clear national framework of standards and accountability. Devolution to front-line NHS organizations must be matched by devolution within front-line NHS organizations. One example of this is to 'bring back matron'.

Turning to the providers, the history of the NHS has largely been one of increasing the size of production units. In general practice, there has been a trend away from single-handed practitioners towards larger group practices. In secondary care, there has been a trend from smaller cottage and specialized hospitals towards large general hospitals. Probably the best example of this may be seen in the Hospital Plan of the 1960s, where larger hospitals were advocated because of economies of scale and a pooling of medical expertise (Klein 2001: 56–8). The main reason may be medical politics, with clinicians wanting to work in larger, better equipped hospitals and in teams rather than in professional isolation. As Harrison and Dixon (2000: 132–3) note, the relationship between hospital size and the quality of care remains one of our knowledge gaps. A neglected dimension of this debate is the accreditation policy of the Royal Colleges that may not allow training in small hospitals to 'count' in terms of medical education. Withdrawal of accreditation has negative effects in setting off a downward spiral or a medical version of the domino theory. For example, if the A&E department closes or is downgraded, then the hospital moves one step closer to a future threat of closure. In other words, it is difficult to attribute changes in organizational size to a narrow, political view of policy or to medical politics of the street-level bureaucrats.

It has generally been claimed that both Conservative and Labour governments have favoured operational decentralization within a tight line management structure (Powell 1997, 1999, 2000; Klein 2001). Saltman and Figueras (1997: 49) claim that the UK represents an example of decentralization – a hybrid of deconcentration and delegation – without devolution. In addition to the old slogan of power to the people, now termed consumers, more power is also promised to clinicians, independent inspectorates, the new strategic HAs, not to mention the Secretary of State, who remains the ghost at the NHS power feast. If power can be seen in zero-sum terms and is limited in quantity, then more power to everyone is impossible. As Klein (1998: 124) perceptively predicted, as governments wish to avoid the problem of centralizing blame, a future White Paper might therefore unveil plans for a devolved NHS.

It is more difficult to give a clear summary on organizational size compared to the other ends of competition and performance measurement. The Conservatives created smaller Health Authorities. Since the purchaser–provider split of 1991, it is necessary to focus on two distinct sets of arguments associated with organizational size. For providers, the long-term trend towards larger hospitals has generally continued, with the closure of small units. Turning to purchasers, the Conservatives favoured decentralized purchasing based on GPFH and its variants. Labour replaced GPFH with the larger units of PCGs/PCTs, and the newly-proposed SHAs. While both governments have stressed the importance of devolution, most commentators suggest that operational devolution has been accompanied by *de facto* centralization associated with clearer lines of top-down performance management.

Summary

It is difficult to specify a clear policy direction on the main public choice theory variables. The Conservatives broadly favoured competition. However, the discourse of competition generally weakened over time, and competition on the ground was less than advocated on paper. On the other hand, New Labour was committed to abolishing the internal market. However, it favours consumerism and incentives, and the degree of competition may increase again in the future. Both governments have favoured performance information, with a general increase of quantity and quality over time. Indeed, there is probably now a profusion of performance indicators. However, the nature of indicators and the use to which they are put may vary between governments. PIs under the Conservatives concentrated on a narrow dimension of efficiency, while they have broadened to other dimensions under New Labour. While the Conservatives aimed many of their PIs towards the consumer but gave them few mechanisms to use them, New Labour's PIs tend to be aimed at political and managerial rather than consumer policy levers. Verdicts on organizational size are even more problematic. The Conservatives stressed devolution to smaller units such as fundholding practices. New Labour supports an intermediate size between HAs and GPFH that delivers the best of both worlds, but this is balanced by larger strategic HAs. Under both governments 'devolution' has occurred within a clear vertical line management structure. To sum up, public choice prescriptions were strongly adopted but relatively weakly implemented by the Conservatives. Initially Labour followed the public choice line only for more performance on information, although it is possible that it is rediscovering competition in its second term. The best attempt to capture this complexity is given in Table 4.3.

Table 4.3 The impact of public choice reforms on health reforms, 1979–2001

	Competition	Performance information	Organizational size
Conservatives	More	More	Smaller
New Labour	Less	More	Larger

The impact of health reforms: a review of the evidence

This section examines changes in efficiency, responsiveness, and equity in the period 1979–2001.

Efficiency

The traditional NHS was always said to be efficient, although the term was not always defined. The evidence for this was largely seen in terms of administration costs being a relatively low proportion of total costs, and Britain produced relatively good health outcomes with a fairly parsimonious health service. However, much (but not all) of the latter may be explained by the low wages of doctors and nurses compared to other countries (Powell 1997).

As explained in Chapter 2, this section focuses on technical efficiency, leaving the wider discussion of allocative efficiency for the topic of responsiveness. One of the most significant claims made by marketeers was that the Conservatives' internal market NHS reforms would increase efficiency (see Robinson and Le Grand 1993; Scott 2001; Holliday 1995; Powell 1997; West 1997; Klein 2001).

A major criticism aimed at the traditional NHS was that it lacked incentives to control expenditure (West 1997). This was particularly the case for GPs who issued prescriptions and referred patients to hospital at no cost to themselves. In other words, they could shunt costs to other parts of the NHS. The GPFH scheme was intended to secure greater value for money (Coulter 1995; Dixon and Glennerster 1995; Petchey 1995). Goodwin (1998: 44) claims that GPFH was intended to encourage greater technical efficiency, yet this measure of 'value for money' has not been examined directly. This is because GPs carry out many diverse activities, and studies have tended to focus on the parts rather than the whole. Goodwin examines prescribing costs, referral rates, savings and transaction costs that relate to technical efficiency. On the topic of prescribing, he lists 17 studies and two reviews. The consensus of these studies is that there was some containment of prescribing costs, but that this may not be sustainable in the longer term. The evidence on referral rates is mixed. There appear to be higher transaction costs, although it is more difficult to say whether any benefits generated outweigh these. Most research has focused on expenditure alone rather than efficiency (Dixon and Glennerster 1995; Robinson 1996), with very limited examination of the quality of care (Coulter 1995). However, Le Grand *et al.* (1998) conclude that fundholders appear to be more efficient purchasers than the HAs.

Turning to secondary care, caution must be exercised when comparing output figures over time (OHE 1999). Traditionally the NHS measured activity in terms of 'deaths and discharges' (D&D), moving to 'finished consultant episodes' and more recently to 'patient spells'. When linked with cost indices, these activity figures give a range of efficiency measures. Examining efficiency in the NHS has led to a new cottage industry, largely associated with the Centre of Health Economics at the University of York (see Soderland and van der Merwe 1999; Dawson and Street 1998, 2000). A number of very broad conclusions may be drawn from this work. First, a number of different efficiency measures exist. Second, different conclusions may be drawn from the different indices. Third, while some indices may be better than others, all are problematic to different degrees. In particular, they tend to be point estimates that are not accompanied by any range of uncertainty, meaning that it is impossible to say whether the differences in efficiency between trusts are 'real'. Moreover, most of this work is intended to guide future policy, and compares efficiency between trusts rather than over time. The latter task is associated with a rival cottage industry associated with the King's Fund (Le Grand *et al.* 1998). They examine changes in efficiency over time by linking the 'official' measure of activity of the cost-weighted activity index (CWAI) to changes in real resources. The CWAI has risen at a faster rate since the start of the internal market than have real resources, and has risen at a faster relative rate than before the reforms. In other words, in crude terms, efficiency increased at an average rate of about 1.5 per cent before and about 2.0 per cent after the reforms (Mulligan 1998: 23–5). However, due to problems of validity and reliability (Dawson and Street 1998, 2000; Mulligan 1998), conclusions about changes in efficiency are heavily qualified. For example, Le Grand *et al.* (1998: 120) refer to 'apparent improvement in efficiency in a crude sense'. More recent figures suggest that efficiency gains seem to peter out in 1996–97 and then fall in the two subsequent years. In other words, the efficiency gains made in the mid-1990s are now in danger of not being sustained (Le Grand 2002).

Responsiveness

Responsiveness can be viewed in the wide sense of allocative efficiency as the match between outputs and preferences. The term has been used in a variety of ways in accounts of health reform (Harrison *et al.* 1990; Powell

1997; Saltman and Figueras 1997; Le Grand *et al.* 1998; Lupton *et al.* 1998; Scott 2001). As Chapter 2 argues, the term needs to be unpacked to clarify responsiveness of what and responsiveness to whom. In principle, it can involve examining a wide range of dimensions such as inputs, outputs, outcomes, probity, cost-effectiveness and efficiency for the stakeholders of direct users, indirect users, taxpayers, and staff. In practice, only some of these combinations have been examined (Powell 1998b). There has been little discussion of responsiveness to indirect users, taxpayers and staff. The two main foci of the literature are responsiveness to consumers and responsiveness to local preferences.

It is generally claimed that the traditional NHS was an excellent example of producer dominance where the professionals made decisions for passive clients. Experts were trusted largely to regulate themselves (Wilding 1982; Klein 2001). A number of accounts (see Ham 1999a) have applied the framework of Alford (1975) to the NHS. This claims that health politics may be seen in terms of structural interest groups, with a power battle between the dominant interests (the medical profession) and the challenging interests (managers) with repressed interests (the community) barely entering the game. As Klein (2001) argues, the language of consumerism was inappropriate in the traditional NHS, where professionals attended to patients' needs rather than consumers' wants or demands: patients were expected to be patient.

The traditional NHS has also been characterized as a 'command-and-control' hierarchy, with Parliamentary accountability to the Minister (later the Secretary of State) of Health. This is an oversimplification (Powell 1997; Exworthy *et al.* 1999; Klein 2001), but, unlike the other services of education and housing examined in this book, there is little electoral or democratic input into the NHS below the Parliamentary level. The NHS has been run by appointed boards rather than elected councils, with critics raising concerns of legitimacy and 'democratic deficit'.

The Conservatives argued that their reforms would lead to a more responsive system. This was largely through the mechanisms of choice and competition, but there was also some stress on responding to local preferences and focusing on the needs of patients rather than producers (Le Grand and Barlett 1993; Robinson and Le Grand 1993; Le Grand *et al.* 1998). In an economic sense money would follow the patient, and in the political sense the system should respond to local voices.

As we saw above, the Griffiths Report (DHSS 1983) argued that the NHS should be more responsive to consumers. As Griffiths later put it, 'the hallmark of the truly great organizations in the private sector is that they have placed quality and customer satisfaction first' (in Klein 2001: 128). This 'supermarket model' involved a change of culture from producer to consumer values: 'If management in the NHS was all about satisfying consumers instead of keeping the doctors happy, then the implications were indeed profound' (Klein 2001: 128–9). However, it is generally claimed that the Griffiths reforms did not lead to a cultural revolution (Harrison *et al.* 1990; West 1997). As Klein (2001: 129) puts it, unlike supermarkets, there were few clear incentives and sanctions in the NHS: the Griffiths model 'lacked an engine to drive it'.

In principle, the engine was provided by the quasi-market reforms. An unresponsive producer that failed to satisfy its customers would lose income. However, as we have seen, customers were managers of purchasing organizations rather than individual consumers, and competition was far from being red in tooth and claw. The 1990s saw increased consumerism associated with the 'Citizen's Charter' series of initiatives. The Patient's Charter promised a series of 'entitlements' that largely fell short of legally enforceable rights. Some, such as the right to be registered with a GP, simply repeated existing entitlements. Others were vague, and yet more resulted in little more than an apology (Powell 1997; Lupton *et al.* 1998; Klein 2001).

The Conservatives also attempted to increase political responsiveness. The White Paper, *Working for Patients* (DH 1989a: 4), stated that in order 'to make the Health Service more responsive to the needs of patients, as much power and responsibility as possible will be delegated to the local level'. They emphasized managerial rather than democratic responsiveness. As the Cabinet Minister, William Waldegrave, put it, what is important is whether public services are 'producer-responsive or consumer-responsive. Services are not necessarily made responsive to the public simply by giving citizens a democratic voice' (in Walsh 1995; Lupton *et al.* 1998: 35). The government stressed that HAs should be more responsive to the needs, views and preferences of local people. They were encouraged to listen to the public or 'local voices' through consultation exercises, opinion polls, and citizens juries. These initiatives have been criticized as being 'the unaccountable in pursuit of the uninformed' (see Cooper *et al.* 1995: 46–74; Walsh 1995; Lupton *et al.* 1998). It is particularly difficult to take account of the views of the silent majority as opposed to the vocal minority.

New Labour follows some of these directions, stressing, at different points, responsiveness to consumers, clinicians and national government (see above). Although Tony Blair has claimed that dealings with the 'forces of conservatism' in the public sector have left 'scars on his back', local professionals are to be placed in the 'driving seat' of local health services through PCGs/PCTs and through clinical governance (DH 1997). Joining them in an increasingly crowded driving seat are users. The *NHS Plan* (DH 2000) stressed that the experience of users and carers is central to the work of the NHS. To this end, a new NHS charter would be developed, moving from narrow measures of process to the things that really matter. Another development was a new annual national survey of patient and carer experience. For the first time ever in its history there will be systematic evidence to enable the NHS to measure itself against the aspirations and experiences of its users, to compare performance across the UK and to look at trends over time. The survey will give patients and carers a voice in shaping the service. However, the mechanisms to achieve this greater responsiveness are less than clear. It is still hard to resist the conclusion that, even with consumers and producers contesting the driving seat, the views of the back-seat driver in the shape of the Secretary of State remain paramount.

Although most commentators address responsiveness as an objective of the reforms, they tend to have few empirical studies of substance to report (Le Grand 1993; Goodwin 1998; Le Grand *et al.* 1998; Mulligan 1998). Le Grand *et al.* (1998: 127–8) sum up that there was little evidence of increased responsiveness to consumers by fundholders, HAs or trusts. Their conclusion about the quasi-market that no 'exit' was possible by dissatisfied users and that methods of expressing 'voice' were limited and little altered, if at all, by the reforms appears still valid.

Some indications on public satisfaction with the NHS can be gauged from the annual British Social Attitudes Survey (Le Grand *et al.* 1998: 124–6). The general levels of dissatisfaction rose during the 1980s, falling in the early 1990s before rising again to highest ever level of 50 per cent in 1996. The figure for 1998 showed a sharp fall to 36 per cent under Labour – the lowest level during the past decade. However, more recent evidence from other polls suggests mixed views on the current government's performance (Mulligan 2000). Demographic factors such as age and class also appear to have an important impact on levels of satisfaction (Harrison *et al.* 1990; Judge and Solomon 1993; Mulligan 2000). There may be some differences between the direct experience of patients and the 'hearsay' information received through the media. Moreover, Harrison *et al.* (1990: 138) argue that the questions posed in the surveys are seldom precise enough to allow us to distinguish between the different evaluation criteria such as efficiency, responsiveness and equity. However, anecdotal evidence suggests that public concerns appear to focus on the two 'gold standard' indices of NHS expenditure and the waiting list (Harrison *et al.* 1990; Powell 1997).

It may be difficult to square the circle between the views of the public as patients and the public as taxpayers. While all the opinion polls say that the public are willing to pay higher taxes, a persistent unwillingness to vote for 'tax and spend' parties (i.e. Old Labour) at least suggests that this claim should be interpreted with some caution.

Similarly, some of the dimensions have received more attention than others (see Figure 4.1). Everyone wants more inputs, except when they have to pay for them. The public is probably more concerned with the output indicator of waiting lists than is the profession. The public wants better outcomes in the sense of more 'years of life and more life to years' (the quantity and quality of life). Although survival rates for many conditions lag behind those in other European countries, health outcomes are clearly

Stakeholder groups

Organizational activities and achievements	Direct users	Indirect users	Taxpayers	Staff
Expenditure	Yes	Yes	No	Yes
Outputs	Yes	Yes	No	Yes
Outcomes	Yes	Yes	No	Yes
Efficiency	Yes	Yes	No	No
Cost-effectiveness	No	No	No	No
Probity	No	No	No	No

Figure 4.1 Data availability for evaluating the impact of public management reforms on service responsiveness

linked with broader material and behavioural factors outside the NHS. The public as direct users are probably not particularly concerned with efficiency or cost-effectiveness *per se*, and staff may feel that prolonged efficiency drives are having negative effects on their working conditions.

Equity

Equity has always been regarded as one of the major principles of the NHS, and there has been a great deal of attention directed at the issue of the extent to which the service has achieved equity (Le Grand 1982; Whitehead 1993; Powell 1995, 1997; Dowling 2000). As we saw in Chapter 2, there are many possible equity objectives. We have very limited and partial information in many of the cells of an equity matrix (Powell 1997), and so the 'baseline' measure of equity before the reforms is problematic.

It is generally claimed that the objective of equity at best tended to be neglected and at worst exacerbated by the Conservatives reforms. However, the accusation that the reforms created a 'two-tier service', implying that the NHS before the reforms was a perfectly equitable, one-tier service, is nonsense. The NHS has always been a multi-tier service, with complex inequalities based on diverse dimensions such as social class, gender, race, client group and geography. The reforms certainly exposed inequalities, whether or not they created or exacerbated them (Powell 1996, 1997). Much of the attention has been focused on inequalities of outcome by social class (Townsend *et al.* 1992; Acheson 1998). These studies argue that health inequalities increased under the Conservatives, but recognize that this was largely due to factors outside rather than inside the NHS. Although there are many studies that point out different types of inequality in the NHS (Townsend *et al.* 1992; Powell 1997; Acheson 1998; Goddard and Smith 1998; Shaw *et al.* 1999), there are few that focus on the equity impacts of the reforms. There are two main areas of debate: GPFH and 'postcode prescribing'.

GPFH was probably one of the most studied aspects of the reforms, and probably the greatest attention has been given to the equity dimension of GPFH (Whitehead 1993; Dixon and Glennerster 1995; Robinson 1996; Goodwin 1998; Dowling 2000). Early predictions that patients of fund-holding practices would be disadvantaged because the practices would run out of money gave way to claims that such patients were treated more quickly, creating a 'two-tier service'. The overall or catch-all term of a 'two-tier service' contains a number of possibilities (Glennerster *et al.* 1994; Coulter 1995; Goodwin 1998; Dowling 2000). First, access: patients of fundholding practices had shorter waiting times for hospital appointments. Second, budget allocation: fundholding practices were more generously funded than non-fundholding practices. Third: cream skimming: fundholding practices may not wish to have 'expensive' patients on their lists. However, many accusations relied on anecdotal evidence rather than controlled studies (Coulter 1995; Dowling 2000), and it is difficult to come to clear conclusions (Dixon and Glennerster 1995; Robinson 1996; Baggott 1997). Dixon and Glennerster (1995: 729) write that although fundholding has been studied more than any other aspect of the NHS reforms, empirical evidence on the impact of the scheme is still lacking. Conclusions from the published research remain limited because either the study designs have not included a control group or the control groups later decided to join the scheme and were likely to be contaminated. There were some gains, some drawbacks, and alongside this scanty balance sheet are a long list of don't knows. Similarly, Petchey (1995: 1139) concludes that 'few reliable con-clusions about fundholding, either positive or negative, can be drawn from existing research'. Le Grand *et al.* (1998) conclude that two-tierism did occur, but it is unclear whether this arose because fundholders were better purchasers or because they were better resourced. One of the more optimistic conclusions was given by Glennerster *et al.* (1993, 1994) who claimed that 'systems in competition will be good for patients' (1994: 183). As Dowling (2000: 222–3) points out, critics were unsure whether to condemn GPFH from the point of view of the frying pan of efficiency or the fire of equity. GPFH was in a 'lose–lose situation': either it did not make a difference, or it created a two-tier service. The wider view is that the verdict of many studies was a static one, and from a dynamic view it was possible that a temporary phase of inequality was necessary before the benefits of GPFH would spread more widely over time (Glennerster *et al.* 1994; Organisation for Economic Co-operation and Development 1995; Audit Commission 1996).

Goddard and Smith (1998) give a useful review of equity of access to health care. They note that most studies suffer from methodological weaknesses and tend to examine inequality in treatment rather than access. However, their remit did not include examining the impact of the reforms. Despite concerns in the media, the literature on the reforms contains surprisingly little on postcode prescribing – that it is possible within a *National* Health Service to obtain a treatment in one part of the UK but not in another (Powell 1998b; Powell and Boyne 2001). A fuller discussion is available within the rationing literature (see Klein *et al.* 1996), but this tends to include little on the impact of reforms. It is clear that there are differences in purchasing plans, and there has been some increase in the number of services that some HAs will not purchase such as cosmetic surgery or IVF. The development of capitation allocation formulae should reduce financial inequity (Mulligan 1998: 32), but, as Bevan (1998) stresses, this may still leave differences in how the money is spent. There are a few high-profile cases such as 'Child B' and some HAs that will not purchase high-cost drugs (Klein *et al.* 1996). It is clear that choice of treatment depends on postcode, but one could easily argue that such inequities always existed in the NHS (Powell 1997: 141–5; Mulligan 1998: 33). Mulligan (1998: 32) states that purchasing so far has not *eliminated* geographical inequities in access to some procedures, and she reports that some doctors *believe* that the introduction of the purchaser–provider split has had an adverse effect on general equity of provision.

New Labour places great emphasis on equity, stressing the importance of 'fair access' and narrowing the health gap (Shaw *et al.* 1999; Exworthy and Powell 2000). One of the six principles of the 'new NHS' (DH 1997) is to renew the NHS as a genuinely national or 'one-nation' service characterized by 'fair access' to services, ending the unfairness, 'unacceptable variations' and 'two-tierism' of the Conservative internal market. It has established NICE to set national standards and CHI to enforce them. It seeks to improve the health of the population and to improve the health of the worst off in society in order to narrow the health gap. The *NHS Plan* (DH 2000) set out for the first time national targets to reduce health inequalities by 2010. These targets involve action inside the NHS, but also in the wider social and economic environment, are necessarily long-term, and so cannot be directly linked with our impact measures. If these measures are successful, inequalities will reduce in the future, but at present it is too early to detect any effects. In particular, we know very little about 'equality

Table 4.4 Academic journal articles on dimensions of management reform
and health

	health AND	health AND reform AND
effici*	143	9
equit*	191	7
responsive*	33	0

Source: Web of Science

of access' or 'fair access' which is a stated aim of the New Labour government (Goddard and Smith 1998).

It follows that most of the cells in the matrix are empty, and we can say
little about most types of equity impacts. The best 'guesstimates' from the
consensus of the literature is that equity probably declined to some extent
under the Conservatives, but may increase under New Labour if its policy
intentions translate into policy in action.

Management reform outcomes: a product of public choice prescriptions?

A survey of the literature examining the impact of the reforms gives the
paradox of too much and too little evidence. A Web of Science search
of the Social Science Citation Index on terms in the title is shown in
Table 4.4. However, the full titles indicate that many of these 'hits' are
not relevant to our criteria as they do not focus on the reforms considered
here. Similarly, a search of the *British Medical Journal* website archive
for the period 1994–2001 with the terms efficiency, equity, equality, and
responsiveness gave 30, 40, 5, and 12 references respectively, with full
titles indicating no relevant references for our purposes in the last two
categories.

Fortunately, there are a number of studies that have summarized the
evidence (Robinson and Le Grand 1993; Robinson 1996; Le Grand *et al.*
1998; Mays *et al.* 2000). In addition, there are a number of broad commentaries on the reforms (Baggott 1997; Powell 1997, 2000). All these
sources agree on two very broad conclusions. First, evaluation of the reforms
is problematic, partly because it represents a formidable evaluative challenge,
and partly because many of the studies are methodologically weak. Second,
it is very difficult to draw clear conclusions on the impact of the reforms.

According to Ranade (1998: 110), the difficulties of assessing the reform
outcomes are considerable. Similarly, Dowling (2000: xiii) points to the

problems of evaluating the reforms. More generally, Øvretveit (1998: 182–5) points to some common problems in evaluation: fuzzy boundaries; wobbly interventions; ghostly goals; gate-crashing confounding variables; prior information; chalk and cheese; the police car effect; and distant outcomes. Many commentators point to factors that can be linked with our summary of evaluation problems in Chapter 3. First, there is an absence of data, which can be seen in terms of missing data, missing the target, missing connections, and missing organizations. It is clear that the data have gaps in that it has proved difficult to operationalize the six concepts of competition, performance measurement, organizational size, efficiency, responsiveness and equity. Similarly, data for these concepts may be inaccurate. Data sets are rarely connected in that they tend to refer to different time periods, services or organizations. Finally, much information comes from examination of diverse case studies, which makes it difficult to generalize to the wider picture. Most of the studies focus on particular elements within the reforms: on the trees rather than on the wood. As we are unsure of the evaluation of these individual elements, it is premature to attempt to produce an overall assessment as the balance between the different elements is uncertain. Dowling (2000: 225–8) discusses the trade-off between efficiency and equity. It is unclear how a balance sheet could reach an overall verdict based on a weighting between efficiency, responsiveness and equity (cf. Klein 2001).

Second, it is difficult to separate the impact of the reforms from other potential influences on efficiency, responsiveness and equity. In particular, the socio-economic context such as changes in economic prosperity, cultural change and technological advances, and other policy changes makes it difficult to differentiate the 'gross' and 'net' effects of the reforms. According to Robinson (1996: 337), the main problems encountered by researchers seeking to assess the impact of the NHS reforms have been the scale, diversity and evolutionary nature of change. Studies have rarely considered the counterfactual of what might have occurred in the absence of reform. For example, linking public satisfaction figures to the reforms is problematic as it is possible that factors such as public expectations, media coverage and the level of funding are more important in shaping satisfaction than any direct impact of the reforms (see Powell 1997: 106–8).

Third, the methods used by some of the studies are problematic. The government did not commission any evaluations. Displaying an impressive knowledge of the Hawthorne effect and of public choice theory, Kenneth Clarke rejected a trial on the grounds that 'you buggers [the medical profession] will sabotage it'. Coulter (1995) points out that evaluation studies fall into three basic types. The first is concerned with monitoring, and most of the work falls into this category. Much of it is qualitative or impressionistic. It is not analytical and is sometimes purely anecdotal in nature. The second involves theory-testing. This 'indirect' work compares whether the conditions or prerequisites for markets to work effectively occur in practice. The third is empirical evaluation. There are very few published studies. They are usually quantitative in nature, requiring some type of quasi-experimental design with control or comparison. These studies are the most rigorous but are also the most difficult to conduct, involving problems of clarifying objectives, choosing controls, eliminating selection effects and attributing causation. Baggott (1997: 296) points to a number of biases within the debate. Supporters of internal markets have emphasized the pre-reform weaknesses of the NHS, while critics stress its strengths. Complex concepts such as efficiency and equity are difficult to measure. Supporters of the reforms have tended to focus on particular measures of activity which are quantitative and open to manipulation to back up their interpretation. On the other hand, the critics' case depends often on anecdote and 'hard cases' that may not accurately reflect the broader experience. Similarly, while the supporters stress efficiency, the critics stress equity. Le Grand *et al.* (1998) have examined the literature with specified search terms and sorted the evidence into a hierarchy. In other words, they do not simply go with the crowd, but place greater stress on the better quality studies. They presented 169 studies, but put greater stress on the 38 studies that contain controls and so are placed towards the top of their hierarchy.

As outlined in Chapter 3, we take greater account of certain types of evidence than others. There has been no shortage of verdicts on the reforms but, based on the discussion in Chapter 3, many 'evaluations' melt away to show a great deal of input but few valid and reliable outcomes. In short, we lack evidence that is based on a large sample of organizations, compares performance before and after the reforms, and takes account of the influence of other socio-economic and policy variables.

Second, given the difficulties outlined above, it is hardly surprising that there is little agreement on the magnitude and direction of the impact of the reforms. An early verdict by Le Grand (1993: 243) was that: 'Anyone who has come to this book hoping to find a definitive answer to the simple question as to whether, overall, the NHS reforms have had a positive or negative impact will be disappointed'. Similarly, Whitehead (1993: 215, 239) considered that many questions remained unanswered. There is no overall picture, which shows how painfully incomplete our information is, and that the studies so far have covered only fragments of the total package of policy interventions, and even then from only certain angles. The early view of the World Health Organization (1993: 57) was that little evaluation of managed market reform has taken place, mainly because these developments are fairly recent. However, in spite of the longer time period, there is little sign of a consensus developing. Klein (1998: 119) considers that the available evidence is incomplete and inconclusive. He claims (1998: 125, fn) that a book by Le Grand *et al.* (1998) provides the 'first comprehensive review of the available research evidence'. Unfortunately, summarizing that book, Le Grand (1999: 30–2) states that 'the first point to make about the evidence concerning the working of the quasi-market is that there is not very much of it, and that what there is, with one or two exceptions, is not very helpful'. He goes on to say that 'it is hard not to agree with Klein (1998: 115) that the outcome was less catastrophic than its opponents feared and less radical than its proponents hoped'. Most commentators agree on the difficulty of reaching clear conclusions. Holliday (1995: 79, 83) points out that it is 'difficult to make a conclusive judgement'. Any assessment of the strengths and weaknesses of the new NHS does not produce a clear reckoning in both positive and negative ways. Baggott (1997: 283) claims that there is much disagreement about the effects of the reforms, and there remains continuing controversy. Caldwell et al. (1998: 121) consider that the empirical evidence is mixed, inconclusive and unclear. West (1997: 154, 155, 181) states that 'there is no convincing evidence that the Reforms have produced a substantially better NHS', but adds that 'there is no reason to believe that the NHS has got manifestly worse under the Reforms'. He later concludes that the reforms 'have probably brought about some limited improvements in health care funding and delivery, and that these improvements are difficult to demonstrate scientifically'.

According to Le Grand et al. (1998: 129–30), the apparent absence of obvious change attributable to the internal market may be because there indeed was little change. Or it may be because there was change, but the studies concerned either focused on the wrong indicators, or focused on the right indicators but their deficiencies of technique were such that they could not pick up the relevant changes in the indicators. It is clear that in some unmeasurable ways the NHS has changed fundamentally since 1991. They conclude that 'although the problems with the published evidence are legion, there do appear to have been a sufficient number of competent studies that would have picked up changes and differences, had they been large'.

Bearing all these problems in mind, Figure 4.2 presents our best estimate summary of the impact of the reforms.

Conclusion

We are now able to return to the three basic questions posed towards the beginning of the book. The first question is whether reforms compatible with public choice theory occurred in principle and in practice. Public choice prescriptions were not consistently and coherently pursued in health care. The Conservatives advocated greater competition, performance information and smaller organizational size to varying degrees in the hope that they might result in greater efficiency and responsiveness. New

Consequences of reform

	Efficiency	Responsiveness	Equity
Competition	Positive	Little	Negative
Performance measurement	Little	Little	Negative
Organizational size	Positive	Little	None

Figure 4.2 Matrix of evidence on the connections between reforms and their consequences

Labour wishes to abolish competition, is increasing the size of the main purchasers, but is pursuing a more rounded system of performance assessment. It retains efficiency and responsiveness as goals, but views these within a wider picture that also places great stress on equity. In short, the period under review saw a muddled and partial version of public choice theory, emphasizing some of its means and ends, but ignoring or even contradicting other elements. Some elements of public choice theory are compatible with the reforms, but it is a pick-and-mix cafeteria rather than the full *à la carte* version. No Health Secretary appears to have had a complete copy of Niskanen (1971) in their red box. Frank Dobson's copy had many pages ripped out, with only the sections on performance measurement remaining. However, the section on competition may have reappeared in Alan Milburn's copy (perhaps pasted in by Tony Blair?). Moreover, a simple examination of both governments' intentions is insufficient as 'policy as adopted' did not always translate into 'policy in action'. Whether viewed from the perspective of dominant interests (Alford 1975), professional dominance (Wilding 1982) or the 'street-level bureaucrats' (Lipsky 1980), the 'implementation gap' (Marsh and Rhodes 1992) looms large in the NHS. As Le Grand (1999: 37) puts it: 'In one view, the British quasi-market in health care neither succeeded nor failed, simply because it was never tried'. Similarly, much performance information was produced, but the extent to which it was used, and the ways in which it was used, are less clear.

The second question is concerned with whether performance changed. It is difficult to establish clear trends in the major variables of efficiency, responsiveness and equity. Few studies have operationalized these concepts and measured them over time. The few studies that have achieved this stress that the measures may suffer from problems of validity and reliability. Our best estimates from the available studies suggest some gains in efficiency in the early years of the internal market which seem to have subsequently levelled off. There have probably been some limited increases in responsiveness. There were probably some decreases in equity under the Conservatives, and there may be some increases under New Labour.

The final question of the impact of reform is the most difficult to answer. There are fewer clear, unambiguous impacts than proponents have claimed or critics feared. It is not fully clear whether this is due to limited impact or simply that studies failed to detect much impact. However, while it is easy to criticize the design of some studies, it probably is more a reflection of the problems of evaluating complex and multiple policy changes. Perhaps as the sharper edges of the legislative changes became blunter on the ground, the resulting outcomes – for better or worse – became less detectable. Our best estimate is that it may be possible to link some efficiency gains and equity losses to greater competition. More performance information may have had some small positive effects on efficiency and responsiveness. Smaller organizational size (mainly in the form of devolved purchasing) may have had some small positive impacts on efficiency and responsiveness. While an overall agnostic or nihilist conclusion is very tempting, a forced verdict suggests that public choice reforms in the NHS may have resulted in some gains on the 'internal' criteria of efficiency and responsiveness, but in some losses in the 'external' criterion of equity.

five

Housing reforms

In this chapter we demonstrate that public choice principles have been at the centre of reforms in the social housing sector. However, given that the sector has two main providers, local authorities and housing associations, it becomes clear that these reforms have differentially impacted upon them, as have other programmes of reform (Walker 2001). As with the other areas of public policy explored in this book, there are fundamental problems in attempting to assess the impact of these reforms. We are able to show that the housing sector has moved beyond policy as adopted to policy in action, and that some changes in efficiency and responsiveness are in the anticipated direction. However, there are a range of areas where equity has been reduced. Given that there are methodological problems in the evaluation and that longitudinal data on reform are somewhat sparse, we are not able to reach clear conclusions on the impact of reform. Nevertheless, the evidence on balance suggests that the impact has been negative on efficiency and equity and positive on responsiveness. Our judgement for the housing sector is that public choice theory has failed to deliver all of its anticipated outcomes.

Housing reforms and public choice theory

In this section we analyse the extent to which reforms in the social housing sector have been consistent with public choice principles. Table 5.1 summarizes the main features of housing policies between 1979 and 2001 and links these to public choice theory. The first two columns indicate the relevant legislation and the nature of the social housing reforms. The next three columns identify whether the reforms resulted in greater competition, more information on performance and smaller housing organizations.

Table 5.1 Social housing policy reform in England and Wales and public choice theory

Legislation	Key reforms	More competition?	More information?	Smaller organizations?
Housing Act 1980	Right to buy (discounts extended and deepened in subsequent legislation)	Yes	No	Partial
	Tenants' Charter	Partial	Partial	No
	Low-cost home ownership	Yes	No	No
Local Government Act 1980	CCT for repairs services	Yes	No	Yes
Social Security and Housing Benefits Act 1982	Introduction of Housing Benefit (subsequently modified through legislation and circular)	Yes	No	No
Building Control and Housing Act 1984	Right to repair, right to exchange	Partial	Partial	No
Local Government Act 1985	Abolition of GLC and metropolitan counties	No	No	Yes
Housing and Planning Act 1986	Section 16 funding for tenants groups (local authority)	Partial	Yes	Partial
	Disposal of local authority estates to the private sector	Yes	No	No
Housing Act 1985	Voluntary transfers for local authority housing departments	Yes	No	Yes
Housing Act 1988	Tenants' Choice	Yes	Yes	Yes
	Housing action trusts	Yes	Yes	Yes
	Tenants' Guarantee	No	Yes	No
	Mixed public–private finance for housing associations	Yes	No	No
	Rent setting/major repairs funding for housing associations	Yes	No	No
	Section 96 funding for tenants groups (housing association)	Partial	Yes	No

Legislation	Provision			
Local Government and Housing Act 1989	Capital control for local authorities	No	No	Yes
	Revenue controls for local authorities	Yes	No	Yes
	Performance indicators for local authority tenants	No	Yes	No
	Strategic enabling role for local authorities	Partial	No	Yes
Leasehold Reform, Housing and Urban Development Act 1993	Rent to mortgage	Yes	No	No
	Right to manage	No	Yes	Yes
	CCT for local government housing management services	Yes	Partial	No
Local Government Act Reform Acts of 1994	Restructuring of local authority housing departments in Wales and some English areas	No	No	No
Housing Act 1996	Local housing companies	Yes	Partial	Yes
	Tougher regulatory framework	No	No	No
	Housing association performance indicators	No	Yes	No
	Statutory basis given to the ombudsman service for housing association tenants	No	Yes	No
	Homelessness and allocation reforms	No	No	No
Wales Act 1999	Establishment of the National Assembly for Wales	No	Yes	No
	Merger between Housing for Wales and National Assembly for Wales	No	No	No
Local Government Act 1999	Best Value regime	Yes	Yes	Partial
	Best Value Inspectorate	No	Yes	No
Summary	Yes	15	12	10
	Partial	5	4	3
	No	13	17	20

Sources: Boyne and Walker (1999), Bramley (1993), Malpass and Murie (1990) and relevant legislation and government papers

A range of polices have been adopted covering changes to finance and resource allocation, various forms of internal and external decentralization, and changes in the management and organization of social housing. These reforms, commencing with the Housing Act 1980, marked a major departure from previous national housing polices. The period prior to 1979 is characterized as a bureaucratic, needs-based system of housing provision and management, dominated by local government. Little information on rights or performance was available to tenants; exit options, through for example the right to buy, only existed in a small number of local authorities; and some of the larger local authorities owned and managed over 100,000 homes (see Malpass and Murie 1990; Cole and Furbey 1994).

Our categorization of key housing reforms highlights the radical nature of policy change and the central role of public choice principles in this – through, for example, the influence of the Adam Smith Institute (Butler *et al.* 1985). What is particularly noticeable is the continuity of many reforms under the Labour administration. All but four of the 33 specific reforms are consistent with at least one element of the public choice model. Indeed, 14 reforms reflect two public choice principles, and four reforms (Tenants' Choice, housing action trusts, compulsory competitive tendering and local housing companies) are in line with all three principles (though the former three reforms have now been repealed). Table 5.1 only refers to policy as adopted. However, it indicates the range of reforms that are derived from public choice theory. The predominant public choice theme is more competition (20 of the 33 reforms), followed by more information on performance (14) and smaller organizational size (12 reforms). There are four cases where reforms are in the opposite direction to the prescriptions of public choice theory. These relate to legislation under the Major and Blair administrations. They are: the recent reorganizations of local government in Britain that have led to an increase in the size of local authority housing departments; the Housing Act 1996 that gave the Housing Corporation and Housing for Wales greater power over supposedly independent organizations; the homelessness reforms under the 1996 Act which reduced choice for homeless households; and, more recently, the absorption of Housing for Wales into the National Assembly, which clearly increases organizational size by disbanding a smaller organization. The reforms identified as consistent with public choice theory are now considered in more detail. In this discussion we explore the extent to which policy as adopted has become policy in action.

More competition

More competition has been brought into the housing sector and the bridge between policy as adopted and policy in action has been crossed in a number of cases. Initial polices to privatize the local authority sector through

Table 5.2 Compulsory competitive tendering of housing management services in England

Number of local authorities	69
Number of units	1,115,481
Number of contracts	318
Average contract size	3,508
Number of external contracts	16
Contracts managed by housing associations	6
Contracts managed by private sector bodies	10
Number of local authorities with external contractors	7
Number of voluntary competitive tenders	3

Source: *Public Housing News* (1996/97)

the right to buy and other home ownership routes imposed a competitive threat on social landlords: tenants who are dissatisfied with the service may choose to take their custom elsewhere (in this case, into the owner-occupied sector). However, the competitive effect is diluted in mixed tenure forms (for example, shared ownership or rents to mortgages) or in leasehold tenures (purchase of flats by tenants). In these forms of tenure the previous landlord–tenant relationship was redefined as a contractual one for specific services such as external maintenance on leasehold flats.

Management reforms brought competition to local authority housing departments in 1980 when the repairs service, traditionally provided by an in-house team, was put out to tender along with other blue-collar services. This was extended in 1993 when CCT for housing management was introduced, though never fully implemented. In England, 69 local authorities had let contracts for all or part of the stock by July 1996 (*Public Housing News* 1996/97), of which the overwhelming majority were won in-house (see Table 5.2). Only two local authorities let contracts voluntarily ahead of statutory requirements. No contracts were let in Scotland or Wales. This outcome suggests that there were few changes to market structure and behaviour. This argument can also be directed at blue-collar services where the market was sometimes 'managed' with disastrous results. For example Ashworth *et al.* (2002) cite the case of the failure of the local authority direct labour organization in Rhondda Cynon Taff, where one of the driving forces was not high-quality and efficient services, but securing local jobs in an area of high unemployment. In order to secure the work the authority underpriced the contract. It subsequently ran into major financial difficulties and the contracts were retendered with the local authority disbarred from the competition, resulting in the loss of the very jobs it had initially sought to protect.

The Labour government's Best Value regime, introduced from 1 April 2000, repealed the CCT legislation and introduced new competitive mechanisms

(Department of the Environment, Transport and the Regions (DETR) 1999c). Though there has been much debate about the 'test of competitiveness' every local housing authority has to pass, there are as yet no data on the consequences for market structures and behaviour (Boyne *et al.* 1999).

Major injections of competition came through the redesignation of housing associations as the providers of new social housing by the Housing Act 1988. Simultaneously, the position of local authorities was weakened and their role in producing new housing restricted through the Local Government and Housing Act 1989, such that by 1999 English local authorities only completed 79 new homes. The Housing Act 1988 deregulated the private rented sector, introduced Tenants' Choice and housing action trusts, and changed the financial system for independent housing associations. Local monopolies were to be weakened in several ways: by the inability of local authorities to increase in size, by the creation of tenant-led organizations, and by the promotion of housing associations as the providers of social housing. Associations would raise finance in the private market, compete for government resources, set their own rents and manage their internal finances, all of which would in turn bring market disciplines to the organization. Furthermore, tenants or potential tenants were to be given more choice as the number of providers of new housing was to increase allowing them to shop between different suppliers.

The extension of markets into social housing has continued through internal and external decentralization. The right to manage (tenant management organizations (TMOs), which include tenant management co-operatives and estate management boards) is a form of internal decentralization, but TMOs have not been numerically significant (Scott *et al.* 1994a). This policy builds upon the decentralization of services within a normal bureaucratic framework. Though it is thirty years since these models were first experimented with (Cole and Furbey 1994), decentralization is now seen as essential for any landlord to attract and retain tenants (Cole *et al.* 2001). External decentralization was promoted by the Conservative government through Tenants' Choice and housing action trusts. These reforms only became policy in action in a small number of cases. However, the most extensive external decentralization has come from local authorities themselves: 143 local authority housing departments have transferred all or part of their housing stock into the housing association sector (Table 5.3). Just over 100 authorities have transferred all their stock through the 'large scale voluntary transfer' (LSVT) route, with a smaller number being supported by the now defunct Estates Renewal Challenge Fund scheme for local housing companies. Larger transfers are usually to a new organization, whilst smaller ones are often to existing associations, increasingly as part of 'group structures' (see below), therefore having a neutral impact on market structure. Though government has suggested an upper limit of

Table 5.3 The number of dwellings transferred out of public ownership to housing associations in England, 1989/99–2000/01

Year	Number of authorities transferring[1] LSVT	Number of dwellings	Mean number of dwellings transferred	Number of Estates Renewal Challenge Fund supported partial stock transfers	Number of dwellings	Mean number of dwellings transferred
1988/89	2	11,176	5,588	–		–
1989/90	2	14,405	7,203	–		–
1990/91	11	45,512	4,137	–		–
1991/92	2	10,791	5,396	–		–
1992/93	4	26,325	6,581	–		–
1993/94	9	30,103	3,345	–		–
1994/95	10	40,234	4,023	–		–
1995/96	11	44,871	4,079	–		–
1996/97	5	22,248	4,450	–		–
1997/98	6	24,405	4,068	9	8,577	953
1998/99	11	56,072	5,097	12	17,828	1,458
1999/2000	14	80,405	5,743	10	16,980	1,698
2000/01	22	295,552	13,434	3	3,804	1,268
Total	109	702,139	6,441	34	47,189	1,388

[1] LSVT and local housing company rules.

Source: Wilcox (2000) and Housing Today, 20 January 2000: 2

12,000 units per newly transferred organization (DETR 2000) during 2000/01 the Housing Corporation registered new transfer associations with 20,000 and 36,000 units (Housing Corporation 2001). However, these mechanisms, and transfer in particular, have a neutral impact on competition unless these new organizations change their behaviour to expand their market share in other areas, thereby offering consumers power to switch between providers.

The legislative changes of the late 1980s restructured subsidy systems and altered behaviour in the housing association sector, though the overall finance system for associations is still reliant on the allocation of resources to areas by needs-based formulae. Subsidy, in the form of Social Housing Grant (SHG), was allocated to associations through a competitive process – won by housing associations that could provide the most units at the lowest cost. In Wales, competition between associations was introduced in 1994 (Walker and Smith 1999). SHG levels fell in England from 80 per cent in 1989 to as low as 20 per cent as associations bid against one another to develop new schemes. As some associations expanded their market share through this programme so their stock became geographically dispersed. Government and the regulator now question the rationale behind numerous landlords with small stock holdings, sometimes away from a local office, in one area. The regulator now seeks to transfer this stock to more local associations, not on the grounds of competition but in pursuit of efficiency and responsiveness.

Government sought to further enhance consumer power by raising local authority and housing association rents and placing emphasis on personal subsidy rather than by the historic approach of investing in bricks and mortar. These policy changes were introduced to give tenants a level playing field and hence a choice of landlord between the social and private sector. A greater reliance on Housing Benefit also allowed low-income or unemployed households a choice of landlord as Housing Benefit could then be viewed as a voucher offering tenants, or prospective tenants, the opportunity to search for their optimal housing solution. There is now evidence of tenants making and exercising their choices (Cole and Robinson 2000). However, as the costs of housing subsidy were transferred from the then Department of the Environment to the Department for Social Security, concerns about the total level of Housing Benefit led to a range of cuts and restrictions in its availability. These changes saw the cost of Housing Benefit rise from £5.401 billion in 1986/87 to £14.066 billion in 1996/97 and subsequently decline in real terms (Wilcox 2000). Part of the strategy to reduce these costs has been to increase producer subsidies once more to alleviate the negative impacts that were seen to arise from these public choice inspired reforms (see below). However, as we discuss below, changes in the social housing sector have offered tenants real choices between landlords.

Though competition has been extended into the social housing sector in a number of ways, the overall framework of finance remains formula-driven. The majority of resources are allocated by formula in the local authority sector. There are, nonetheless, examples of changes in this area: increasing discretion is given to regional office controllers to allocate a proportion of resources based on organizational performance; a range of competitive measures has been introduced to top-slice funding for particular programmes; and local authorities are also being encouraged to plan the use of their own resources more strategically, over a three-year period, with the gradual introduction of resource accounting (DETR 1999b). Housing associations, though individually competing for subsidy, work in a formula-driven framework. Over recent years, this has been increasingly needs-focused, based on a policy agenda of regeneration and the provision of social housing in the high-demand South East of England. The government resources available to housing associations have not grown substantially over the 1990s, and in response to this they have explored new non-housing subsidy forms of activity. This diversification of funding sources has led to a diversification of activity, including regeneration, care and support, and private finance initiatives (PFI) for 'key workers' (Mullins *et al.* 2001). This once again pits housing association against housing association in a new era of competition.

In Chapter 3 we identified nine conditions that need to be met if the public choice prescriptions of competition and customer choice are to be achieved. We may summarize our conclusions in terms of those conditions as follows:

1 There has been a marginal increase in the number of service producers as local authorities have transferred their stock into the housing association sector.
2 The balance between producers has become more equal and shifted away from local authorities to housing associations.
3 Consumers have more choice as competition has led to an increase in the number of public suppliers.
4 Consumers have greater choice between public and private suppliers because of the growth in the private rented sector.
5 There has been no change in direct choice because 'third-party' intermediaries have not played a role in the sector.
6 Exit has not fundamentally altered; though local authority housing departments may have exited to the housing association sector, the overall impact on market structure is limited.
7 The outcome for entry is similar to that for exit.

In addition to these changes in market structure, change has also been witnessed in the behaviour of social landlords.

8 Local authorities have a large number of constraints placed upon them, which means that they are unable to defeat rivals and expand market share. Many have overcome these obstacles by transferring to the housing association sector where there are greater freedoms, notably financial ones. Housing associations are in competition with one another, and have been for some time. This was initially for subsidy, but now extends to a range of other activities as they seek to expand revenues and market share in a variety of settings.

9 Reforms have increased the power of consumers, who can and do shop around between different public and private landlords. They are also able to exercise more control over their existing landlord when a transfer is proposed, by voting on the transfer and thereby ensuring that the landlord takes account of their wishes.

A large number of Conservative policies have been left in place by the Labour government, which has promoted a range of pilots to enhance competition and choice. For example, choice-based allocations (R.S.G. Smith 2000) shift power away from the landlord in the allocation process to the applicant, who can choose which vacancies to apply for rather than be offered a property by a prospective landlord. However, these more recent changes remain policy as adopted rather than policy in action, because they are still pilots or demonstration projects and have not been fully transferred to the policy mainstream. Table 5.1 indicated that more competition was the dominant public choice theme adopted. However, our review of policy in action suggests that though competition has increased the extent to which this is consistent with public choice theory is more limited. Thus changes to market structures and behaviour are not as profound in practice as policy as adopted would suggest.

More information on performance

As with the enhancement of competitive mechanisms within the social rented sector, the provision of information on organizational performance gathered pace during the late 1980s. The Tenants' Charter for local authority housing tenants, introduced in the Housing Act 1980, gave tenants information on a range of issues (such as security of tenure) and the right to be consulted on major changes in housing management. These rights have subsequently been extended, and tenants have been given access to independent funding to support tenant participation and stock transfers. Some rights, such as the right to repair which allowed tenants to undertake repairs and charge the costs back to the landlord, also had implications for competition by allowing a tenant to shop around for a service.

Table 5.4 Performance information published for tenants in 2000/01

Dimensions of organizational performance	Current performance	Past performance	Performance of other organizations
Expenditure	0	0	0
Outputs	4	4	4
Outcomes	6	6	6
Efficiency	1	1	1
Cost-effectiveness	0	0	0
Probity	0	0	0

The systematic provision of performance measures to tenants has come through four reforms. First, the report to tenants regime was introduced in 1989 to provide information which would help local authority tenants make decisions about their landlords' performance whilst also opening up channels of communication between landlords and tenants (Smith and Walker 1994). Second, the Tenants' Guarantee, introduced in the 1988 Housing Act to increase the range of housing association tenants' rights under the then newly introduced assured tenancy, contained a requirement to provide performance information to tenants. Though initially on a permissive basis, action by regulators turned this into an expectation that has subsequently been given a statutory footing in the Housing Act 1996 under the 'Social Housing Standard'. Third, local authority tenants, and indeed housing association tenants, received Citizen's Charter performance indicators. These were published some time after the report to tenants and contained different performance measures, though similar information is often differently defined (Smith and Walker 1994; Symon and Walker 1995). Neither set of housing indicators provided a substantial amount of information on performance but rather consisted mainly of management information (Smith and Walker 1994; Boyne 1997a). Best Value seeks to address the weaknesses of these past performance regimes. This fourth performance information reform provides a clearer and more focused set of performance measures that place more emphasis upon outcomes and consumer satisfaction than prior regimes (Boyne 2002). The Best Value regime requires these to be published annually in a performance plan that also includes data on past and comparative performance.

The number of measures for the local authority sector is indicated in Table 5.4. The ongoing process of improvement to the measures of performance in the social housing sector has resulted in the use of the same measures for housing associations who are required to comply with the Best Value framework (though housing associations' performance indicators are more extensive, covering issues of corporate governance and finance). This now offers comparability between the two sub-sectors, giving tenants comparable information between different providers, which may influence their behaviour and enhance competition.

The information that has been made available to tenants in the local authority sector since 2000/01 under the auspices of the Best Value regime is audited to verify its accuracy. In the housing association sector data are not formally audited. However, regulators make site visits to associations and part of their remit includes an assessment of information and its systems. The regulatory function also includes the collation of a range of organizational performance indicators (Housing Corporation 1997). These are used to promote best practice, to analyse the relative performance of associations, and to highlight regulatory issues. Thus another agency works on behalf of consumers whilst making available information on associations which may be in direct competition with each other. In the local government sector there was little evidence of the systematic use of comparative data amongst the majority of landlords (see Boyne *et al.* 2000 on Welsh landlords) though benchmarking has been recently promoted by the Chartered Institute of Housing through Housemark, a benchmarking club. Though performance data have been made available to tenants for over a decade, little is known about its use in decision-making. The limited research evidence that does exist suggests that information has not been used in systematic ways (Symon and Walker 1995).

In addition to the receipt of information, complaints mechanisms have been formalized within the housing association sector and are promoted as best practice within the local authority sector (Welsh Office 1992). The advent of tenant participation also gives tenants routes to raise grievances, though this is dependent upon individual landlord practices. The right to information and to be involved in housing management issues has been enshrined in legislation since the 1980s. Every local authority and housing association now has to develop a 'tenant compact' that identifies at a neighbourhood level the information tenants are entitled to and ways that they can influence the management of the organization (DETR 1999a). These policies have to be adopted by all social landlords during 2001/02, therefore we know little about their impact on behaviour.

In summary, there has been a growth in the number of performance measures and rights available for tenants. Given that the baseline for performance measures was zero in the late 1970s, the provision of this information is judged to have been beneficial – something is better than nothing. However, the limited evidence that is available suggests that they are not used systematically by consumers, though consumers are now shopping between different providers in some parts of the UK. They are clearly used by landlords and regulators to monitor the performance of housing organizations, and this may have positive effects on performance.

Table 5.5 Housing completions in England, 1980–99

	1980	1989	1994	1999
Local authorities	67,337	14,012	1,094	79
Housing associations	19,299	10,651	30,848	17,523

Source: Wilcox (2000)

Table 5.6 Levels of unfitness in English local authorities and housing associations

	1991		1996	
	000s	%	000s	%
Local authorities	265	6.9	227	6.8
Housing associations	41	6.7	35	3.9

Source: Wilcox (2000)

Smaller organizations

Reforms have reduced organizational size, in many cases to create single-purpose organizations out of multi-purpose local authorities, whether through disaggregation, capital and revenue controls, the promotion of local authorities as strategic enablers, or the privatization initiatives that were discussed above. For example, the right to buy has had a substantial impact on the size of local authority housing departments: over 1.5 million local authority homes have been sold since 1980, netting in excess of £50 billion at 1997/98 prices. This reduced the overall size of the sector by a third and cut the total tenure share of local authorities in England and Wales by over ten percentage points. Government capital investment in social housing has declined as the sector has shrunk. Total gross investment has fallen from £7.7 billion in 1980/81 to £3.3 billion in 1998/99, though is projected to rise during 2000–02 (Wilcox 2000). As inputs have reduced, so have the number of social housing units completed (Table 5.5). However, whilst overall resources have fallen within the social rented sector the number of unfit properties has fallen 14 per cent in both the housing association and local authority sectors (Table 5.6).

The right to buy has not been the only reform to result in smaller organizations. For example, local authority housing management CCT led to smaller operational management units (Table 5.2). Stock transfers can also reduce organizational size, if the previous landlord's stock has been divided up at transfer (Table 5.3). Such reforms can be classified as consistent with public choice principles. As with data on changes in behaviour

Table 5.7 The average size of housing associations in England and Wales

Number of units	1979	1996	2001
England	136	438	683
Wales	122[1]	469	1986[2]

Notes:
[1] Data for 1981.
[2] 2001 data for the 29 developing associations in Wales.

Sources: Housing Corporation (1979, 1981, 2001), Housing for Wales (1996), National Assembly for Wales (2001a) and Wilcox (1992, 1997)

in relation to markets and performance information, there is again little systematic information on organizational size issues. Walker (2001) provides some evidence. He argues that there is greater managerial freedom in the housing association sector, compared to the local authority sector, where associations can adopt new strategies. However, three in four social rented homes remain in the local authority sector.

Contrary trends in organizational size have emerged. Table 5.7 shows that the promotion of housing associations has led to substantial increases in the average size of housing associations. This has been a product of individual organizational growth and stock transfers from the local authority sector. The number of associations with over 2500 homes was 60 in 1992, but by 1996 this figure had increased to 105. This is a perverse effect of establishing single-purpose organizations: LSVT associations are decoupled from the overall bureaucracy of the local authority yet represent large organizations within the housing association sector. Furthermore, typically as a result of financial pressures, housing associations are merging and developing group structures. Around 20 per cent of the housing association stock is currently owned or managed by associations that have merged over the last decade. These mergers are a result of pressures emanating from the private finance regime – associations need a greater asset base or a more balanced stock portfolio (Mullins 1998). In the group structures model a holding company is established which deals with key strategy issues, including finance, information technology and personnel. Attached to this are a number of associations, each of which is separately registered with the regulator. This model is seen to be flexible and allows for growth whilst gaining economies of scale. In April 2000, 77 per cent of associations were in a group, and two-thirds of all groups have two or three members (Audit Commission and Housing Corporation 2001). The largest association, Places for People, is now a group that owns in excess of 60,000 homes, more than the entire stock holding of development-active Welsh associations and bigger than most local authority housing departments.

Table 5.8 Average stock size before and after local government reorganization in Wales

Type of authority	Before LGR		After LGR	
	Number of LAs	Average	Number of LAs	Average
Rural	17	2,990	9	6,511
Urban	7	10,634	6	12,992
Valleys	13	6,917	7	11,510

Source: Walker and Williams (1995)

Table 5.9 The impact of public choice reforms on social housing in England and Wales, 1979–2000

	Competition	Information on performance	Organizational size
Local authorities	More	More	Reduced
Housing associations	More	More	Increased

The gradual reduction in local authority organizational size has been stalled by the reform of local government in the 1990s. This has served to increase local authority organizational size through merger of neighbouring districts into new unitary authorities (though local government reform in 1986 broke up the Greater London Council, a substantial landlord). Table 5.8 clearly indicates that the overall impact of reorganization in Wales was to substantially increase the stock and staffing levels of individual departments (Walker and Williams 1995). In England the impact of structural reform has been less dramatic, but still produced a net increase in the average size of councils' stock from 12,193 in 1995 to 13,040 in 1998 (Boyne and Walker 1999).

Summary

The general direction of social housing reform in the UK since 1979 is clearly consistent with public choice principles and there is evidence of policy in action, not just adoption (see Table 5.9). In both the local authority and housing association sectors, competitive pressures have increased and more information on organizational performance has been produced. However, although organizational scale has declined in local government, the average size of housing associations has risen. Therefore, if public choice theory is correct, and if changes in competition and performance information are roughly equal in the two sectors, then improvements in organizational performance should be greater in local authority housing departments than in housing associations. In the latter sector, any positive effects from competition and performance indicators may be offset, at least in part, by organizational growth.

The impact of social housing reforms: a review of the evidence

In this section we present a comprehensive analysis of the research evidence on housing reforms. The evidence is drawn from the extensive range of government, research council, charitable foundation and academic research undertaken over the last two decades. Our evaluation is based upon the three criteria of technical efficiency, responsiveness and equity.

Efficiency

Public choice theory predicts that the costs of constructing a 'standard' dwelling should fall over time as a result of social housing reforms since 1979. Available data do not provide a clear picture of the changing costs of production in the housing association sector, but do suggest that costs have reduced (see Table 5.10). Even though the average size of associations

Table 5.10 The costs of producing housing association units in England

Year	Number of units completed[1]	Investment[2] (£000s)	Cost per unit[3] (£s)
1990/91	21,560	1,602	73,995
1991/92	49,640	2,151	43,331
1992/93	76,030	3,605	47,415
1993/94	64,078	3,231	50,423
1994/95	59,513	2,911	48,914
1995/96	41,974	2,537	60,442
1996/97	47,320	2,305	48,711

Notes:
[1] Out-turn figures are for rented, housing market package (1992/93), short-life and low-cost home ownership.
[2] Investment is derived from Housing Corporation, local authority and private sector finance. Disaggregated data are not available for the private finance element which might also be used for stock improvements and transfers.
[3] Real prices. Variations are due to construction lags, new programmes and changes in the construction market.

Source: Wilcox (1997)

has increased they may still be too small to achieve economies of scale in production, except in the case of the largest associations (Bramley 1993). The absence of major productivity gains may in part reflect the nature of the housing and land market and costs in the construction industry and labour market. Competition between associations for government subsidy has 'bid down' the amount of grant requested by housing associations year on year. As noted above, in 1990 subsidy rates were 80 per cent. By 1997 government set the SHG rate at 52 per cent. Inter-association competition during the 1990s resulted in the average subsidy dropping further to 42 per cent and in some areas of England it fell to as low as 20 per cent. Alongside reductions in subsidy, quality has diminished as space standards have fallen (Karn and Sheridan 1994).

Comprehensive and systematic time-series data on housing management costs are not available. Housing associations and local authorities, though providing similar services, vary in their definitions of housing management tasks and the costs attached to them (Jackson *et al.* 1992). Housing associations have traditionally been more expensive than local authorities (Maclennan *et al.* 1989) and continue to be so (Bines *et al.* 1993). This has been attributed to their smaller size and higher-quality services (Maclennan *et al.* 1989), and to the fact that they are more likely to be working in difficult areas, which historically received an additional subsidy (Bines *et al.* 1993). There is research evidence pointing towards reduced costs within housing associations (Walker 1998a, 1998b), a result of regulatory activity as much as market pressures from private finance institutions (Walker and Smith 1999).

Longitudinal data indicate that local authority housing management costs have actually risen in absolute terms. CIPFA housing revenue accounts show that they have moved from £2.21 (per week per unit) in 1986 to £8.64 in 1992 and stood at £12.50 in 2000. There are, however, a number of factors which influence the interpretation of these data. These include accountancy practices that mean that differing services and elements of services are charged against housing management costs over time (Jackson *et al.* 1992; Kemp 1995). Cost pressures in this part of the public sector have come through government action and control over rents as much as from competition. Indeed, more recent evidence suggests that there is no market to test the costs of housing management services (*Public Housing News* 1996/97). There is no evidence on the costs of housing management under CCT, or comparisons with non-tendered housing management, though cost comparisons between housing associations and local authorities are becoming more common (Housing Corporation 1998b). In addition, local authorities tender differing amounts and types of services. The impact of competition on the costs of housing management services is a complex area. Disputes are ongoing about the nature and scope of housing management (for example, Franklin and Clapham 1997) and what can be charged to the housing revenue account. Extensive government research (Maclennan *et al.* 1989; Price Waterhouse 1992; Bines *et al.* 1993) has not been able to identify housing management costs, though government continues to explore this issue.

The relationship between organizational size and technical efficiency is also complex because a number of contradictory forces are in operation across the local authority and housing association sectors. Housing associations as the externalized providers of new homes have grown substantially in size through new building. Much of the expansion of individual housing associations has come through their increased public sector expenditure. Local authorities have become smaller as they have lost stock through the right to buy. There are, however, cross-sectional studies that compare large and small organizations (Bines *et al.* 1993). These studies suggest that the size of housing stock managed by 'mass landlords' (councils and housing associations) is negatively related to performance (Clapham 1992). Such results may be taken to imply that all housing agencies should be disaggregated into small units. However, other research shows that the picture is more complex. Boyne (1996a) analyses the relationship between the size of the housing stock in 401 English and Welsh councils and three measures of performance: the number of weeks taken to relet vacant dwellings, the percentage of the total stock that is vacant, and the percentage of tenants owing over 13 weeks' rent. In all three cases, the effect of scale is non-linear: performance at first declines with the size of the housing stock, but improves again in the largest authorities. This pattern is inconsistent with the public choice assumption that the largest organizations are the poorest performers. Indeed, the results imply that the optimum scale is either large or small, and that the worst performers occupy the middle of the range.

Bines *et al.* (1993) analyse housing performance on the basis of a combined indicator derived from response time to reactive repairs, the number of weeks taken to relet vacant dwellings, the rate of transfers and the percentage of tenants in arrears. Their results for high-, medium- and low-performing local authorities indicate that smaller organizations (up to 5000) were more likely to be better performers, with only a small percentage of larger organizations (over 30,001 units) being classified as high performers. For housing associations the picture is less clear. It is, however, important to note the impact of the use of different performance measures. If the Audit Commission's indicator of rent arrears (that used by Boyne) is adopted within the housing association sector, the quality of performance falls across all sizes of organization (Bines *et al.* 1993). In relation to housing associations as the externalized providers of new social housing and their small mean stock size, research evidence suggests that their intrinsic organizational form as single-purpose housing organizations does not substantially influence efficiency (Birchall 1997).

Table 5.11 Performance change on measures of efficiency

	Average relet time[1] (days)	Rent collection[2] (%)	Rent arrears[3] (%)	Void rate[4] (%)
1993/94	35	98.4	n/a	0.89
1996/97	37.8	98.5	3.8	1.2
1999/00	41.8	96.9	3.8	2.3
Change	−19.4%	−1.5%	0	−158.4%

Notes:
[1] Average time taken to relet dwellings available for letting or awaiting minor repairs.
[2] Rent collected as a percentage of rent due.
[3] Rent arrears as a percentage of the rent roll.
[4] Management voids as a percentage of stock.
Source: Audit Commission performance indicators

Whereas the effects of competition and organizational size are unclear, performance measurement regimes have had a profound impact on social housing organizations and the nature of housing management, which has become increasingly driven by performance criteria (Walker 2000). Maclennan et al. (1989) noted that performance measurement systems were rudimentary in the sector, though the National Federation of Housing Associations (NFHA 1987) has promoted the use of performance measurement for over a decade. During the early 1990s the performance of social housing organizations increased. Rent arrears were lower, property allocated more rapidly and repairs were undertaken more quickly (see Bines et al. 1993; Housing Corporation 1997). These increases in performance have happened whilst local authorities have become smaller and many housing associations larger. However, following a decade of improvement there is now evidence of deteriorating performance in these areas in housing associations and local authorities. For example, Pawson (2001), using Audit Commission data, shows how performance has fallen in all local authorities over the period 1996/97–1999/2000 for all types of authorities for rent collection, rent arrears, relet times and void rates. It is possible to track these data over the period 1993/94–1999/2000 and arrive at the same conclusions (Table 5.11). Change in performance deteriorates in three areas – marginally for rent collection, by nearly a fifth for relet times, and over one and a half times for empty properties – and remains unchanged for rent arrears (the indicator was not collected in the same format in 1993/94). For these core indicators of housing management performance the judgement on efficiency is negative.

The evidence presented above indicates that public choice principles have played an important role in the changes to efficiency that we have discussed. The impact of these reforms on efficiency is roughly in proportion to the number of reforms noted in Table 5.1. Competition processes have introduced a market structure and led to changed behaviour – for example, the costs of new dwellings in the housing association sector fell and organizations became much more aware of their costs. The introduction of performance measurement regimes has affected the performance of social housing organizations. The evidence on organizational size is mixed. Some results suggest that smaller organizations were better performers, but the evidence also indicates that larger organizations are good performers. Some changes are a product of the actions of others – for example, the regulator in the housing association sector is a powerful influence on performance (Mullins *et al.* 2001), and the external organizational context, as we discuss later, is a further important influence on efficiency.

In summary, the evidence that is available does not allow us to draw a clear-cut conclusion on the impact of public choice reforms on costs, quality and quantity. Some costs have been reduced whilst others have risen. Initial gains in performance in the key areas of housing management tasks have been reversed as performance has fallen. Key measures for housing management performance do, however, indicate that performance has deteriorated through the 1990s. We therefore conclude that public choice theory reforms have not had a positive gross impact on efficiency.

Responsiveness

There is sufficient published evidence to argue that social housing organizations have become more responsive to the needs of their users over the last few decades. This has arisen from competitive pressures, the provision of information to tenants and the creation of smaller organizations; however, other factors have also played an important role. Though hard performance data are limited, evidence from the Audit Commission shows that responsiveness, as measured through the percentage of repairs completed within government time scales, improved for the period 1996/97–1999/2000 (Pawson 2001), in contrast to the efficiency changes noted above. Indirect service users, for example applicants or people seeking information about the local housing market, know more about rehousing possibilities through the availability of information and the growth of housing advice. The question of responsiveness to taxpayers more widely is less clear – performance information is now at hand, though we know little about its use. For our final group of stakeholders, staff, even less is known. No research since the early 1990s (Bines *et al.* 1993) has examined staff issues. Their concerns are highlighted in relation to proposed policy changes (e.g. CCT or transfers) but not researched. The Best Value regime potentially alters this by gathering their views during reviews; however, this is 'policy as adopted' and limited evidence exists on behaviour (Boyne *et al.* 2000). This section therefore focuses upon direct service users.

The power of the bureau has been successfully challenged – indeed this process has been supported by the professional institute, the Chartered Institute of Housing (Walker 1998b). One facet of this has been the debate about the nomenclature of public sector users (Symon and Walker 1995). The term 'client' is no longer judged appropriate because it has connotations of patronage and professional power. Many organizations now call their tenants 'customers', indicating that they are valued and their views will be taken on board (Caincross et al. 1996). The use of the term 'consumer' has not as yet developed, reflecting the realities for many social housing tenants – their choices may be limited. One explanation of these changing attitudes is found in the growth of competition, for example through exit routes, brought about by the Housing Act 1988. This produced a substantial response from local authorities and they adopted a range of market-based research strategies (Satsangi and Kearns 1992). For example, by 1990/91, 56 per cent of English local authority housing departments had undertaken tenant satisfaction surveys (Bines et al. 1993). All local housing authorities are now required to undertake surveys of customer satisfaction as part of the Best Value regime, whilst housing associations have to report levels of tenant satisfaction to their regulator.

The provision of performance data has been an important aspect of growing responsiveness. It has allowed government and its agencies to ask questions about the performance of social housing landlords, as noted above. These were not previously issues of concern, simply because the data did not exist. Much of the impact of the rhetoric about the introduction of performance has been to increase the accountability of housing services. However, tenants are given little say in the construction and identification of performance measures – they are set by government or its agencies or representative organizations (see Chartered Institute of Housing 1997) – though they are now consulted on them through their national consultative organizations. When performance indicators are provided to tenants the research evidence suggests that this information has not been used in a systematic way to extract effectiveness from bureaux or to open up a dialogue (Symon and Walker 1995). Consequently, accountability is typically upwards towards government and not downwards to the service users (Clapham and Satsangi 1992; Smith and Walker 1994; Symon and Walker 1995).

The Best Value regime makes information available on outputs, outcomes and efficiency to all stakeholders. However, information about housing organizations is not tailored to the needs of particular groups, nor necessarily easily accessible, particularly in the case of housing associations. We noted earlier that some groups of stakeholders, such as staff, need to be treated heterogeneously. However, the data that are made available on the performance of organizations treat all stakeholders homogeneously. Figure 5.1 presents our evaluation of public choice reforms on service

Stakeholder groups

Organizational activities and achievements	Direct service users	Indirect service users	Taxpayers	Staff
Expenditure	No data			
Outputs	Standard data			
Outcomes	Standard data			
Efficiency	Standard data			
Cost-effectiveness	No data			
Probity	No data			

Figure 5.1 Data availability for evaluating the impact of public management reforms on service responsiveness

responsiveness. It is also important to stress that this indicates if data are available because it is not possible to indicate levels of satisfaction with services provided by a landlord. It shows that the emphasis is on outputs, outcomes and efficiency. No measures of cost-effectiveness have been developed, nor have issues of probity been addressed. Information on expenditure was previously available, but is now no longer so because it is seen as management information rather than performance data. However, proposed changes could reduce the data that are available. For example, in Wales efficiency measures (cost per unit of management) will no longer be collected (National Assembly for Wales 2001a).

To overcome the weaknesses of performance regimes, whilst reflecting the limited choices available to tenants, the search for responsiveness has been extended beyond new definitions of tenants, market-based research strategies and performance indicators. Social housing landlords, with the support and encouragement of government (e.g. Housing Corporation 1998a), have promoted voice mechanisms – a varied range of strategies to involve tenants in decision-making and thereby improve their knowledge about the landlord and its services.

Tenant involvement in social housing pre-dates searches for responsiveness via information on performance (Ward 1974; Birchall 1992; Caincross *et al.* 1996). Tenant involvement, or voice mechanisms, range from information provision (consultation) through to the full delegation of responsibility to tenants' organizations (tenant control) (Burns *et al.* 1994). The right to be consulted on major changes in housing management has been enshrined in legislation since 1980, and now tenants have progressed to establish a range of TMOs which extend tenants' rights and interest in the performance of the landlord. The most extreme example of tenant management in England is the establishment of a TMO for the entire stock in the Royal Borough of Kensington and Chelsea (Darke and Rowlands 1997).

The emphasis upon voice and involvement has led to an 'industry' based around tenant participation: there are innumerable 'good practice' guides (see Scott *et al.* 1994b; Chartered Institute of Housing 1997); government in part funds the Tenant Participation Advisory Service and national tenants' organizations; and independent funding and advice exists for tenants where the landlord wishes to transfer its stock. However, the existence of advice, government action and funding tells us little about responsiveness in action.

Research in the early 1990s indicated the ongoing development of tenant involvement (Bines *et al.* 1993). For example, over 80 per cent of all social housing landlords had consulted their tenants on at least one or more issues in 1990/91; 35 per cent of housing associations had tenants on their committees, as against 16 per cent of local authorities. However, the promotion of participation and the existence of tenants' groups was seen more in larger organizations and large urban local authorities. Evidence presented by Bines *et al.* (1993) indicates that participation was more common where the degree of difficulty was higher.

Local authorities may develop participation strategies for particular purposes, notably transfers and area-based initiatives, both historically (e.g. Estates Action) and for current pilots (e.g. neighbourhood renewal). In the case of transfers, early research evidence indicated the limited extent to which tenants were involved in the decision-making process (Mullins *et al.* 1993). However, the need to consult tenants on the transfer and seek their approval in a ballot serves to develop an ongoing dialogue, whilst local housing companies' constitutions require tenant membership of the board and are leading to the development of more successful tenant involvement strategies (Hull 1997). Indeed, it is likely that local authority housing departments will not exist in a decade (Walker 2001) as stock transfer grows apace. This, in turn, will result in many more tenants becoming involved in the management of their landlords and further enhancing responsiveness.

Though notions of collective participation do not sit comfortably within a public choice framework, they were developed because of the limited choices faced by public sector tenants, and because of a realization that the provision of performance information alone does not increase responsiveness. However, research evidence indicates that officials have substantially more power in the tenant participation framework than tenants (Caincross *et al.* 1996; Sommerville 1998). Attempts to increase the responsiveness of social landlords to their tenants partly developed because demand exceeded supply, resulting in reduced choice. However, changes in the external environment now mean that supply exceeds demand in many areas (Cole and Robinson 2000). Social landlords now see information on their users as essential to ensure that they can tailor their services to users' needs. They recognize that this is also in their own interests. Dissatisfied tenants now have alternatives – other social housing providers, low-cost home ownership and private renting. Landlords therefore need to ensure that they are able to provide the services that will retain the users, thus market processes are also influencing responsiveness.

In our assessment of organizational size it was noted that some smaller organizations were seen to achieve better performance. Clapham (1992; Clapham and Kintrea 1992, 2000) has consistently argued that smaller organizations are able to be more responsive, and thus that all organizations should be reduced in size. Much of this evidence is derived from his work on housing co-operatives and community-based housing organizations in Britain, especially Scotland (Satsangi and Clapham 1990; Clapham and Kintrea 1992, 2000). However, higher tenant ratings of services were achieved in co-operatives which 'were operating in a more favourable environment' (Satsangi and Clapham 1990: viii) than in local authorities and housing associations. Some small-scale research does, however, support the view that responsiveness is higher in smaller organizations or organizational units. Glennerster and Turner (1993) indicate the ways in which locally based housing management solutions which involve tenants can raise satisfaction and the quality of life on estates. This evidence supports much of the rhetoric surrounding tenant participation (Ward 1974; Power 1987). Many organizations have adopted models of internal decentralization to be 'closer to the customer' (Cole and Furbey 1994). However, the large geographical areas covered by some housing associations can still mean that they are distant from their tenants. An innovative response by some associations has been to develop call centres to respond to customers' needs over the telephone (Walker 2000). This serves to provide a highly responsive service to tenants and a continuous flow of information about tenant attitudes towards the service as 'outbound' calls are made to assess aspects of satisfaction. Some housing associations are seeking to address the issue of size by establishing group structures or core and periphery organizations rather than mergers. These aim to provide more sensitive local services, often based around local authority areas.

In summary, we argue that responsiveness has increased, through tenant participation or 'voice' mechanisms as much as public choice principles that would lead to 'exit'. However, public choice reforms have clearly played a role in the successful search for enhanced responsiveness. In particular, changes to market structure have resulted in landlords working to ensure

Table 5.12 Average weekly incomes of household heads by tenure in Great Britain

Tenure	1976	1980	1984	1988	1992	1995	1998
Owners							
Outright owner	59	81	107	157	194	236	220
With mortgage	96	142	195	267	320	361	401
Tenants							
Local authority	58	68	76	93	110	122	130
housing association	54	66	88	94	120	137	142
Private – unfurnished	48	60	77	110	149	173	231
Private – furnished	57	87	89	161	170	223	250

Source: Wilcox (1997, 2000)

that they can retain tenants, to collect information on their users and to disseminate information about themselves. Additionally, much of the evidence suggests that smaller organizations result in higher levels of responsiveness.

Equity

The application of public choice principles to the social housing sector has impacted upon technical efficiency and responsiveness. However, there are a range of unanticipated outcomes from the reform programme, raising questions about equity and market processes in the public sector. Equity criteria of use, access, outcome and final income, discussed in Chapter 2, are closely interconnected in the housing sector. Therefore, we focus on four illustrative areas central to public choice reforms. We begin with the impact of housing those in greatest need in the social housing sector and the way in which the equity issues of use, access and final income are interconnected. Then we show how raising rents to a 'market level' has exacerbated problems of final income. Next, we reveal the impact of competition and information on performance as affecting outcomes and access issues in housing management. Finally, we use stock sales to illustrate issues of access.

Changes to the subsidy systems, the new role for housing associations and the option to exit the sector through the right to buy mean that social landlords now house those in greatest need. Table 5.12 indicates the general decrease in incomes of social renters as against owner-occupiers. (However, those in the lowest income decile are no longer renters but owner-occupiers (Burrows *et al.* 2000).) Within the social rented sector this implies a more equitable distribution of government subsidy. However, there are countervailing effects on equitable use. The targeting of social housing to those in greatest need has resulted in a process of residualization (Forrest and Murie 1991). Local authorities now hold poorer-quality stock and house the poorer sections of society who cannot afford to purchase their home. This then increases the proportion of tenants who are welfare-dependent. An additional countervailing outcome is that these tenants are also more likely to need more welfare and personal intensive housing management services in addition to property management (Walker 2000). The same residualization processes of the population, rather than the stock, have been seen in the housing association sector, which has increasingly housed those in greatest need since taking on the role of provider of new social housing. The outcome of residualization processes has been to leave social housing a stigmatized tenure of last resort. Its populations are welfare-dependent, crime is often high and some social housing estates can be 'no-go areas'. Processes of competition and reduced organizational size have marginalized large sections of society – from the labour market and from the mainstream of society (Clapham *et al.* 1995). Housing associations have acted against these movements through the development of 'local lettings policies' where they do not seek to house those in greatest need but take a view of the social needs of an estate (Griffiths *et al.* 1996). Perversely, these attempts to alleviate the adverse equity outcomes from public choice reforms could potentially lead to less equitable access to the stock as those in greatest need are no long housed as a first priority.

Second, Table 5.13 illustrates that there have been substantial increases in rents. These have arisen from the shift in housing finance policy towards personal subsidies and the movement of social housing rents towards the market level (Walker and Marsh 1998). However, substantial equity problems associated with final income have arisen. This is partly because changing rent policy in the social housing sector has impacts in other policy areas. Many tenants are now in unemployment or poverty traps and are unable to take advantage of employment opportunities (Clapham *et al.* 1995). These traps are a product of the interaction of taxation and welfare benefits, including Housing Benefit. The unemployment trap refers to the hurdle a household has to face to increase its income from work as against benefit. The poverty trap refers to the reduction of benefits and the payment of taxation as extra income is earned. In the worst-case situation the poverty trap can lead to a household facing a 97 per cent marginal tax rate as their earnings increase. Though there are limited behavioural studies, the action of many households is to choose benefits rather than employment (Bradshaw and Millar 1991). This process is exacerbated by the low earnings capacity of many social housing tenants and the increasingly low paid employment open to them (Ford and Wilcox 1994). Thus, final income of social housing tenants can be inequitably affected by these market-based reforms.

Table 5.13 Average weekly local authority and housing association rents in England (£)

Year	Local authority	Housing associations	
		Fair rents	Assured rents
1989	20.70	26.83	24.50
1990	23.74	29.94	28.97
1991	27.29	32.73	33.93
1992	30.57	36.48	39.03
1993	33.62	38.50	44.87
1994	35.68	42.15	45.90
1995	38.31	44.46	48.42
1996	40.10	48.25	50.24
1997	41.18	51.35	51.40
1998	42.24	54.51	53.16
1999	43.82	–	53.84
% change	112	103	120

Source: Wilcox (2000)

Inequities also emerge from the changing subsidy system in the local authority sector, though by the action of government. As rents have risen to reflect the market, local authorities' revenue accounts have been controlled by government, which has developed a system of internal cross-subsidy. This means that tenants in employment and paying their own rents subsidize the rents of welfare-dependent tenants. This leads to the poor subsidizing the poorer (Malpass *et al.* 1993) with resultant negative impacts on use and access.

Governments have put in place polices to respond to these unanticipated outcomes. From the late 1990s policies were devised, initially by the Welsh housing association regulator and then the English, to restrain rent increases (Walker and Smith 1999). Table 5.13 indicates that increases between 1998 and 1999 in England were less than 1 per cent for assured rents. Labour government welfare benefit reforms are designed to address some of these issues, but whilst housing benefit remains unreformed their impact is uncertain. The impact of these public choice inspired reforms has not been to bring final incomes into line with those of the rich. However, as Table 5.12 illustrates, the income of social housing renters has always been lower than that of owners. Following periods of rapid rent increases, which reduced access, attempts have been made to overcome these problems, but the remedies offered by public choice theorists have not been used. Rather the market has been managed to achieve this outcome – in the housing association sector the regulator has taken action to force rents down.

Third, competition and performance pressures have also changed the nature of housing management, with implications for access, use and outcomes. Competition and the associated cost pressures have reduced welfare provision in the housing association sector. The use of private finance led associations to build large peripheral low-risk estates on greenfield sites. The more equitable distribution of social housing to those in greatest need led associations to concentrate lower-income households in their stock. There are contradictory processes at work – a more equitable distribution of resources but the creation of low-income areas. The outcome is a tension about the nature of housing management. Housing management has been driven towards a 'bricks and mortar' approach focusing upon core housing management services by reforms in the spheres of competition and information on performance reforms. Simultaneously, housing organizations have been housing those in greatest need, which has led to more demands for welfare provision. Housing organizations have historically filled the welfare gaps left by other agencies – for example, helping someone with a welfare benefit claim or going shopping for an older person. If housing management does not provide these services the organization might be ineffective: if full benefits are not claimed, a tenant could fall into arrears and face eviction. Not only is this costly and time-consuming, but also the association's performance on rent arrears deteriorates. The response of housing associations to these tensions has been to attempt to reverse some of the negative outcomes that have arisen from the implementation of reforms based around competition, information on performance and organizational size. This is referred to as 'housing plus' or community development, a function traditionally undertaken by some associations. This involves associations providing a greater range of services to tenants (e.g. furnished tenancies for households who cannot purchase these goods, employment and training opportunities through construction work when new investment takes place or care and support packages). This may work to increase the equity in the sector; however, there are internal cross-subsidies because the services are paid for out of associations' overall rental income but benefits may only be reaped in one location (Clapham and Evans 1998). The development of housing plus has also been a response to the unanticipated outcomes of the introduction of market-like mechanisms in the housing association sector and seeks to address equity issues following the identification of a range of problems. Consequently, the merits of smaller and single-purpose organizations can be contested. Though associations may be better able to focus upon their tasks, the processes of residualization raises questions about the capacity of single-purpose bodies to manage people in poverty. These people may have a range of needs for services from different agencies which could, in the main, be served by one organization, for instance a local authority, thus the equity outcomes for a tenant of a single-purpose body such as housing association are reduced.

The final example of inequality is the sale of local authority stock. Stock sales have exacerbated the geographically uneven distribution of social rented housing affecting the equity criterion of access. Sales have been highest in the South East of England, where housing demand is greatest (Wilcox 1997). Thus choices for applicants for social housing are constrained both by historical decisions of local authorities and now the actions of individual tenants. Yet it can be argued that if a tenant buys a home and lives there another 30 years it makes little difference what tenure they are in. However, with high demand in areas such as the South East and homes being sold in the open market when a right-to-buy owner-occupier dies, rather than being available for social housing purposes, sales further affect access to social housing. In addition, other organizational responses such as stock transfers may mean that there are increased opportunities for access to social housing. The new housing association is able to develop (using its asset base, government subsidy and private finance) whereas a neighbouring local authority can only rely upon the existing housing associations.

New provision by housing associations led to building on greenfield sites and a reduction in rehabilitation work, resulting in homes in inappropriate places and thereby affecting access and use (Bramley 1993; Page 1993). By the end of the Conservatives' term of office this was beginning to express itself in some localities through a lack of demand. The most famous example of this was a new estate being demolished in the North East without ever being occupied. One response to these problems, and associated with the emphasis upon area-based projects, has been to invest in rehabilitation again. This example further illustrates how access varies by area. In some areas tenants may have choice as there are a number of housing associations, including the stock-transfer local authority, all providing new homes. In another area the local authority has sold most of its stock through the right to buy and tenants are left to choose from a residualized stock in short supply.

The application of public choice principles has resulted in resources being directed to those in greatest need. However, in relation to the evaluation criteria of use, access, outcome and final income, our examples suggest that equity has been reduced. In relation to the groups of the population illustrated in Figure 2.2 no systematic information is available. It is possible to point towards the availability of sheltered housing to improve the housing and care conditions of older people. The Housing Corporation has developed a 'black and ethnic minority strategy' to increase their access to decent housing. Though many groups may have seen increases in equity – see Harrison with Davis (2001) on disability, gender and ethnicity – it is uncertain if these are the result of public choice reforms. What is undeniable is that there have been a number of unanticipated outcomes from a reform programme based upon competition, performance and organizational size. These reforms have resulted in problems, difficulties and tensions. Aspects of these issues are rooted in government action in other areas, for example, the operations of the welfare benefits and taxation system.

Management reform outcomes: a product of public choice prescriptions?

That the origins of many of the management reforms to the social housing sector were a product of public choice theory is undeniable. Table 5.1 and the evidence above demonstrated that the majority of reforms correspond to the prescriptions of public choice theorists. Government documents from the Conservatives' terms in office during the 1980s and 1990s draw upon the framework. For example, the new role for markets and choice for tenants was clearly signalled in the Conservative manifesto of 1987 where a choice-of-landlord scheme was promoted (Conservative Party 1987). More recently, the Labour government has continued these themes, emphasizing choice, disaggregation and information (DETR 1999c, 2000).

Thus far we have only been able to demonstrate in broad terms that there is more competition, more performance information and smaller local authorities and larger housing associations. We are less clear on performance, but in the broadest terms we can argue that there have been increases in responsiveness, increases followed by decreases in efficiency, and decreases in equity. In Chapter 3 we noted general problems in the evaluation of any programme of reform. In addition to these technical problems, housing researchers have not been preoccupied with the impact of management reform on the sector. A Web of Science search (Table 5.14) found only 213 articles in total. Further analysis of these papers shows that the preoccupation of housing research has been with changes in tenure and efficiency in, for example, mortgage markets rather than the delivery of public services. This is clearly seen in the electronic literature search which included the 'AND reform' search category. This produced only one

Table 5.14 Academic journal articles on dimensions of management reform and housing

	housing AND	housing AND reform AND
effici*	159	1
equit*	31	0
responsive*	2	0

Source: Web of Science

article, concerned with reforms to the efficiency of the Chinese urban housing market rather than any aspects of management reform in the UK. Thus attempts to be more precise in the housing sector are no different and are clouded by methodological limitations and the presence of other variables.

Methodological limitations: the absence of data

The four data absence problems discussed in Chapter 3 are present in the housing literature. Overall the research evidence presented is derived from small-scale and *ad hoc* research. There are no longitudinal studies of the effects of policies to promote efficiency, responsiveness or equity. The large-scale surveys undertaken by Maclennan *et al.* (1989) and Bines *et al.* (1993) have built upon each other, being funded by the same government department, asking the same substantive research questions and adopting comparable methodologies, rather than being longitudinal. The data from these studies are now over a decade old and no recent research has been as extensive. Any current evidence is then flawed because organizations are missing. Furthermore, little work has examined the housing sector from a public choice perspective, therefore it has not considered issues of competition, size, performance indicators, efficiency, responsiveness and equity collectively to make the connections between the different parts of the framework. If studies have considered one of these facets they have typically done so from a different perspective. For example, work on competition has focused upon quasi-markets, which includes issues of equity but not, for example, size (Bramley 1993), thereby missing the target and resulting in missing data. Similarly, when studies have examined performance they have not considered all the sub-dimensions of performance (Clapham and Satsangi 1992; Smith and Walker 1994).

The presence of other variables

The evidence presented has indicated the interconnection of the three public choice principles. Notably, it is possible to suggest that efficiency improvements have been generated by the combined introduction of competition and performance indicators. Changes to market structure and behaviour have had adverse affects on organizational size in the housing associations sector. However, factors outside the public choice framework can act against its theoretical effects. In particular, organizational collusion, government action and the environmental context can have effects on technical efficiency. For example, competition within the housing association sector is internal and associations worked together to ensure that the private sector could not enter their market (Mullins 1997), thus protecting themselves from further competitive pressures. Consequently, the exposure to competition is tempered. Government action in one area can have unanticipated consequences in other spheres of government. The *laissez-faire* approach to housing association rents in the early 1990s had profound impacts on the costs of welfare benefits for tenants and on the Exchequer. This has led to efficiency drives to reduce rent levels (Walker and Smith 1999), rather than a search for additional efficiency through alterations to the competition framework, performance regimes or organizational size.

The pressures for increased performance are not, however, necessarily derived from systems of performance management alone. Housing associations and local authorities are subject to sanctions if they do not meet key performance measures which are now enshrined in legislation. The Best Value Inspectorate is able to take action if, for example, local authorities' rent arrears or management costs are seen as too high or their management is judged to be 'failing'. The Housing Corporation or the National Assembly for Wales will take particular interest in an association that it perceives to be performing poorly. Housing associations can lose government subsidy for new home building if their performance is poor. In these examples performance is driven by a regulator or inspector (a new bureaucracy), which public choice theory would see as a 'second best' compared to market pressures.

Key indicators of performance for housing associations are those set by the private finance institutions from whom they borrow. Thus liquidity ratios, gearing ratios and net interest cover are critical. If these indicators are not met loans can be withdrawn. This pressure on financial performance is emphasized through the regulators to ensure probity and value for money in the expenditure of public resources (Clapham and Satsangi 1992; Walker 1998b). Within the housing association sector the introduction of greater competition for government grants, competition for private finance (and the associated business rigour that is required to satisfy these lenders) and performance regimes highlight the interdependent nature of the reforms and the elements of public choice theory itself. Competition and performance measurement bring pressures for good-quality management to ensure that loans are repaid. The measurement of 'good-quality management' is demonstrated through performance indicators (see Audit Commission and Housing Corporation 1997; Housing Corporation 1998b). These confounding factors also illustrate the impact of other programmes of reform. Public choice theory was not the only set of ideas implemented to improve performance. Walker (2001) notes, in particular, how private sector management practices have been adopted in the housing association sector, and less so in the local authority sector. Practices include business process re-engineering, zero-based budgeting, benchmarking and risk assessment strategies (see Shah 2000).

Much of the housing research literature also places emphasis on the external organizational environment as a determinant of performance (Maclennan *et al.* 1989; Jackson *et al.* 1992; Bines *et al.* 1993; Walker 1994; Kemp 1995). The external environment is expressed through the concept of the 'degree of difficulty' of the housing management task. This concept encapsulates stock condition, geographical location of the stock and aspects of socio-economic deprivation. It is suggested that the 'degree of difficulty' is a key determinant of organizational performance. Kemp (1995: 785) argues for the significance of the environment in housing management performance research:

> The concept of the degree of difficulty of housing management is important because it draws attention to the fact that housing management performance is not only a function of ownership or organisational size and structure, or of the policies and practices of housing managers – yet these are the features that are frequently stressed in critiques of public-sector performance.

These examples illustrate the breadth of ways in which other factors are able to influence the efficiency of social housing organizations, and temper conclusions on the gains made through the adoption of public choice principles.

In relation to responsiveness, we again see interconnected impacts from the implementation of public choice principles. Local authorities have developed consumerist approaches in response to threats of competition and the imposition of performance regimes. In relation to organizational size, the evidence presented here would suggest that social landlords are able to provide responsive services. However, concepts of responsiveness have extended beyond public choice notions of competition and performance to consumer involvement. Tenants are able to express voice, thus creating opportunities to temper the power of the bureaux. Nonetheless, it is important to recognize that voice has been developed, in part, by local authority housing departments to reduce the possibilities of exit. However, the success of involvement strategies and the development of modes of responsiveness is seen to be dependent upon the changing basis of power relations (Caincross *et al.* 1996; Sommerville 1998) and the capacity of organizations to adopt responsive modes of management (Glennerster and Turner 1993; Price Waterhouse 1995). Critical influencing factors have been residualization and the move towards market rents in the social rented sector. This has resulted in responses which draw upon the residents of local estates to help resolve their own problems (Taylor 1995).

Conclusions

It is clear from the evidence presented in this chapter that public choice reforms in the housing sector clearly move beyond notions of policy as adopted to policy in action. For the two social housing sub-sectors the public choice prescriptions of more competition and information on performance were adhered to. Competition entered the everyday workings of most social housing organizations, though government did not fundamentally alter its resource allocation mechanisms, and needs-based formulae drove investment decisions. Given the limited amounts of performance data available prior to the Conservative governments of the 1980s and 1990s, increases in information on performance were quite easily achieved. The amount of information on the performance of social housing organizations has continued to grow. The effects of public choice reforms on organizational size have not been as straightforward. The promotion of housing associations as the providers of new social housing in a highly competitive environment has resulted in their growth. Local authorities have, by contrast, become smaller through sales and other policies.

Although the broad direction of social housing reforms is fairly clear, their impact is much less so. In the first place, data on changes in housing performance are incomplete, therefore it is difficult to establish the temporal trends in variables such as efficiency, responsiveness and equity. Second, reforms that reflect the three strands of public choice theory have been introduced together, so it is difficult to disentangle the separate effects of changes in competition, performance indicators and organizational scale. Third, the performance of housing organizations is affected by an array of social and economic variables. Therefore, the impact of public choice principles cannot be easily isolated.

Nevertheless, it is possible to make some judgements on the basis of the available empirical evidence. Efficiency increased during the period but subsequently fell off and declined. Figure 5.2 shows that where there is evidence the impact of public choice theory has been negative. Earlier in the chapter we argued that if public choice theory were correct, improvements in organizational performance would be greater in the local authority sector. Where evidence does exist it does not support this claim. Indeed efficiency has deteriorated in this sector (Table 5.11). Much of our discussion of responsiveness has focused on tenant participation. This was enhanced through public choice theory reforms, though it is now driven by other factors. Our overall assessment of changes to responsiveness is nonetheless positive (Figure 5.2). The judgement for equity is particularly complex, given other intervening variables and the interactions between access, use, outcomes and final incomes. However, the level of equity in the housing system has declined: resources in social rented housing may be better targeted on households in greatest need, but the evidence presented suggests

Consequences for:

Reform	Efficiency	Responsiveness	Equity
Competition	No evidence	Positive	Negative
Performance Indicators	Negative	Positive	Negative
Size	No evidence	Positive	Negative

Figure 5.2 The consequences of public choice reform in social housing for efficiency, responsiveness and equity

that equity in use, access, outcomes and final incomes have all deteriorated (Figure 5.2). It can be argued that this is, to some extent, the result of reforms that reflect public choice principles. If this reading of the evidence is correct, then an overall assessment on the impact of public choice reforms suggests that public choice theory loses 2–1 in the housing sector – improvements have been seen in one area and a deterioration in two.

six

Education reforms

Introduction

The principles of public choice theory have been central to the reforms which have been pursued in education since 1979. Whilst there are key differences of approach and strategy, the New Labour government has generally continued the reforms of the previous Conservative governments (Coffey 2001). We examine the nature of the public choice reforms in primary and secondary education and evaluate evidence on the extent to which they have had an impact. Specifically, we examine the three elements of reform considered in Chapter 1 – competition, performance information and organizational size – and evaluate their consequences for efficiency, responsiveness and equity in education.

Education reforms and public choice theory

In this section, we analyse whether the education reforms have been consistent with the principles of public choice theory. Table 6.1 provides a summary of the legislative reforms (column 1), the key elements (column 2) and highlights policy as adopted in the three areas of competition, performance and organizational size (columns 3–5). Our analysis includes all major legislation relating to education between 1979 and 2001.

The education system in England and Wales has been subject to considerable reform since 1979. Major structural, policy, financial and managerial reforms were put in place to promote competition, provide enhanced performance information and create smaller educational organizations. The new Conservative government's reform strategy in the early years has been described as incremental and not coordinated (McVicar 1996). Following the passing of the 1988 Education Act, reform gathered pace and was much more focused on enhancing competition and markets and weakening the position of local education authorities (LEAs). Levačić (1994: 35) argues that the reforms aimed to replace 'LEA administrative allocation of pupils and resources to schools within a system of quasi-markets whereby each school manages its own budget which primarily depends on its success at attracting pupils'. Further, the reforms put in place the main elements of the quasi-market in which 'providers (schools) are separated from purchasers (ultimately parents) whose choices between alternative schools are reflected in the funding delivered to the school by the funding formula' (Levačić 1998: 332).

Coffey (2001: 22) suggests that with the election of New Labour, there 'has been some change of emphasis away from individualization and a "free market" towards a strengthening of the merits of cooperation, diversity, choice and partnership in a market environment'. Similarly, Power and Whitty (1999) say that Labour's education policies suggest a more confined role for markets and greater state involvement and investment. Public choice theory suggests that more competition, better performance information and smaller and more autonomous organizational units will lead to improved performance. An examination of the reforms in Table 6.1 suggests that most are consistent with at least one of the elements of public choice theory that we are examining. Fourteen of the reforms are concerned with increasing competition, and three, enacted by the Labour government, reduce the extent of competition. Seven involve more performance information. Eleven reforms relate to the issue of organizational size. Table 6.1 illustrates the relevant primary legislation. In the sections that follow, we also take into account secondary legislation and circulars. We now move on to examine the nature of these reforms within education in more detail. In each section we first examine policy as adopted and then assess the extent of policy in action.

Competition

The focus of educational policy in the Thatcher governments was to establish a quasi-market within education to distribute services (Le Grand and Bartlett 1993). In 1980, the key element of the market environment was the newly established Assisted Places Scheme (Education Act 1980), designed to give children from low-income backgrounds an opportunity to attend private school, provided they passed an entrance examination. The reform of school governing bodies in the Education Act 1986 began the process of making schools autonomous units. Governing bodies were placed in a management role in each school, capable of making decisions relating to entry and exit of pupils, and operating within a market environment.

The major elements of the market environment were put in place by the Education Reform Act 1988. Parental choice was introduced to make schools

Table 6.1 Education Reforms in England and Wales and public choice theory

Legislation	Key reforms	More competition?	More information?	Smaller organizations?
Education Act 1980	Publication of school performance information: prospectus	Yes	Yes	No
	Assisted Places Scheme	Yes	No	No
	Parental 'preference' of school	Yes	No	No
Education Act 1986	Reform of school governing bodies	No	No	Yes
Education Reform Act 1988	Parental choice	Yes	No	No
	Local Management of Schools	Yes	No	Yes
	Formula Funding	Yes	No	No
	Grant-maintained (GM) schools	Yes	No	Yes
	City technology colleges	Yes	No	Yes
	Abolition of the Inner London Education Authority	No	No	Yes
Local Government Act 1992	Audit Commission	No	Yes	No
Education (Schools) Act 1992	Publication of league tables	No	Yes	No
	Establishment of Ofsted	No	Yes	Yes
Education Act 1993	Extension of GM status	Yes	No	Yes
	Encouragement of specialist schools	Yes	No	No
Local Government Act 1994	Local government reorganization	No	No	Yes

Act	Policy			
Nursery Education and Grant-Maintained Schools Act 1996	Introduced nursery education voucher	Yes	No	No
Education Act 1997	Baseline assessment introduced	No	Yes	No
	Inspection of LEAs	No	Partial	No
School Standards and Framework Act 1998	Limit to class sizes	No	No	Yes
	Abolition of GM status	No	No	No
	Abolition of Assisted Places Scheme	No	No	No
	LEA role in school improvement	No	No	No
	Abolition of nursery education voucher	No	No	No
	Standards and Effectiveness Unit	No	Yes	No
	Introduction of educational associations	Partial	No	Yes
	Inspection and takeover of LEAs	No	No	No
	Option for private schools to enter state sector	Yes	No	No
	Introduction of selection in schools	Yes	No	No
Local Government Act 1999	Best Value regime	Yes	Yes	No

more responsive to the wishes and demands of parents (Power 1992; Woods 1992). According to Ball (1996), parental choice was facilitated by other policies, including:

- open enrolment, which permitted parents to select schools of their own choice – rather than having this imposed on them by LEAs;
- per-capita funding, or formula funding, which meant that schools received the majority of resources on the basis of the number of pupils enrolled (LMS);
- the introduction of new status schools – grant-maintained (GM) and city technology colleges (CTCs) – which was intended to provide parents with more choices concerning the school their children attend. In the case of grant-maintained schools, parents had an active role to play in the process of changing the status of their school. CTCs were financed from both public and private sector sources.

In essence, the quasi-market in education was driven by the notion that schools which were unpopular with parents would be starved of resources and would, in an effort to stave off closure, improve. Levačić (1994: 37) highlights the key ideas behind the reforms:

> competition between schools will force schools to improve standards and differentiate their product in order to attract pupils. Schools which fail to do this will be closed because of lack of funds. Published performance indicators aid parental choice by exposing 'good' and 'bad' schools. LMS gives schools the means to improve educational standards, respond to consumers and use resources more efficiently than LEA bureaucracies did.

Later legislative reform also drove the competition agenda. The Education Act 1993 changed the system by which schools became grant-maintained: now every school had to consider GM status annually and the balloting process was simplified. The introduction of the nursery education voucher in 1996 was intended to promote competition and facilitate the establishment of a market in the nursery sector. The reintroduction of selection in schools in the 1998 Act was partly intended to enhance competition and diversity in the schools system. This policy permitted LEA schools to select a proportion of pupils on the basis of a curriculum speciality. CTCs were also allowed to recruit part of their intake on this basis, and GM schools over half of their entry. It is argued that the selection policy was popular with parents because it was regarded as 'parent-driven' and also encouraged schools to 'play to their strengths' (T. Edwards et al. 1999). The key reforms introduced by Labour in the School Standards and Framework Act 1998 indicate an inconsistency of approach towards competition. At one level the increased selection in schools enhanced competition, whilst the abolition of both the nursery education voucher and the option for schools to become grant-maintained undermined it.

In order to assess the extent to which there is more competition and consumer choice in the education market in 2001 than before the reforms, the first seven criteria identified in Chapter 3 will be used.

On the basis of public choice theory, competition should be associated with an increase in the number of producers. In the quasi-education market, more producers were created with the establishment of CTCs. Therefore, in those locations which had a college, there were more producers and hence more choice for education consumers. However, this did not apply in other areas. Across England and Wales, a total of 15 colleges were established (Hill 2000). This figure is small compared to the total number of schools across England and Wales (30,233), CTCs representing 0.05 per cent of the schools provision. In relation to schools overall, the actual number of secondary schools in England fell by 20 per cent between 1989 and 1999, despite an increase in the pupil population. The decrease in the schools total was largely due to school closures and amalgamations (Taylor *et al.* 2000). Taylor *et al.*'s (2000: 36) evaluation of the impact of the market reforms on both the actual number of schools and their pupil population leads them to conclude that LEAs, Ofsted inspectors and natural population changes play a key role 'in determining changes to pupil recruitment'. Further, they argue that 'to some extent the lack of change as a result of introducing a policy of increased school choice is hardly surprising . . . it is easy to exaggerate the significance of national policies in education, and important to retain a model in which such changes are heavily mediated by the actions of local agencies' (2000: 37). Neither this study nor information on the number of CTCs established produces evidence supporting the public choice prescription that the number of providers has increased.

In relation to the second element, the extent to which competition made the market share between schools more equal and weakened the dominance of major suppliers, the reforms changed the nature of schools provision. The introduction of GM schools, funded centrally, with much greater market flexibility than LEA-provided schools, reduced the dominance of LEA schools as the sole choice for consumers. In this sense, competition had the potential to equalize market share between GM and LEA schools and also to undermine the major role which LEAs had played in education. The creation of CTCs had the same effect, this time with the input of private as well as public sector funding. Permitting schools to recruit a proportion of their pupils on the basis of a curriculum specialism, in addition to promoting diversity, undermined the dominance of the traditional LEA school which recruited all children. However, whilst the education legislation was driving the establishment of the new institutions, as highlighted above, few CTCs were created. Further, the number of schools which secured GM status was relatively small. By 1997, there were 514 primary schools (2 per cent of the total) and 680 secondary schools (15 per cent of the total) with GM status (Hill 2000). The majority of these were in England. In Wales, only 5 per cent of all eligible schools became grant-maintained (Farrell and Law 1994). In this sense, although the new institutions threatened to undermine the role and position of local government in education, in practice their lack of take-up may not have affected LEAs to this extent. However, the *threat* of competition may have been enough to change the behaviour of service providers.

There is also evidence that the market share among all schools changed relatively little over the period of the reforms. Stillman (1990) suggests that there has been minimal active choice of schools amongst parents, with few selecting schools out of their own catchment areas. According to Forrest's (1996) study, despite the 1988 Act, 41 per cent of LEAs continued to operate a system of allocating children to schools on the basis of catchment areas. This may be because once schools were full, new rules on admission, including sibling enrolment and proximity to a school, for example, were applied by many LEAs (Whitty 1996).

Third, public choice theory suggests that consumers should have more choice among schools provided by the public sector. Taylor *et al.*'s (2000) evidence indicates that with the actual number of schools decreasing, parents are likely to have had less choice of school. The creation of GM schools offered existing consumers choice over the status of their school. Where GM schools did exist, consumers had more choice of suppliers, but only in situations where another LEA school was also an option. There is limited evidence available on whether the creation of GM schools resulted in greater competition or not. Woods *et al.* (1998) claim that in one of their case-study areas, the creation of the GM school did not result in competition – one structure was simply replaced with another. Choice of schools is dependent on local markets. Glatter and Woods (1994: 57) argue that 'competition in schooling (where it exists) is characteristically local in nature'. This therefore undermines the public choice prescription that consumers should have more choice between schools – essentially, choice is tied to locality.

Levačić's (1994) study of parental choice in one LEA indicates that there is some evidence of greater competition for places amongst parents, with the number of applications for out-of-catchment-area schools rising along with increases in the numbers of appeals against the final choice allocated. However, her study also finds that a number of schools with surplus places did not actively compete with each other for pupils, but 'colluded in "gentlemanly" agreements not to recruit from each other's catchments' (1994: 40). In addition, some LEAs attempted to minimize the extent of competition between schools as this conflicted with their political and professional values (Farrell and Law 1999a). Evidence such as this therefore undermines the opportunity of choice of school for parents.

Fourth, to be consistent with public choice theory, the reforms should also have led to consumers having more choice between public and private providers. The establishment of CTCs, funded partly by the private sector, delivered this choice for some consumers. However, in addition to the low take-up of these, evidence provided by Whitty *et al.* (1993) suggests that the private sector was reluctant to fund CTCs and that the majority of the resources actually came from the public sector. The creation of the Assisted Places Scheme in the 1980 Education Act also had the potential to enhance consumer choice (Walford 1988). However, evidence on the impact of the scheme shows that whilst many children from low-income backgrounds benefited, the majority of places were taken up by the children of professional and middle-class parents (Edwards *et al.* 1989). Walford (1994: 41) emphasizes that whilst 'parents may have been given the chance to choose to *apply* for an assisted place . . . it is the schools that *select* which children are to be given this advantage' (emphasis in original). Overall, whilst mechanisms for choice between the public and private sector were put in place with both the establishment of CTCs and the Assisted Places Scheme, the evidence suggests that CTCs were not funded by the private sector to the level anticipated and the Assisted Places Scheme did not attract the expected numbers of low-income families. Choice for consumers between public and private sectors was therefore not evident.

Fifth, public choice theory suggests that consumers should have more direct choice of providers – the establishment of consumer choice in the 1988 legislation placed parents in this consumer role. However, it has to be recognized that, despite a language of consumer 'choice', parents were only provided with an opportunity to express their 'preference' for a particular school (Kenyon 1995). If schools were full, parental choice could not be met. A specific problem in education is the 'lumpiness' of the good – the difficulty of providing choice when schools are overcrowded and of reducing school places in schools that are not popular (Kenyon 1995). Delivering choice in the education market therefore presents specific problems. It is unclear if this issue affects health and housing in the same way.

Finally, competition and consumer choice rely on free entry to and exit from the market, the sixth and seventh elements of competition identified in Chapter 3. The issues highlighted above relating to the 'lumpiness' of education make both entry and exit difficult, particularly in the short term. A school cannot easily exit from the market one year and enter it the next. However, despite these problems, the education reforms have attempted to implement the free market entry and exit characteristics. In terms of exit, a mechanism for implementing exit was put in place with the appointment of educational associations. After a given length of time in which to put right particular problems, those schools which had not improved were eventually closed. P. Edwards *et al.*'s (1999) evaluation of LMS in three case-study LEAs leads to the conclusion that, despite their poor performance, schools have not been forced to exit from the market. This was due to the geographical proximity of schools and an absence of any other choice for parents.

In relation to entry, the establishment of new school providers is heavily regulated and controlled (Levačić 1995). Whilst new providers can enter the market, they must meet specific standards of operation identified by central government. These relate to the quality of service, levels of investment and the curriculum, for example. It is interesting to note that entry to the market was limited by government to only new LEA schools. According to Westoby (1989: 75), 'an important limitation of the [Education Reform Act] reforms is that opting out is not paralleled by any mechanism whereby new grant-maintained schools can come into existence, using central government funds to satisfy a perceived demand'. New entry to the education market is therefore not as straightforward as entry into a free market (Woods and Bagley 1996). New regulations enabling private schools to become publicly funded foundation schools were part of the 1998 Act. This policy raised the number of state schools but did not change the number of schools overall. As such, the initiative did not promote new entrants to the market, but only changed the status of existing suppliers.

This discussion highlights the wide range of policy reforms introduced to promote competition in education. It can be concluded that whilst the mechanisms were put in place for more enhanced competition and greater consumer choice, policy in action has been much weaker than policy as adopted.

More information on performance

Public choice theory suggests that more information on performance will influence the efficiency, responsiveness and equity of services. Once politicians and users have data they can put pressure on service providers to be more responsive and efficient. This process becomes more effective when consumers can use 'exit' as well as 'voice' to encourage producers to respond to their preferences. In theory, performance indicators covering the criteria of expenditure, outputs, outcomes, efficiency, effectiveness and probity, compared over time and against the performance of other organizations, would indicate that the reforms have led to more performance information. These criteria will be used to evaluate the extent of the reforms in the education service. First, we examine policy as adopted, and then assess the extent to which policy operates in practice.

Throughout the whole period 1979–2001, there was a substantial increase in the provision of performance indicators in education. Whilst it can be argued that this aspect of the reforms in part developed out of concerns expressed in the late 1970s over the poor performance of schools in relation to the needs of the economy (Broadbent and Laughlin 1997a), another element of the drive towards greater performance information was that of facilitating consumer choice and enhancing competition in the education market. Public choice arguments about the role of performance information in providing data for consumers and politicians can be seen in much of the legislation passed by the Conservative governments and to some extent continued by the Labour government.

Examination results have been made available since 1981, when schools were first obliged to publish them in their prospectus under the 1980 Education Act. However, there was no requirement to include comparative information. Performance data became much more significant after the 1988 Education Reform Act. Now parents could use the data to inform decisions on the choice of school for their children. The development of performance indicators was pushed forward with the publication of the Parent's Charter in 1991. This stated that parents would have:

- an annual written report about each child;
- regular reports on schools from independent inspectors;
- publicly available 'league tables' comparing the performance of local schools;
- a prospectus or brochure about individual schools;
- an annual report from each school's governors.

The Department for Education (DfE 1991) claimed that 'under the government's reforms you should get all the information you need to keep track of your child's progress, to find out how the school is being run, and to compare all local schools'. The data were more widely available after 1992, when results for individual schools were not only provided by the DfE but also published by the national press. The Labour government has continued the policy of producing 'league tables' of examination results, but appears to have inconsistent views on their value. Whilst in opposition David Blunkett seemed to indicate that information could have negative consequences, warning that 'it is important that league tables are used to help to lever up standards in schools that are underperforming and not damage them' (cited in Demaine 1999: 19). However, in the 1997 White Paper it was stated that 'the publication of performance data benefits parents and acts as a spur to improve performance. We will publish more such data than ever before' (Department for Education and Employment (DfEE) 1997: 25). Interestingly, since devolution a different approach has been adopted in Wales. In July 2001, it was announced that examination results would no longer be published in 'league tables' but simply produced by individual schools in their prospectus (Davidson 2001). After consultation with schools and parents, it was concluded that 'it would serve the best interests of both the teaching profession and the general public to discontinue the publication

Table 6.2 Data provided in the school performance tables in 1998

- Number of 15-year-old pupils in 1997/98
- Percentage of above achieving 5 or more GCSE grades A–C and equivalent
- Percentage of above achieving 1 or more GCSE grades A–G
- Number of above taking other specified vocational qualifications and percentage achieving all the qualifications or units studied
- Average point score per 15-year-old (included for the first time in 1997)
- School progress measure (included for the first time in 1998)
- Number of pupils in year 11, regardless of age
- Percentage of above obtaining 5 or more GCSE grades A–C
- Number of pupils aged 15 with 'statements' of special educational needs

Source: West and Pennell (2000)

of the current Secondary Schools Performance Information for Individual Schools' (National Assembly for Wales 2001b: 9).

There has been a great deal of concern expressed over the quality of the data provided, particularly the issue of whether examination results reflect school performance or socio-economic factors. Fitzgibbon (1996: 31), for example, states that 'the league tables were of course based on raw data and were therefore widely acknowledged to be of limited value – if not indeed positively misleading – if one wanted to assess the effectiveness of schools'. Over the years, the quantity and quality of performance indicators have improved and the data provided have expanded to cover other dimensions not previously measured. The data have been developed by the Labour government, mainly by requiring 'better' measures of outcome. For example, a measure of average GCSE score was included in 1997, and in 1998 a school progress measure was included. This was intended to ensure that 'school performance tables will be more useful, showing the rate of progress pupils have made as well as their absolute levels of achievement' (DfEE 1997: 6). The data included in the 1998 league tables are shown in Table 6.2. Of the indicators listed, six refer to outcomes and the remainder provide information on context. The other dimensions of performance indicated in Chapter 3 are not covered. The approach of publishing league tables which enable comparisons between schools fits clearly with public choice theory. In 1997 new data were included which compared performance over time.

In addition to the provision of information for parents, there have also been attempts to encourage the wider use of performance indicators. In the late 1980s, strategies were adopted to promote their contribution in school evaluation. These were the CIPFA 'blue book' (1988), the pilot project from the DES (1989) and a report from Coopers and Lybrand (1988). As Gray and Wilcox (1995) highlight, these produced lists of criteria, many unquantifiable, such as 'how does the school receive visitors?', which were suggested for use in evaluating schools. Reforms of the role of LEAs indicated that they should also be using performance indicators. The Education Reform Act 1988 gave LEAs a new role in improving standards. This was further developed by the Labour government in the 1998 School Standards and Framework Act, which identified a role for the LEA in school improvement. This required the LEA to evaluate test, examination and inspection data for each of its schools and to compare results and progress with other schools. The framework for inspection of LEAs (Ofsted 2000) requires authorities to show the Ofsted inspectors a range of information, including examples of the performance data that they provide for schools.

The 1998 Act also set up the Standards and Effectiveness Unit in the DfEE, which was to 'promote the analysis and use of performance data to measure pupils' progress at national, local and school level' (DfEE 1997: 33). This unit provides an extensive range of data for schools to access for self-evaluation. The data are provided annually, partly in the form of what is described as the 'Autumn Package' (see www.dfes.gov.uk), and partly through individual performance and assessment reports (PANDAs) sent to each school. These enable individual schools to evaluate the performance of their school against national standards, other comparable schools and over time. They also allow schools to consider the influence on educational performance of factors such as gender and the number of children taking free school meals. In addition, individual departments within some schools are provided with performance information through their involvement in projects such as the ALIS (A Level Information System). Fitzgibbon (1996) suggests that the reforms promoting competition and the publication of examination league tables have encouraged increasing numbers of departments to 'sign up' to the initiative.

The Audit Commission has played a significant role in the provision of performance indicators in education. Since 1992, LEAs have been required to collect and publish a set of indicators that the Commission specifies. These indicators focus largely on economy and efficiency rather than quality of service or outcomes. In addition, since April 2000, LEAs have been subject to the Best Value regime which requires the annual publication of a range of performance information in a performance plan, including comparisons over time and against other organizations. The Best Value PIs are set by government and supersede many of the Audit Commission PIs. The PIs have been amended over the years and now include a wider range of dimensions of performance (Boyne 2000). Table 6.3 indicates the dimensions of performance covered by the Best Value performance indicators for primary and secondary education in 2000/01. Although the Audit Commission does not present the data in 'league tables', it is possible to compare the performance of one authority with another, and, using the previous year's publication, to compare performance over time. Therefore stakeholders

Table 6.3 Dimensions of performance assessed in the Best Value indicators, 2000/01

• Expenditure	5
• Efficiency	4
• Outputs	0
• Outcome	5
• Cost-effectiveness	0
• Probity	0

Source: DETR (1999d)

can make more informed judgements about the relative performance of their LEA.

More recently, the performance management reforms indicate a link between teacher appraisal and the examination results of pupils. Teachers and their appraisers are expected to use this information. One of the benefits of performance management is said to be that it will 'meet the needs of children and raise standards' (Department for Education and Skills (DfES) 2000: 1). Teacher appraisal will involve 'an assessment of the results achieved by pupils in a teacher's care' (DfEE 1997: 49). This policy was resisted by the National Union of Teachers (NUT), which legally challenged the scheme. The arguments put by the NUT were that the policy would lead to difficulties in teamworking, and that pupil performance was influenced by factors outside the control of the school and hence they should not be held to account for it.

The analysis above indicates that a number of policies were introduced which attempted to increase the amount of performance information available and encourage its use. However, we need to examine not just policy as adopted, but also policy in action. We therefore go on to assess whether the information was accurate and actually provided, and whether it was used by the intended recipients. For some of the reforms it is comparatively easy to assess whether the information was produced. For example, information on examination results is publicly available on the DfES website (since 1994). However, many parents access this information when it is published by national newspapers, and research indicates that although all the main broadsheets include information on the percentage of pupils who pass with five or more A–C GCSEs, not all include performance defined as GCSE grades A–G or the measure of school progress (West and Pennell 2000).

In terms of the role of the LEA in providing performance information to schools, a study of 27 LEAs indicated that 'on balance the level of feedback activity from the analysis and evaluation of examination results is small and uncoordinated' (Her Majesty's Inspectorate 1989). Gray and Wilcox (1995: 24) claimed that little progress had been made: 'LEAs

Table 6.4 Quantitative measures reported by LEAs as being available to them in 1990/91 to inform the judgement of secondary schools' performance

	% of all LEAs
Possible outcome measures	
Public examination results	78
Post-16 destinations	55
Attendance	52
Exclusions	4
Possible contextual measures	
Incidence of free school meals	42
Incidence of special needs	44
Reading tests	12
English tests	9
Arithmetic/mathematics	8
Verbal reasoning tests	8
Non-verbal reasoning tests	5
Ethnic backgrounds of pupils	7
Other measures of pupil attainment	5
Other pupil characteristics	8
Possible school characteristics	
Staff	10
School	6
Finance/resources	3
Parents/community	3

Source: Gray and Wilcox (1995)

have only recently begun to develop procedures for systematically sharing information about school's performance'. They indicated that in 1990/91 comparatively few LEAs had a range of PIs available to them to judge performance (see Table 6.4).

More recent comprehensive research on the type and amount of performance information provided by LEAs is not available. It is therefore difficult to assess whether there has been significant improvement. There is some very limited case-study evidence on LEAs' role in producing data for schools. Strand (1997), for example, describes the approach of one LEA which used a number of key performance indicators as part of a broader school improvement strategy. The study indicates that in one school, the Key Stage 1 results subsequently improved markedly in most areas. However, the validity of this evidence is limited as there is no attempt to isolate the impact of performance indicators from that of other strategies put in place.

It is also important to assess the *use* of the performance data. There is a range of evidence on the use that parents make of examination league tables. David *et al.* (1994) argue that most families in their study chose schools on criteria which they described as the three Ps: academic results, or performance; ethos, or pleasant feel; and proximity. They indicate that 76 per cent of the parents they surveyed had read a brochure about individual schools within the borough. However, one-third of these parents had not seen the section on examination results. Of those who had, 17 per cent found them very useful, 29 per cent quite useful and 17 per cent not useful. Whilst 29 per cent felt that examination results 'added to the overall picture', 27 per cent found them 'confusing and difficult to understand'. This conclusion is based on a sample of 70 families in two inner London boroughs. The results of this study must be treated with some caution as it was conducted before the examination results were published in comparative form. In a later study of the parents of 107 children in London, only 8 per cent indicated that they had not seen the results (West *et al.* 1998). However, only 55 per cent felt they had understood them. Similarly, Woods *et al.* (1998) showed that parents were increasingly using performance information, but very few identified 'league tables' as the most important factor in making their choice of school. They also suggested that the emphasis placed on examination results did not correspond to the values held by parents.

There is limited evidence on the extent to which other groups use performance information. In part, this reflects the recent nature of many of the reforms. There are very few studies on the use that schools are making of the data. MacBeath and Mortimore (2000), for example, suggest that schools are increasingly becoming more skilled at using data for self-evaluation and are also *likely* to have attitudinal data from parents, students or staff. However, they provide no data to confirm the validity of this statement. Increasing numbers of schools use ALIS. Fitzgibbon (1996) indicated that by 1993, 368 institutions were using the system which had been set up in 1983. Tymms (1995) shows that ALIS reports were read far more by heads of department than by other teachers.

There has been criticism of the extent to which LEAs themselves use performance data. For example, in relation to unauthorized absences and exclusions, the Audit Commission (1999) suggests that fewer than half of LEAs use data to identify pupils at risk, their problems, and the schools that need the most help. Similarly, in relation to Best Value, research has indicated that local authorities are finding the development and use of performance information particularly difficult (Boyne *et al.* 1999). There has been very little research on the extent to which politicians themselves use the data. Day and Klein (1987) interviewed 22 members of an LEA and concluded that there was a general view that it was not possible to measure the outputs of the education system by examination results. Instead of using measures such as examination results, most of the politicians they spoke to preferred to assess the performance of schools by visiting them.

To summarize, there is evidence that the quantity of performance information provided has increased. Both the Conservative and Labour governments introduced policies to produce more data on school performance, although recently in Wales this has been reversed. There is less evidence on the provision of data by LEAs for schools. The quality and the range of data have improved since 1979. The main indicators are concerned with outcomes, as defined by examination results, and this measure has been amended and improved over time. However, there are many dimensions of performance for which there are no data. Overall, more use is being made of the information. For example, examination results are increasingly used by parents. However, there is little evidence on the extent to which schools use the data to undertake self-evaluation or, as yet, teachers use the data for performance appraisal. Similarly, we have limited empirical data about the ways in which LEAs use performance information. Overall, policy as adopted is consistent with public choice theory, but policy in action is less so. This is because whilst more performance information was produced, its use is difficult to enforce.

Organizational size

Many of the reforms in education have impacted on the size of organizations. This has occurred at a variety of levels. The structure of LEAs has been reorganized, some LEA functions have been devolved to schools under LMS, there have been some changes to the size of schools, and policies have been put in place to reduce the size of classes.

A number of structural reorganizations have changed the size of LEAs. The rationale behind these has often been vague. However, there are hints that the government was concerned with issues of responsiveness, economy, efficiency and effectiveness as well as criteria such as community loyalty and democratic accountability (Boyne and Law 1993). In London, the Inner London Education Authority (ILEA) was abolished in 1990, and its education functions were allocated to the smaller London boroughs. Riley (1993: 57) suggests that 'the central government case against the ILEA was that it was too big, too expensive and too unresponsive to local needs'. A further reorganization of LEAs occurred in 1996. In Scotland and Wales, the two-tier system of regions/counties (which provided education) and districts (which provided services such as refuse collection and leisure) was replaced by unitary authorities. In Wales, there are now 22 LEAs where there had been 8, and in Scotland the corresponding figures are 32 and 12. The system of local government in England was also subject to reform in 1996. In some areas, new unitary authorities replaced the county and district councils. In others, the existing two-tier system was retained. As prescribed by public choice theory, these structural reorganizations of local government led to education functions being delivered by smaller organizations.

In addition to suggesting that organizations should be smaller, public choice theory also indicates that they should have more autonomy. However, since 1979 there have been an increasing number of mechanisms of central control and less autonomy for LEAs. Size can also be considered in terms of the functions or responsibilities that an organization has. The Conservative governments, in particular, have attempted to reduce the functions of LEAs, whilst Labour has introduced legislation which specifies that the functions of an underperforming LEA can be taken over by the private sector. Local authorities lost a number of functions, such as responsibility for staff appointments, under the 1988 Act. These were given to smaller organizations, including school governing bodies. The creation of Ofsted also reduced the significant role that LEAs had played in school inspection. Walford (1994: 100) argues that 'the 1988 Education Reform Act was not simply concerned with education, but marked part of central government's desire to reduce the importance of local authorities'. The reforms were expected to reduce the role of LEAs to a marginal and residual one (Whitty 1996). Although the Labour governments have added to LEA functions in terms of responsibility for school improvement, in many ways they have continued to undermine them. For example, they have introduced policies requiring LEAs to delegate even more resources to school governing bodies and also permitted schools further opportunities to purchase school services outside the LEA.

In contrast to the reduced autonomy for LEAs, legislative reform has sought to enhance the autonomy of schools since 1979. Under the LMS initiative, and with the enhancement of the governing body as the key decision-making body, schools have in principle been empowered to operate as autonomous units. Key responsibilities relating to staff appointments and expenditure decisions, for example, have been devolved to schools from LEAs.

Further aspects of this issue are the actual size of schools themselves and the classes within them. As highlighted above, the intention of legislative reforms since 1988 has been for popular schools to expand and for unpopular schools to contract in line with the competitive forces of the market. However, this policy conflicts with the strategy of reducing the surplus capacity within the education system. The need to reduce surplus capacity resulted from the dramatic decline in birth rate in the 1960s and 1970s. The policy of reducing surplus capacity has been followed by all governments since the mid-1970s. The rationale for this was that a strategy of closure and amalgamation would lead to both financial savings and increased educational effectiveness (Ranson 1990). Whilst reducing surplus places may enhance efficiency, it would also limit the possibilities for parents to choose a school for their children. In addition, after the 1988 Education Reform Act, LEAs found it difficult to attempt to close schools as many which faced closure opted for a ballot on GM status (Halpin *et al.*

1991). As part of the debate on school rationalization, the issue of the optimum size for schools was examined. Ranson (1990) suggests that after 1979 professional opinion had turned away from large schools. However, concerns were also being raised over the costs of small schools. The *Better Schools* White Paper (DES 1985) indicated that small schools had a higher per-pupil cost than large schools and that the preferred minimum roll for secondary schools was 900. It also stated that sixth forms should have at least 150 pupils. The issue of optimum size involved consideration of both the cost and the quality of schooling. According to Richmond (1992: 272), from this time 'optimum school size was now clearly being considered in terms of curriculum delivery and size of enrolment coupled to cost-effectiveness'.

In relation to class size, whilst the Conservative governments intended this to be driven by market forces, thus resulting in schools expanding and contracting class sizes in line with demand, the Labour party came into power in 1997 with specific policies. As part of its 'education, education, education' pledges in the election campaign, its intention was to ensure that class sizes, at least in the infant age range, did not exceed 30. This policy, therefore, undermined the operation of the demand and supply agenda of the previous administrations (Power and Whitty 1999) and has since been extended to cover the junior age range in schools.

To what extent have these policies relating to size been implemented? The structural reorganization of LEAs has led to education being delivered by smaller organizations. However, despite this, policy in practice indicates that reorganization into smaller units led to the development of partnership arrangements for some specialist services such as subject advisers. Services were still provided at the same organizational size as before reorganization. Using the number of staff employed as a measure of size, Howlett (1991) indicates that the abolition of ILEA actually led to an increase in numbers of inspectors, from 152 under the ILEA to 203 under the London boroughs. This evidence suggests a gap between the policy as adopted and policy in practice.

The intention of the reforms has been to reduce LEA responsibilities. Despite a series of reforms undermining them, the evidence suggests that LEAs continue to perform a key function in education locally. Whitty (1996: 8) argues that 'schools have so far been much more reluctant to opt out of their LEAs than the government anticipated', leaving local government with the responsibility for these schools. One reason for LEAs retaining a significant role has been that schools, especially primary schools, have 'bought back' many of the functions devolved to them through LMS. P. Edwards *et al.*'s (1999: 139) findings suggest that despite legislative reform reducing their responsibilities, LEAs continue to 'exercise a strong influence over their schools based on their accounting, personnel and legal expertise'.

Although self-management brought with it opportunities for schools to operate autonomously, there are a number of constraints on them (Russell *et al.* 1997). The legal determination of the National Curriculum has led to a more unified approach to classroom practices, greater management and control of teachers' work, and a more focused evaluation of targets achieved by pupils. Further, there is the constraint of resources – schools gained their financial responsibilities at a time when the availability of public sector resources nationally was curtailed. There has been pressure on schools to operate within their allocated budgets. Russell *et al.* (1997: 246) argue that whilst schools can increase their budgets by recruiting more pupils, 'schools do not have the freedom that commercial organizations do, to enter new markets or to determine pricing strategies'. Despite such constraints, LMS brought with it the opportunity for governing bodies to play a strategic policy-making role, assisted by headteachers, who became responsible for putting policy into action within the school. However, there is much evidence that governing bodies do not operate in this way (Farrell and Law 1999b; Farrell 2000). The reality is that headteachers undertake both the strategic and operational decisions within the vast majority of schools. Further, despite their potential for autonomy in purchasing decisions, as discussed above, schools bought the majority of their services back from LEAs under service level agreements.

Taylor *et al.*'s (2000) evidence on changes in school size shows that whilst some increased in size, others decreased. This study, based on secondary schools in England between 1989 and 1999, does not find that changes in size are the result of the introduction of market forces. Rather, the explanation for change lies in the programme of school closure and amalgamation which government pursued in the early 1990s.

Evidence on the implementation of Labour's class size policy shows that in general the policy has been implemented. Table 6.5 indicates that only 0.5 per cent of infant pupils in England were in classes of 31 or more in 2001. The data between 1998 and 2001 clearly show that the drive to have children in smaller classes is working.

In conclusion, the key issues relating to size and autonomy are that organizational size decreased with the creation of smaller units of delivery, and LEA autonomy was undermined as that of schools increased. Although

Table 6.5 Percentage distribution of infant class sizes in England, 1998–2001

	1998	1999	2000	2001
30 or fewer pupils	78	89	98	99.5
31 or more pupils	22	11	2	0.5

Source: DfES (2001)

there was a policy to reduce the size of infant classes, the policy on school size was much less clear. In practice, despite these changes, some services continued to be delivered by the same size organization – LEAs retained a powerful role due to schools both buying back services and not opting out on a large scale. Whilst the potential existed for school governing bodies to run their schools, much of the power for this was taken by headteachers. The evidence to date indicates that the policy of reducing infant class size has been widely implemented. The policy on reducing the surplus capacity within schools has not been in line with public choice theory. Overall, these changes point to a reduction in organizational size and, in many cases, an increase in organizational autonomy.

Summary

The central public choice elements of competition, the provision of more performance data and the reduction in size of organizations have all been pursued within the education reforms. However, despite legislative reforms which have put the principles of public choice theory in place, the implementation of policy in practice is not as evident. In the next section we examine the extent to which the reforms have impacted on efficiency, responsiveness and equity.

The impact of education reforms: a review of the evidence

This section evaluates the impact of the education reforms with reference to the three criteria of efficiency, responsiveness and equity. In each of these areas, we are seeking to evaluate two issues: whether changes have occurred since the reforms; and whether these changes can be attributed to the reforms.

Efficiency

Public choice theory suggests that the introduction of markets, more information on performance and a reduction in the size of organizations will lead to greater efficiency. We assess the evidence and identify whether any changes in efficiency are a result of the reforms. The definition of efficiency used here is technical efficiency – the ratio of service inputs to service outputs or, in other words, the relationship between the money spent and the quantity and quality of the service produced with these resources. There are a number of outcomes which would be consistent with a judgement of increased efficiency. A school becomes more efficient, for example, where unit costs are decreasing and quantity and quality remain the same. It may also be more efficient in situations where unit costs are increasing, the percentage increase in quantity is higher than the percentage increase in cost, and the quality remains the same (see Table 2.1 for further combinations). There is scarcely any research which provides a good assessment of the impact of the reforms on efficiency. One of the reasons for this is the difficulty of measuring the outputs of public services. It is argued that this is particularly difficult within education. Levačić (1998: 338) states that

> if a well-specified production function existed it would be possible to estimate school efficiency utilizing the standard economics concept of efficiency. But the absence of such knowledge concerning the technical relationship between resource inputs and educational outputs is compounded by the multi-dimensional nature of educational outputs and differences in the subjective value placed on these outputs. This state of affairs makes the traditional economic definition of 'efficiency' (the highest value of output achieved with a given value of inputs) non-operational.

However, others such as Mayston and Jesson (1991) argue that efficiency can be measured for schools and LEAs using the technique of data envelopment analysis. They suggest that it is important to use available measures of output, whilst recognizing that they are contestable.

One possible measure of efficiency within education is the percentage of unfilled places in schools. If schools have surplus capacity then the fixed costs such as buildings and heating remain constant, whilst the output (number of pupils taught) is lower than its possible maximum. The attempts to reduce surplus capacity were considered in the previous section. There is a large variation among English LEAs on this measure of performance in 1999/2000, from 0.8 per cent to 25.2 per cent. The data in Table 6.6 indicate that performance on average has improved from 1996/97 to 1999/2000 (the only time period for which consistent data are available).

There is some speculation in the literature that the market reforms have had a positive effect on efficiency within the schools system. However, the evidence which is available focuses on the lower costs of funding education, and this provides data on spending rather than efficiency. Levačić's (1993, 1998) studies fall into this category. Whilst arguments are advanced in both of these studies that delegated budgets are encouraging

Table 6.6 Average percentage of unfilled places in English schools

	1996/97	1997/98	1998/99	1999/2000
Primary schools	9.5	9.5	9.2	9.3
Secondary schools	11.6	11.5	10.4	8.2

Source: Local authority performance indicators, Audit Commission

schools to think about the use of their resources and become more efficient, there is no direct evidence on whether efficiency levels have improved. Simkins (1994) also indicates that schools are placing more emphasis on efficiency in relation to school premises and grounds, although he does not provide any data to confirm this. The unavailability of evidence on the existence of efficiency within schools is surprising given that an essential component of Ofsted inspections following the 1992 Act was an assessment of the link between the details outlined in a school's development plan and the school budget. This requirement goes some way towards encouraging school managers to think about the use of resources in a framework of outputs. However, despite the need to consider these issues, the evidence shows that schools were not strong in this area (Glover *et al.* 1997; Levačić and Glover 1997, 1998). In the vast majority of schools researched in these studies, inspectors recommended that schools should consider the management of their resources in the light of the objectives and specifically address the efficiency of their use of resources.

There is no evidence that performance information has had any effect on efficiency in education. Whilst in theory more data should enable politicians, the public and other stakeholders to put pressure on educational organizations to be more efficient, in practice there is no evidence available on this effect.

There has been no research undertaken on LEA size and efficiency, but the limited information available on local authority size suggests that efficiency is weak at small scale and improves as scale increases (Boyne 1996a). The reduction in the size of some LEAs following reorganization is therefore unlikely to have had a positive effect on efficiency. Although the finding that LEAs continue to provide some services (such as subject advisers) at the same organizational size as before reorganization suggests that there may be opportunities for efficiency gains, there is no evidence that these were achieved.

Although there are no data on school size and efficiency, there is some limited research which examines the relationship between school size and expenditure. Butel and Atkinson (1983), for example, found that although there were economies of scale, these were often very small. Evidence indicates that small schools are less efficient than larger ones. The Audit Commission (1991) indicates that primary schools with fewer than 80 pupils on the roll cost between £2000 and £3800 per pupil, against £1000 for schools with more than 120 pupils.

There is no evidence on the link between Labour's policy that infant class sizes should not exceed 30 pupils and efficiency. However, limiting class sizes in this way is unlikely to promote efficiency. Power and Whitty's (1999: 537) evaluation of Labour's policies in education classifies this as part of the 'old left elements' of a 'renewed state involvement and investment, a confined role for markets, reference to egalitarian principles and some indication that the welfare state should provide support for education, at least from the cradle, if not to the grave'. The promotion of efficiency has not traditionally been part of this agenda.

Responsiveness

The reforms discussed earlier in the chapter were introduced partly to enhance the responsiveness of the education service. For example, Woods *et al.* (1998: 147) argue that 'the general case for enhancing the market elements of the system is that it leads to greater responsiveness to those the schooling system serves and to educational practice that better meets their needs and preferences'. In order to assess whether the reforms have been successful we need to consider first which stakeholders (direct service users, indirect service users, taxpayers, staff) public officials should be responsive to. Defining responsiveness is problematic as it is often unclear which elements of performance different stakeholders value most. For example, do parents value examination results (outcomes) more than cost per hour of teaching (efficiency)? What do taxpayers value? We also need to examine responsiveness at different levels. We consider the responsiveness of central government, local education authorities and individual schools. Our discussion is limited by the fact that the majority of the evidence concentrates on school responsiveness to parents' wishes (e.g. Woods 1992) and there is only limited information on other stakeholders.

At a national level, it is clear that central government has highlighted parents as the primary stakeholders in their education policies. Its views can be illustrated by the following statement: 'parents know best the needs of their children – certainly better than educational theorists or administrators, better even than our mostly excellent teachers' (DfE and Welsh Office 1992: 2). Government policies on competition and performance information have focused on giving power to parents. In theory, parents can use the information to make choices of school for their children and market forces will ensure that schools are responsive to them as customers. LMS gives schools the freedom to respond to parental preferences. In addition, reforms such as parental representation on governing bodies and the annual governing body meeting give parents opportunities to express 'voice' which schools can then respond to. However, how responsive was central government to the wishes of parents and other stakeholders in introducing these reforms?

Demaine (1999: 28) suggests that the government has been responsive to the wishes of the general voting public. He makes the assertion that 'there can be little doubt that the new forms of management of schools and the policing of teachers' work [go] down well with the voters of "middle England" whose electoral support new Labour must secure in order to win general elections'. However, no evidence to support this claim is provided.

Some evidence from a three-year study of 138 families in one LEA (Hughes *et al.* 1994) sheds some light on the issue of what parents value and helps address the question of whether the government was responsive to parents. In this study, it is reported that 51 per cent of parents thought that a good school was one which had positive relationships within the school, and just 16 per cent identified academic results as being important. Only 48 per cent thought is was a good idea to publish results, with 19 per cent having mixed feelings and 31 per cent disapproving. In addition, whilst 49 per cent did not see themselves as consumers at all, 34 per cent did to some extent and 12 per cent did to a large extent. Hughes *et al.* (1994) conclude that it was doubtful whether politicians could claim that the reforms were what parents wanted. However, this study was based only on primary school parents in one LEA, which is a significant limitation in interpreting the evidence. In addition, the study was conducted over three years from the late 1980s to the early 1990s. Ideally, data would be available from a representative sample of parents across different LEAs and over a longer time frame.

Interestingly, in Wales, the National Assembly indicated that it was responding to parents' views by reversing the policy on the publication of examination results in 'league tables'. Their analysis of responses to their consultation on this shows that whilst parental and governing body responses were fairly evenly split between the two options of abolishing the tables and improving the data, teacher responses were strongly in favour of the former (National Assembly for Wales 2001b). The Assembly also conducted focus groups of parents to obtain more informed perspectives on this issue. However, it is difficult to evaluate this evidence due to its qualitative nature. From the consultation responses it appears that the Assembly was more responsive to teachers than to parents.

It has also been argued that national government responds to business in its policies. The launch of the 'great debate' in education by Callaghan in 1976 is widely recognized as being driven by the need to promote a core curriculum in education which recognizes vocational skills required by business (Lowe 1993). There are signs that New Labour's education policies are also responsive to business interests. The emphasis in policy documents on the 'knowledge economy', concerned with knowledge in the work situation, is part of New Labour's strategy of ensuring that education reflects the needs of business (Ozga 2000). Central government is also attempting to make local authorities responsive through the Best Value regime. A Welsh White Paper, *Local Voices*, describes the modern council in the following way: 'they are committed to securing best value. They involve and respond to local people and local interest and listen to local voices' (National Assembly for Wales 1998: 4). Authorities are required to consult not just current users, but also those who will use the service in the future, local taxpayers and those with an interest in the service.

There is limited research on responsiveness at the level of the LEA. One of the few studies to examine this issue is Bullock and Thomas (1997). Their survey of over 70 headteachers in 1992 indicates that the vast majority were happy with both the range and quality of LEA-provided services, and felt that LEAs were responsive to their needs. In a more recent study of the extent to which headteachers and a range of school governors perceive the funding of their foundation school (previously grant-maintained) by the LEA to be fair (Anderson *et al.* 2001), there is the clear view in each of the ten schools that LEAs are withholding resources. One teacher-governor's view about this was that the LEA was funding 'loyal' schools (those which had not previously opted out) more generously. There has been no exploration of whether LEA policies reflect the wishes of other stakeholder groups. There is some limited evidence which indicates that size is not a factor influencing the responsiveness of LEAs. Boyne (1996a) presents data showing, for example, that the speed of response to assessments of special education needs is not related to the size of the organization. There is some initial indication that local authorities are increasingly attempting to find out stakeholder views as a result of the Best Value requirements (Boyne *et al.* 1999). Local authorities are using a range of consultative techniques such as citizen's juries, interactive websites and surveys (Lowndes *et al.* 2000). However, there is as yet limited evidence to show that authorities are responding to the preferences expressed. A limitation of the research on Best Value is that it generally refers to local government as a whole, rather than specifically to the education department.

Research indicates that schools are attempting to be responsive to parents, often as a result of market-based reforms. Woods *et al.* (1998: 168) evaluated the education market in three LEA areas and found that schools were attempting to respond to parents' wishes. In one area, a school adopted a technology focus so as to expand 'its attraction to a certain section of parents in order to obtain a more balanced intake of students in terms of ability and social class'. In other schools, which were undersubscribed, in poorer areas and with a student body skewed towards the lower ability range, the authors found evidence of the development of a school curriculum which was more vocationally oriented. Overall, they found that competitive pressures had led schools to 'privilege academic achievement'. Evidence provided by Gewirtz *et al.* (1995: 126) suggests that within the quasi-market 'schools generally feel a need to try to make themselves more attractive to consumers, to be reflexive about the messages they communicate to the "outside world" and to cultivate images that will appeal to parents generally and especially to *particular sorts of parents*' (emphasis in original). This evidence of responsive schools is, however, limited in that it is a small-scale study of the impact of choice within a number of schools in three London authorities between 1991 and 1994 and may therefore not be applicable to all schools.

Although there is some evidence that schools are trying to respond to what they think parents' wishes are, there is little evidence to suggest that they are attempting to find out what parents want. According to Woods *et al.* (1998: 188), 'finding out the views of parents and pupils and seeking to provide education which meets their needs and preferences was weak and poorly developed'. Further, this has meant that schools have mistakenly perceived academic achievement as the prime parental interest. In reality, parents place equal weight on academic achievement and the personal and social development of children (Woods *et al.* 1998). In addition, the mechanism of 'voice' as a method of finding out parents' views is problematic in practice. Despite this, developing the 'voice' mechanism can give parents an opportunity to more effectively participate in education, and this provides one of the challenges for educationalists (Farrell and Jones 2000).

It is difficult to assess the extent to which the reforms have led to increased responsiveness to staff. In part, this may be because the rationale behind many of the reforms has been to move away from a producer-dominated culture to one focusing on users. Broadbent and Laughlin (1997b) highlight an example of responsiveness to producers – the reorganization of the National Curriculum in 1993 is widely believed to have been driven by the trade unions in education, which had long argued that the system was unworkable. In Wales, since the establishment of the National Assembly, policies, on the whole, are seen as being responsive to teachers. Gethin Lewis, secretary of the NUT in Wales, commented that Jane Davidson, Minister for Education and Lifelong Learning, was 'a listening minister, listening to the concerns of teachers and the NUT in particular' (The *Guardian* 2001). However, the recent introduction of performance-related pay for teachers is not widely supported by the teaching profession in Wales (Farrell and Morris 2001).

Changes in LEA size also had an impact on some staff; for example, the abolition of ILEA meant that services valued by staff were no longer provided. Riley (1993: 59) indicates that 'there was common agreement across the boroughs that the loss of the information and research base of the ILEA research and statistics branch has substantially reduced the quality of the information on which educational decisions and judgements are made in London'. Paradoxically, one public choice reform, to reduce the size of organizations, had had a negative impact on another element, to increase the amount of information on performance.

Overall, parts of the education system are becoming increasingly responsive to stakeholders (primarily parents). However, there is not enough good evidence to make a conclusive statement on this issue. Research indicates that there are increasing attempts to assess what criteria stakeholders are interested in. For example, there are some attempts at the LEA level to engage with stakeholders and assess their preferences. In relation to schools, however, it appears that most respond to what they think parents want, rather than assessing what they are actually interested in. Whilst teachers' concerns have largely not been addressed in the past, it seems that this is changing somewhat, particularly in Wales.

Equity

As identified in Chapter 2, the central question with regard to equity is whether the recipients of education get what they need. We now examine evidence on the extent to which equity within education has changed, and, if so, whether this is due to the education reforms. The four criteria of use, access, outcome and final income will be used in order to evaluate changes in equity.

Equity of use is concerned with ensuring that educational resources are distributed on the basis of the individual's level of need for these. This requires, for example, that children with the lowest ability receive more teaching support than children with the highest ability. From a number of studies there is evidence of inequity of use as a consequence of the publication of performance data. According to West and Pennell (2000: 434), a consequence of the publication of the information is that schools seeking to achieve the best possible results fail to provide additional support for pupils at the bottom end of the performance scale. The use of education resources for these pupils is therefore inequitable. This conclusion is supported by Gillborn and Youdell (2000). The focus of schools on those pupils most likely to achieve the required grades had led to what the authors describe as the 'A–C economy'. Their study of two schools leads them to suggest that education is rationed and is overprovided to those pupils who may become D–C conversions. This inequity of use, the authors suggest, can lead to inequity of outcome on the basis of social class, gender and ethnic origin. For example, in one of their case-study schools, 47 per cent of white pupils achieved five grade A–C passes whilst only 24 per cent of black students met this standard. Similarly, 53 per cent of those who attained the required grades did not receive free school meals, compared with 30 per cent who did receive them. The validity of this evidence must be set against other relevant factors, including levels of intelligence, which were not taken into account in coming to the conclusion that there is inequity in both use and outcome in education. An additional problem is that they provide no baseline to compare the level of equity before and after the reform.

There are also arguments that the introduction of formula funding under LMS had a negative impact on the extent to which special needs were funded in education. Whitty (1996) argues that formula funding undermined the extent to which LEAs could provide earmarked funding to counter disadvantage, as the vast majority of funds allocated to schools were distributed on the basis of the number of children enrolled. Further evidence on this issue is advanced by Simkins (1994) and Walford (1994) amongst others. Walford (1994: 125) argues that 'the problem with formula funding as currently instituted, however, is that it rests on a very simple idea of equity that implies that fairness involves spending equal amounts of money per child whatever the background of the child or the community it serves'. Simkins (1994: 29) argues further that 'much then depends on how allocations to small schools and to meet the needs of socially disadvantaged pupils and those with special educational needs actually work out.' LEAs differ considerably in the ways that they treat these factors.

The New Labour policy of reducing class sizes for the youngest children in schools may have had a positive effect on equity of use. Arguments advanced by the National Commission on Education (1993) indicate that younger children have greater needs than older children, in that they are more dependent on teaching support. The education system had traditionally been organized with the smallest classes at the A-level stage. There is no evidence available on whether equity of use for the youngest children was actually enhanced by Labour's policy – clearly its impact on children of all ages needs to be assessed before conclusions can be drawn.

Equity of access in education requires that services are accessible to individuals on the basis of their needs. Again, on this criterion, there is evidence of inequity. Ball's (1996) evaluation of the extent to which parental selection of schools is related to social class finds that the schools parents choose for their children are related to their own social class. The study highlights that providing parents with the capacity to select schools for their children has had a differential impact on parents. As a result of the parental choice policy, there are now three groups – the privileged/skilled choosers, the semi-skilled choosers and the disconnected. The finding that there is inequity of access for parents from different social classes is supported in a number of other detailed studies of local education markets (see Echols et al. 1990; Bartlett 1993; Gewirtz et al. 1995; Reay and Ball 1997; Noden et al. 1998). According to Noden et al. (1998: 235), for example,

> by requiring schools to accept applicants up to their physical capacity it appears that middle-class advantage has been extended by enabling greater numbers of children to flee from low scoring inner-city schools. This is because middle-class families are more likely to have the resources to be able to travel further to school and because certain schools have adopted admissions policies which favour more privileged applicants.

Gewirtz et al. (1995) also find evidence of inequity of access to schools. Schools used the criterion of 'unusual talent' to recruit children from middle-class families. The authors indicate that oversubscribed schools used selection criteria, such as a child's performance in music and dance, together with a parent interview, thereby enhancing the entry of middle-class children. The data upon which this evidence is based are drawn from interviews conducted with LEA officials and parents in three LEAs in London between 1991 and 1994. The entry of CTCs into the education market following the 1988 legislation was intended to enhance competition and choice. However, Gewirtz *et al.* (1995) also find that the establishment of these colleges had a negative impact on this aspect of equity. The evidence highlights that one college's selection of children led to it recruiting more than the average proportion of children with the highest reading ability, thereby reducing the access of other children. Whilst the data upon which this evidence is drawn are limited by the fact that only one CTC in one locality was the subject of the research, it highlights a negative impact on equity of the CTC policy.

Studies such as those reviewed above examine the impact of the education market and school choices at a local level. However, the finding that school choices and social class are highly related is not supported in large-scale studies, such as those conducted by Gorard and Fitz (2000) and Taylor *et al.* (2000). Both of these studies fail to find evidence that social class is a determinant of school admissions. Taylor's (2001: 197) evidence suggests that school choices in the education marketplace are generally hierarchical and 'that the position of schools within these hierarchies is largely associated with their relative examination performance' rather than social class. Gorard and Fitz's (2000: 423) evidence relates to the whole of England and Wales. The authors find that the 'introduction of market forces in education has not led to increased social segregation over time for the most disadvantaged sections of society'. These findings are questioned by Noden (2000), who conducted a similar analysis and found that the average level of segregation in English LEAs had increased in the late 1990s. There is sharp disagreement between these studies on the achievement of equity of access. It seems to be dependent on whether the evaluation is undertaken on a small or a large scale, although the division on the level of scale does not, as Noden's (2000) findings indicate, determine the nature of the results. Noden's (2000) evidence supports the findings in the local studies. It is not clear why these differ from those of both Gorard and Fitz (2000) and Taylor *et al.* (2000), nor which conclusion to draw on the link between choice of school and social class. However, the majority of the evidence supports the finding that providing parents with choice has had a negative impact on this aspect of equity.

Some studies find evidence of inequity of access in terms of performance data. West *et al.* (1998), for example, indicate that there are significant differences between mothers who understood the data and that the level of understanding was related to their own educational achievements. According to this study of parents of 107 children, where the mother had at least GCE A levels, 67 per cent of respondents reported that they understood the examination results. This compares with only 31 per cent where the mother had qualifications below this level. Whilst the findings of this study suggest that the use of performance data is not equitably spread across the population, it does not directly provide evidence that the choices mothers make in terms of schooling have inequitable effects on children.

Equity of outcome in education is not a simple concept. Le Grand (1982: 65) says that 'indicators of performance such as educational qualifications are suspect because they measure a limited aspect of educational achievement, and because they do not capture the broader impact of education on society'. The latter includes salaries commanded by school leavers and indicators of occupational mobility. In order to capture educational outcome, all three elements (qualifications, earnings and occupational mobility) should therefore be considered. The majority of evidence on outcomes relates to the achievement of qualifications. West and Pennell (2000) show that the average GCSE score between 1992 and 1997 improved by 2.8 per cent. However, for the bottom decile of the cohort, there is a decline of 0.1 per cent and for the top decile there is an increase of 4.4 per cent. This indicates therefore that equity of outcomes is not being achieved for children at all levels. The limitations of this data are that they do not cover a sufficiently long time period and do not include data before the implementation of the reforms. It is possible, therefore, that the rate of growth in inequity has slowed down.

The public choice reforms have also had a negative effect on equity of final income. The achievement of equity of final income requires that 'services should be allocated in such a way as to favour the poor, so that their "final incomes" are brought into line with those of the rich' (Le Grand 1982: 14). Bartlett's (1993: 149) evidence of the operation of the quasi-market in education in four case-study schools shows that 'those schools which faced financial losses under the formula funding system tended to be those schools which drew the greatest proportion of pupils from the most disadvantaged section of the community'. Further, although parental choice has been enhanced by open enrolment, 'the door is firmly closed once a school [is full]. And by encouraging an increasingly selective admissions policy in [oversubscribed] schools open enrolment may be having the effect of bringing about increased opportunity for cream-skimming and hence increased inequality' (Bartlett 1993: 150).

Overall, on the basis of the four criteria that we have examined, there is evidence of inequity in education. As many of the studies do not evaluate the level of equity before the public choice reforms, it is not clear that equity is worse after their implementation than before. However, it is clear that elements of the reforms such as the publication of performance data have put significant pressure on schools to achieve the best possible results and that, consequently, schools may be more willing to exclude some children from additional teaching sessions. Further, the capacity of schools to select pupils can have a negative effect on the access of some pupils. The policy of reducing class sizes may have had a positive effect on equity of use for the youngest children in schools. However, there is no evidence available on this or the impact of the policy on class sizes at other stages.

Management reform outcomes

It is clear that many of the reforms within education correspond to public choice theories on competition, performance information and smaller and more responsive organizations. For schools, almost all of these policies were enacted. More performance indicators were developed, competition was introduced and schools were given more autonomy. In contrast, for LEAs the policies on the publication of performance data and reduction in size were the most significant. Assessing policy in practice shows that the implementation of many of these policies varies between LEAs and between schools. Studies could assess if performance is better in LEAs where they have encouraged competition between schools. Similarly, research could address the question of whether there is more equity in areas where there is less competition. However, to date little research has been undertaken which uses this approach to assessing the impact of reform. Chapter 3 identifies a number of problems in undertaking evaluations. Many of these were evident in attempting to evaluate the impact of the public choice reforms in education.

A major problem in assessing the impact of the reforms is the lack of systematic empirical studies. This can be illustrated by the results gained from a Web of Science search (Table 6.7). At first, these appear to be promising figures. However, when the searches were refined to include only reforms in the UK, the number of 'hits' reduced dramatically. For example, the search education AND efficiency AND UK produced only 12 'hits', and none of these were relevant in our evaluation. Similarly, the number of studies on equity fell from 588 to 7, of which only three were useful for this chapter.

Table 6.7 Results of a Web of Science search of efficiency, equity and responsiveness

	education AND	*education AND reform AND*
effi*	919	56
equit*	588	81
responsive*	170	4

Source: Web of Science

In order to assess the impact of the reforms the concepts of competition, performance information, organizational size, efficiency, responsiveness and equity must be operationalized. For some aspects, particularly efficiency, this was problematic. Levačić (1998), for example, argued that it was not possible to measure efficiency because of difficulties in specifying the output of education. However, others such as Mayston and Jesson (1991) disagreed. They suggested that it was possible to work with the information already available, whilst recognizing that it was not a perfect and universally agreed measure of output. They argued that 'waiting for ever for perfect data, or disregarding the insights available from improved methods of analysis, is unlikely itself to lead to better decisions' (1991: 107). The problem of operationalizing the relevant concepts was not confined to efficiency, although that was where it was most evident. None of the studies included all of the sub-dimensions considered in Chapter 2, hence there were gaps in the data set needed to assess the reforms.

In some cases it was not possible to assess the impact of public choice reforms as there were 'missing connections'. A minority of the studies explicitly examined the link between particular public choice reforms and outcomes such as efficiency, responsiveness and equity. Despite policies introducing competition, more and better information on performance and smaller organizational size, evidence of their impact on efficiency, responsiveness and equity is limited.

Our conclusions are tentative in some areas as much of the research is small-scale, including very few organizations. For example, Gillborn and Youdell (2000) assess only two schools to determine equity. Gewirtz et al.'s (1995) evidence relates to three LEAs in London, and Bartlett's (1993) to four case-study schools. Clearly, this makes it difficult to assess the general validity of their findings. In contrast, there are a number of large-scale studies of the education market and choices locally (Gorard and Fitz 2000; Noden 2000; Taylor 2001), though the findings of these studies are contradictory and therefore inconclusive.

One of the main difficulties in assessing the impact of reform was in disentangling their effect, first from other reforms occurring at the same time, and second from changes in the external environment. For example, is it a change in the number of performance indicators and their use that leads to improvement in performance or is it the setting of targets for those indicators? There are also a range of factors in the external environment, apart from these reforms, which may have an impact on performance. It is generally accepted, for example, that factors such as the level of deprivation can have an influence on examination results. In addition, many of the reforms were interrelated and introduced at the same time. Little attempt was made in the studies to disentangle these elements. As Levačić (1995: 54) indicates in relation to assessing the impact of LMS, 'one would need to specify an explanatory model in which the effects of the introduction

Consequences of reform

Reform	Efficiency	Responsiveness	Equity
Competition	Small positive	Small positive	Negative
Performance indicators	No evidence	Small positive	Negative
Organizational size	Small positive	Small positive	Negative

Figure 6.1 The impact of the reforms on efficiency, responsiveness and equity

of the national curriculum on the mix of activities and resulting outputs could be separated from the effects of the changes in decision-making brought about by local management'. Similarly, few studies tried to isolate the impact of competition from the influence of increased availability of performance information.

Despite these problems, we are able to attempt some conclusions on the impact of the reforms. Figure 6.1 indicates our best estimate of the impact of more competition, more performance information and smaller organizational size.

Conclusion

In education, all three public choice reforms of more competition, more performance information and smaller organizations were introduced. A quasi-market was developed, information was provided to 'oil the wheels' of the market, and services were devolved to smaller units of delivery. In this chapter, we have highlighted the reforms as they were adopted and evaluated evidence on their implementation. This indicates that whilst competition was promoted in the reforms, competition was not evident in all areas. Whilst parents could send their children to the school of their choice, there were factors, including proximity to schools, which limited that choice. Private sector schooling was not an option for the vast majority of parents, despite the existence of the Assisted Places Scheme and the provision of CTCs. Further, market share between schools did not correspond with parental choice – rather LEAs continued to operate on the pre-reform system of allocating children to schools on the basis of catchment area. More performance information was provided and is increasingly being used, particularly by parents. It is also being used by LEAs and schools, although there is little recent empirical evidence on this from which to draw firm conclusions.

Organizational size decreased, largely due to the delegation of responsibilities from LEAs to schools themselves, and the structural reorganization of LEAs. However, when assessing policy in practice for both reforms, it was evident that it differed to some extent from policy intention. The policy on reducing surplus capacity led to a consideration by both central and local government of the optimum size for schools. It is significant that the policy on unfilled places was driven through official circulars, rather than legislation. Focusing solely on primary legislation may lead, therefore, to important omissions. Interestingly, this policy conflicted with the policy of encouraging competition.

The evidence suggests that there were changes in performance on the criteria of efficiency, responsiveness and equity. Research indicates that some improvements in efficiency levels were made, largely as a result of the formula funding reforms. Efficiency appears to have improved in relation to surplus capacity within schools. Although there is no evidence to assess this, it is possible that it resulted from the measurement of this aspect of LEA performance. Research findings on responsiveness tend to be mixed. Legislative reform attempted to make schools more responsive to their parent body through policies such as competition and the provision of performance information. However, the evidence shows that many parents do not perceive themselves as 'choosers' and do not place the value on examination results that the policies imply. Many schools attempt to be responsive to parents by focusing on academic achievement, but fail to assess first if this is what parents want. The review of the National Curriculum, staged tests and, in Wales, the abolition of league tables together highlight responsiveness to the producer body. Finally, there is evidence of inequity in all of the four areas of use, access, outcome and final income. Education provision clearly does not favour those with particular needs for the highest level of service, nor is the service equally accessible to all. Further, educational outcomes are not equally attained by all children. All three public choice reforms had a negative impact on equity. Our conclusions are tentative, given the number and quality of the studies available. However, we suggest that both efficiency and responsiveness have improved slightly and that equity has worsened.

seven

Conclusion

In this book we have developed and applied a conceptual framework for evaluating the impact of reform on the performance of public sector organizations. In Chapter 1 public management reform was defined as a deliberate change in the arrangements for the design and delivery of public services. Thus resistance and reform go hand in hand, because there would be no need to impose new arrangements if public service organizations were already moving fast enough in the desired direction.

We also noted in Chapter 1 that evaluations of reform must be theory-driven if they are to produce useful results for academic researchers, policy-makers and service managers. In the absence of a theoretical perspective, evaluators would be unable to categorize reforms in a meaningful way or predict their consequences. In this book we have used public choice theory to structure our analysis and conclusions, because policies based on this theory have inspired many public management reforms in the UK and elsewhere. According to public choice theorists, organizations that deliver public services will achieve better results if they are exposed to more competition, forced to publish information on their performance, and disaggregated into smaller units. A core aim of this book has been to discover whether these propositions are valid. Do reforms that are based on public choice principles deliver the service improvements that are sought by politicians and the public?

In order to answer this question, or indeed any question about the impact of reform, it is necessary to identify the appropriate evaluative criteria and methods. In Chapter 2 we identified two intrinsic criteria (efficiency and responsiveness) and one extrinsic criterion (equity) for assessing the impact of reforms associated with public choice theory. We showed that each of these criteria in fact consists of numerous sub-criteria, which substantially complicates an assessment of whether reform has worked.

Furthermore, no weights are available for judging the relative importance of success or failure on each of the sub-criteria. These problems are not unique to public choice theory, but are likely to impede any evaluation of new arrangements for public service provision. We are not aware of any theoretical perspective on organizational performance that assigns clear weights to different dimensions of the impact of reform.

Even if these conceptual issues could be resolved, an evaluation of reform must still confront methodological hurdles. In Chapter 3 we outlined the main questions which need to be addressed by empirical studies that attempt to assess the consequences of reform. The first step is to establish whether reform has actually occurred, both in principle and in practice. Second, it is necessary to track performance over time, and to examine whether there is a significant difference in the periods before and after reform was implemented. Third, the impact of reform needs to be separated from other influences on performance, in order to identify whether its net effect has been positive, negative or neutral. We then proceeded to apply this evaluative framework to reforms in health, education and housing in the UK.

In the remainder of this final chapter we summarize and synthesize the findings in Chapters 4–6. Were public choice reforms adopted and implemented, and what were the consequences for the efficiency, responsiveness and equity of service provision? And what are the broader implications of our analysis for public management reforms?

Policy as adopted

All three of the services that we have analysed were affected by some of the reforms prescribed by public choice theory. The policies adopted by Conservative governments between 1979 and 1987 established a more competitive framework for public service provision. Legislative assaults were launched on the monopoly positions of health organizations, schools and public sector landlords; purchasers and providers were separated; and revenues were linked more closely with the number of users of public services. The emphasis on competition has been reduced slightly by the Labour government since 1997, but remains an important element of policies that promote diversity and plurality in local service markets (e.g. the Best Value regime in local government).

Legislation on performance indicators has also been largely consistent with public choice principles. Much more information has been made available for parents of children at primary and secondary schools, for hospital patients and the general public who may become users of health services, and for tenants in the local authority and housing association sectors. Both the quality and the quantity of performance indicators have grown over time – especially under the Blair governments which have had a particular fascination with monitoring public services and setting targets for future achievements. It seems to be almost an article of faith that measurement is a precondition of improvement. The consequence, in any case, is that policies on the collection and publication of performance indicators have moved in the broad direction desired by public choice theorists.

By contrast, public choice prescriptions on organizational size have been more muted in the reform programmes of the Conservative and Labour governments, at least as far as the three services covered in this book are concerned. Furthermore, the extent of disaggregation (and reaggregation) of service providers altered both over time and between different parts of the same service. Although, on balance, there were moves towards smaller organizations under the Conservative governments from 1979 to 1997, this 'downsizing' has been reversed under Labour. The best estimate is, therefore, that over the period as a whole policies on size have been neither strongly consistent nor inconsistent with public choice theory.

Policy in action

Public management reforms in the UK have not constituted a 'full-blown' adoption of public choice principles. Although there was extra competition, this stopped short of substantially easing restrictions on entry and exit in public service markets, the number of separate suppliers did not greatly expand, and consumer choice was often expressed through intermediaries rather than exercised directly. Similarly, although there was a huge increase in the number of performance indicators, the coverage of significant dimensions of service standards (e.g. quality, effectiveness) developed more slowly.

Thus the reform programme was mainly in the direction prescribed by public choice theorists, but was neither comprehensive nor complete. The extent of reform in practice was further diluted by problems of implementation. In other words, the degree of reform in policy in action was less pronounced than in policy as adopted. The delivery of public services on the ground continued, in many cases, to reflect the 'old regime' that pre-dated the new policies and legislation. In some services, and in some organizations, our review of the evidence suggests that reform did not actually occur.

The existence and degree of these implementation gaps can largely be explained by the difference between changes in structure and behaviour. For example, elements of the NHS were disaggregated and relabelled as 'purchasers' and 'providers', but bureaucratic and monopolistic actions continued to flow through the supposedly competitive channels. Similarly, schools were allocated revenues on the basis of the number of pupils and encouraged to expand their market shares, but some headteachers preferred to collaborate rather than compete. Although a great deal of new performance information was manufactured (sometimes literally so by unscrupulous officials), the *use* of the data by politicians, producers and consumers was much less extensive. And even when the average size of organizations was reduced, this was not always accompanied by a relaxation of central controls, so they were not freed to provide more diverse services.

Setting up new structures and processes may be described as the easy part of public management reform: this can be mandated through legislation. Modifying behaviour, by contrast, is much more difficult and elusive. This gap between structures and behaviour raises important issues for public choice theory and for models of reform in general. Public choice reforms are designed to tackle the supposed inefficiency and lack of responsiveness that result from the pursuit of self-interest by bureaucrats. Yet the reforms partly founder on precisely this problem – public officials buffer or block the new regime by continuing to follow the old policies and behaviour. The outcome is that reforms are eroded, neutralized or reversed. The flaw in public choice theory is that it lacks a sub-model of implementation. How can the very problems that spurred the adoption of new policies be overcome when attempts are made to put these policies into practice? Any successful model of reform must confront and resolve this inherent issue if organizational performance is to be improved. It seems unlikely, however, that resistance to change will crumble completely. In this case, the impact of all reforms will always fall short of theoretical expectations.

Impact of public choice reforms on efficiency, responsiveness and equity

Judgements on changes in performance in the health, housing and education sectors, and on the contribution of public choice reform to such changes, are plagued by all of the methodological problems that were discussed in Chapter 3. For example, data are often absent on the extent of reform and its consequences. In many instances, no 'before and after' data on the performance of health, housing or education providers were available. This problem may be eased in future studies as a result of the recent proliferation of performance indicators – in this respect, at least, public choice reforms have had a positive outcome. Nevertheless, it is clearly important for central and local agencies to collect and disseminate better information on efficiency, responsiveness and equity, otherwise the evaluation of reforms will remain difficult, if not impossible.

Furthermore, estimates of the impact of public choice reforms often fail to take other influences on performance into account. Academics and policy researchers need to make more strenuous efforts to 'filter out' the influence of other variables when examining the impact of reform. Few of the studies of health, housing and education even recognize this problem, let alone take steps that would provide a partial remedy (e.g., selecting case studies that are alike on background variables but different on the extent of reform, or using multivariate statistical models that reveal the separate effects of reform). The impact of further large-scale reforms in the UK public sector may be easier to evaluate because of the establishment of devolved governments in Northern Ireland, Scotland and Wales. These new bodies are already adopting policies that differ from those of the Westminster government, so it should be possible in future to compare different reforms and their consequences in different parts of the UK.

Another issue that our analysis in Chapters 4–6 has highlighted is that the impact of public choice reforms on organizational performance is likely to be small for two reasons: the policies as adopted did not fully reflect public choice principles, and the policies in action suffered from substantial implementation gaps. This raises a number of general questions. First, to what extent must all the elements of a reform programme be adopted if performance is to improve? In the case of public choice theory, can extra competition and more performance indicators have the intended impact even if the third element, organizational size, does not change as required? Second, must reform be completely consistent with an underlying theory in order to work? Is a small step in the desired direction enough, or should reform be radical? For example, in the case of public choice theory, does a 'quasi-market' count for anything or must there be 'real' competition? Whatever the answers to these questions, it is clear that a combination of incomplete reform, incomplete data, and unsophisticated research methods is a major obstacle to the identification of the consequences of new arrangements for public service delivery.

Despite these obstacles to evaluation, it is possible to come to some provisional conclusions about the impact of public choice reforms. The picture may have gaps and be blurred, but it is sufficiently consistent across services and studies to reveal the main contours of the evidence. In two of the three services examined, health and housing, the reforms that we have analysed appear to be associated with higher efficiency, at least in the short term. Similarly, responsiveness to service users seems to have become stronger in housing and education. There is insufficient evidence to draw conclusions on changes in the efficiency of education or the responsiveness of health services. By contrast, in all three of our case-study services, there is enough empirical research to suggest that the level of equity has declined.

The final step in this analysis would now appear to be imminent: that is, to pronounce public choice reforms an unequivocal success or failure. We have, however, gone as far as the evidence will allow. Stronger conclusions are impossible for technical and theoretical reasons. The technical barrier to further inferences is that the magnitude of changes in efficiency, responsiveness and equity remains elusive. All that the evidence has shown, and even then not clearly, is that these aspects of performance have changed.

None of the empirical studies to date has made clear comparisons of the percentage changes in efficiency, responsiveness and equity. It is possible that movements in equity are small while those in efficiency and responsiveness are large, or vice versa. Even if such precise results were available, we would still lack any theoretical guidance on the relative weight to be attached to a 10 per cent growth in (say) efficiency as against a 10 per cent decline in equity, so crisp conclusions would remain beyond our reach. This simply serves to highlight that although public policy-making may be informed by evidence, it can never be determined by evidence. Judgements on the success or failure of public management reforms are, ultimately, inherently and inescapably political.

References

Acheson, D. (1998) *Independent Inquiry into Inequalities in Health*. London: Stationery Office.

Alford, R. (1975) *Health Care Politics*. Chicago: University of Chicago Press.

Anderson, L., Bush, T. and Wise, C. (2001) Is funding fair? Perceptions and experiences from foundation schools, *Educational Management and Administration*, 29(4): 397–409.

Appleby, J., Smith, P., Ronade, W., Little, V. and Robinson, R. (1993) Monitoring managed competition, in R. Robinson and J. Le Grand (eds) *Evaluating the NHS Reforms*. London: King's Fund.

Arnould, R.J., Rich, R.F. and White, W.D. (eds) (1993) *Competitive Aproaches to Health Care Reform*. Washington, DC: Urban Institute Press.

Ashworth, R., Boyne, G.A., McGarvey, N. and Walker, R.M. (2002) Regulating public bodies: the case of direct service organisations in British local government, *Environment and Planning C: Government and Policy*, 20(3): 456–70.

Aucoin, P. (1990) Administrative reform in public management: paradigms, principles, paradoxes and pendulums, *Governance*, 3: 115–37.

Audit Commission (1991) *Rationalising Primary School Provision*. London: HMSO.

Audit Commission (1994) *Protecting the Public Purse 2. Ensuring Probity in the NHS*. London: Stationery Office.

Audit Commission (1996) *What the Doctor Ordered. A Study of GP Fundholders in England and Wales*. London: Stationery Office.

Audit Commission (1999) *Missing Out: LEA Management of School Attendance and Exclusion*. London: Audit Commission.

Audit Commission and Housing Corporation (1997) *House Styles*. London: HMSO/Housing Corporation.

Audit Commission and Housing Corporation (2001) *Group Dynamics. Group Structures and Registered Social Landlords*. London: Audit Commission.

Baggott, R. (1997) Evaluating health care reform: the case of the NHS internal market, *Public Administration*, 75: 283–306.

Ball, S. (1996) School choice, social class and distinction: the realization of social advantage in education, *Journal of Education Policy*, 11(1): 89–112.

Barrett, S. and Fudge, C. (1981) *Policy and Action.* London: Methuen.

Bartlett, W. (1993) Quasi-markets and educational reforms, in J. Le Grand and W. Bartlett (eds) *Quasi-markets and Social Policy.* London: Macmillan.

Bartlett, W., Roberts, J. and Le Grand, S. (eds) (1998) *A Revolution in Social Policy.* Bristol: Policy Press.

Bevan, G. (1998) Taking equity seriously, *British Medical Journal*, 316 (3 January): 39–42.

Bines, W., Kemp, P., Pleace, N. and Radley, C. (1993) *Managing Social Housing.* London: HMSO.

Birchall, J. (1992) Council tenants: sovereign consumers or pawns in the game? in J. Birchall (ed.) *Housing Policy in the 1990s*, pp. 163–89. London: Routledge.

Birchall, J. (1997) Organisational form and performance: observations from opted-out public service agencies. Paper presented to the Housing Studies Association Conference, Cardiff, September.

Blanchard, W. (1986) Evaluating social equity: what does fairness mean and can we measure it? *Policy Studies Journal*, 15: 29–54.

Boschken, H. (1994) Organizational performance and multiple constituencies, *Public Administration Review*, 54: 308–13.

Boyne, G.A. (1987) Median voters, political systems and public policies: an empirical test, *Public Choice*, 53: 201–19.

Boyne, G.A. (1993) Central controls and local autonomy: the case of Wales, *Urban Studies*, 30: 87–102.

Boyne, G.A. (1995) Population size and economies of scale in local government, *Policy and Politics*, 23: 213–22.

Boyne, G.A. (1996a) Scale, performance and the new public management: an empirical analysis of local authority services, *Journal of Management Studies*, 33: 809–26.

Boyne, G.A. (1996b) Competition and local government: a public choice perspective, *Urban Studies*, 33: 703–21.

Boyne, G.A. (1997a) Comparing the performance of local authorities: an evaluation of the Audit Commission indicators, *Local Government Studies*, 27(4): 17–43.

Boyne, G.A. (1997b) Public choice theory and local government structure: an evaluation of reorganization in Scotland and Wales, *Local Government Studies*, 27(3): 56–72.

Boyne, G.A. (1998a) *Public Choice Theory and Local Government.* London: Macmillan.

Boyne, G.A. (1998b) Public services under New Labour: back to bureaucracy? *Public Money and Management*, 18(1): 43–50.

Boyne, G.A. (1999) Processes, performance and Best Value in local government, *Local Government Studies*, 29(3): 1–15.

Boyne, G.A. (2000) External regulation and best value in local government, *Public Money and Management*, 20(3): 7–12.

Boyne, G.A. (2001) Researching public management: the role of quantitative methods, in K. Ross, S. Osborne and E. Ferlie (eds) *The New Public Management: Current Trends and Future Prospects.* London: Routledge.

Boyne, G.A. (2002) Public and private management: what's the difference? *Journal of Management Studies*, 39: 97–122.

Boyne, G.A. and Cole, M. (1996) Fragmentation, concentration and local government structure: top-tier authorities in England and Wales, 1831–1996, *Government and Policy*, 14: 501–14.

Boyne, G.A. and Law, J. (1991) Accountability and local authority annual reports: the case of Welsh district councils, *Financial Accountability and Management*, 7: 179–94.

Boyne, G.A. and Law, J. (1993) Bidding for unitary status: an evaluation of the contest in Wales, *Local Government Studies*, 19(4): 537–55.

Boyne, G.A. and Powell, M. (1991) Territorial justice: a review of theory and evidence, *Political Geography Quarterly*, 10: 263–81.

Boyne, G.A. and Walker, R.M. (1999) Social housing reforms in England and Wales: a public choice evaluation, *Urban Studies*, 36: 2237–62.

Boyne, G.A., Gould-Williams, J., Law, J. and Walker, R.M. (1999) Competitive tendering and best value in local government, *Public Money and Management*, 19(4): 23–9.

Boyne, G.A., Gould-Williams, J., Law, J. and Walker, R.M. (2000) *Wales Evaluation Study on Best Value: Final Report*, Cardiff: Cardiff Business School.

Boyne, G.A., Powell, M. and Ashworth, R. (2001) Spatial equity and public services, *Public Management Review*, 3: 19–34.

Bradshaw, J. and Millar, J. (1991) *Lone Parent Families in the UK*. London: HMSO.

Bramley, G. (1993) Quasi-markets and social housing, in J. Le Grand and W. Bartlett (eds) *Quasi-markets and Social Policy*. London: Macmillan.

Broadbent, J. and Laughlin, R. (1997a) Contracts and competition? A reflection on the nature and effects of recent legislation on modes of control in schools, *Cambridge Journal of Economics*, 21: 277–90.

Broadbent, J. and Laughlin, R. (1997b) Contractual changes in schools and general practices: professional resistance and the role of absorption and absorbing groups, in R. Flynn and G. Williams (eds) *Contracting for Health: Quasi-markets in the NHS*. Oxford: Oxford University Press.

Broadbent, J. and Laughlin, R. (1997c) Evaluating the new public management reforms in the UK: a constitutional possibility? *Public Administration*, 75: 487–507.

Brunsson, N. (1989) Administrative reforms as routines, *Scandinavian Journal of Management*, 5: 219–28.

Bullock, A. and Thomas, H. (1997) *Schools at the Centre? A Study of Decentralisation*. London: Routledge.

Burns, D., Hambleton, R. and Hoggett, P. (1994) *The Politics of Decentralisation: Revitalising Local Democracy*. London: Macmillan.

Burrows, R., Ford, J. and Wilcox, S. (2000) Half the poor? Policy responses to the growth of low-income home-ownership, in S. Wilcox (ed.) *Housing Finance Review 2000/2001*. York: Joseph Rowntree Foundation, Chartered Institute of Housing and Council of Mortgage Lenders.

Butel, J.H. and Atkinson, G.B.H. (1983) Secondary school size and costs, *Education Studies*, 9(3): 151–7.

Butler, E., Pirie, M. and Young, P. (1985) *The Omega File*. London: Adam Smith Institute.

Cabinet Office (1999) *Modernising Government*, Cm. 4310. London: The Stationery Office.

Caiden, G. (1982) Reform or revitalization? in G. Caiden and H. Seidentopf (eds) *Strategies For Administrative Reform*. Lexington, MA: D.C. Heath.

Caiden, G. (1988) The vitality of administrative reform, *International Review of Administrative Sciences*, 7: 331–57.

Caiden, G. (1991) *Administrative Reform Comes of Age*. Berlin: De Gruyter.

Caincross, L., Clapham, D. and Goodlad, R. (1996) *Housing Management: Consumers and Citizens*. London: Routledge.

Caldwell, K., Francome, C. and Lister, J. (1998) *The Envy of the World*. London: NHS Support Federation.

Calnan, M., Cant, S. and Gabe, J. (1993) *Going Private*. Buckingham: Open University Press.

Campbell, D. (1969) Reforms as experiments, *American Psychologist*, 24: 409–29.

Carter, N., Klein, R. and Day, P. (1992) *How Organizations Measure Success*. London: Routledge.

Chartered Institute of Housing (1997) *Housing Management Standards Manual*. Coventry: Chartered Institute of Housing.

Chen, H. (1990) *Theory-Driven Evaluations*. London: Sage.

Child, J. (1974) What determines organizational performance: the universal versus the it-all-depends, *Organizational Dynamics*, Summer: 2–16.

CIPFA (1988) *Performance Indicators in Schools: A Contribution to the Debate*. London: CIPFA.

Clapham, D. (1992) The effectiveness of housing management, *Social Policy and Administration*, 26: 209–25.

Clapham, D. and Evans, A. (1998) *From Exclusion to Inclusion. Helping to Create Successful Tenancies and Communities*. London: Hastoe Housing Association.

Clapham, D. and Kintrea, K. (1992) *Housing Co-operatives in Britain*. Harlow: Longman.

Clapham, D. and Kintrea, K. (2000) Community-based housing organisations and the local governance debate, *Housing Studies*, 15: 533–59.

Clapham, D. and Satsangi, M. (1992) Performance assessment and accountability in British housing management, *Policy and Politics*, 20: 63–74.

Clapham, D., Walker, R.M. *et al.* (1995) *Building Jobs, Building Homes. Housing and Economic Renewal*. London: National Housing Forum.

Clarke, R. (1985) *Industrial Economics*. Oxford: Blackwell.

Coffey, A. (2001) *Education and Social Change*. Buckingham: Open University Press.

Cole, I. and Furbey, R. (1994) *The Eclipse of Council Housing*. London: Routledge.

Cole, I. and Robinson, D. (2000) *Changing Demand, Changing Neighbourhoods: The Response of Social Landlords*. Leeds: The Housing Corporation.

Cole, I., Hickman, P., and Reeve, K. with McCoulough, E., Nixon, J., Slocombe, L. and Whittle, S. (2001) *On-the-Spot Housing Management: An Evaluation of Policy and Practice by Local Authorities and Social Landlords*. London: Department of Transport, Local Government and the Regions.

Connolly, T., Conlon, E. and Deutsch, S. (1980) Organizational effectiveness: a multiple constituency approach, *Academy of Management Review*, 5: 211–17.

Conservative Party (1987) *The Next Moves Forward*. London: Conservative Party.

Cook, T. and Campbell, D. (1979) *Quasi-experimentation*. Chicago: Rand McNally.

Cooper, L., Coote, A., Davies, A. and Jackson, C. (1995) *Voices Off. Tackling the Democratic Deficit in Health*. London: Institute for Public Policy Research.

Coopers and Lybrand (1988) *Local Management of Schools: A Report to the DES*. London: Department of Education and Science.

Coulter, A. (1995) Evaluating general practitioner fundholding in the United Kingdom, *European Journal of Public Health*, 5: 233–9.

Crinson, I. (1998) Putting patients first: the continuity of the consumerist discourse in health policy, from the radical right to New Labour, *Critical Social Policy*, 18(2): 227–40.

Cutler, B. and Waine, B. (1997) *Managing the Welfare State*. Oxford: Berg.

Darke, J. and Rowlands, V. (1997) Are tenants really in control at Kensington and Chelsea? Paper presented to the Housing Studies Association Conference, Cardiff, September.

David, M., West, A. and Ribbens, J. (1994) *Mother's Intuition? Choosing Secondary Schools*. London: Falmer Press.

Davidson, J. (2001) Press release, 20 July.

Davies, H. and Nutley, S. (2000) Healthcare: evidence to the fore in H. Davies, S. Nutley and P. Smith (eds) *What Works?* Bristol: Policy Press.

Davies, H., Nutley, S. and Smith, P. (eds) (2000) *What Works?* Bristol: Policy Press.

Dawson, S. (1996) *Analyzing Organizations*. London: Macmillan.

Dawson, D. and Street, A. (1998) *Reference Costs and the Pursuit of Efficiency in the 'New' NHS*. Centre for Health Economics Discussion Paper 161. York: University of York.

Dawson, D. and Street, A. (2000) Comparing NHS unit costs, *Public Money and Management*, 20(4): 58–62.

Day, P. and Klein, R. (1987) *Accountabilities: Five Public Services*. London: Tavistock.

Dearlove, J. (1979) *The Reorganization of British Local Government*. Cambridge: Cambridge University Press.

Demaine, J. (1999) Education policy and contemporary politics, in J. Demaine (ed.) *Education Policy and Contemporary Politics*. London: Macmillan.

DfE (Department for Education) (1991) *The Parent's Charter*. London: DfE.

DES (Department of Education and Science) (1985) *Better Schools*, Cmnd. 9469. London: HMSO.

DES (Department of Education and Science) (1989) *School Indicators for Internal Management: An Aide-Mémoire*. London: DES.

DfEE (Department for Education and Employment) (1997) *Excellence in Schools*: London: DFEE.

DfES (Department for Education and Skills) (2000) *Performance Management in Schools: Performance Management Framework*. London: DfES.

DfES (Department for Education and Skills) (2001) *Infant Class Sizes in England: September 2001*. London: DfES.

Department for Education and Welsh Office (1992) *Choice and Diversity: A New Framework for Schools*, Cm. 2021. London: HMSO.

DETR (Department of the Environment, Transport and the Regions) (1999a) *National Framework for Tenant Participation Compacts*. London: DETR.

DETR (Department of the Environment, Transport and the Regions) (1999b) *Business Planning for Local Authority Housing with Resource Accounting in Place. A Consultation Paper*. London: DETR.

DETR (Department of the Environment, Transport and the Regions) (1999c) *Implementing Best Value*. Circular 10/99. London: DETR.

DETR (Department of the Environment, Transport and the Regions) (1999d) *Best Value and Audit Commission Performance Indicators for 2000/2001*. London: DETR.

DETR (Department of the Environment, Transport and the Regions) (2000) *Quality and Choice: A Decent Choice for All*. London: DETR.

DH (Department of Health) (1986) *Primary Health Care: An Agenda for Discussion*. London: HMSO.

DH (Department of Health) (1987) *Promoting Better Health*. London: HMSO.

DH (Department of Health) (1989a) *Working for Patients*. London: HMSO.

DH (Department of Health) (1989b) *Caring for People*. London: HMSO.

DH (Department of Health) (1991) *The Patient's Charter*. London: DH.

DH (Department of Health) (1994) *The Patient's Charter: Hospital and Ambulance Service Comparative Performance Guide 1993–1994*. London: HMSO.

DH (Department of Health) (1995) *The NHS Performance Guide 1994–1995*. London: HMSO.

DH (Department of Health) (1996) *The NHS Performance Guide 1995–1996*. London: HMSO.

DH (Department of Health) (1997) *The New NHS*. London: Stationery Office.

DH (Department of Health) (1999a) *Quality and Performance in the NHS: High Level Performance Indicators*. London: DH.

DH (Department of Health) (1999b) *Quality and Performance in the NHS: Clinical Indicators*. London: DH.

DH (Department of Health) (2000) *The NHS Plan*. London: Stationery Office.

DH (Department of Health) (2001a) New pilots to tackle cancelled operations. Press Release 2001/0116, 5 March.

DH (Department of Health) (2001b) Milburn hands power to front-line staff. Press Release 2001/200, 25 April.

DHSS (Department of Health and Social Security) (1983a) Compulsory Competitive Tendering. DHSS Circular, September 1983.

DHSS (Department of Health and Social Security) (1983b) *NHS Management Inquiry* (Griffiths Report). London: DHSS.

Dixon, J. and Glennerster, H. (1995) What do we know about fundholding in general practice? *British Medical Journal*, 311: 727–30.

Dowling, B. (2000) *GPs and Purchasing in the NHS*. Aldershot: Ashgate.

Downs, A. (1957) *An Economic Theory of Democracy*. Boston: Little, Brown.

Downs, A. (1967) *Inside Bureaucracy*. Boston: Little, Brown.

Downs, G. and Larkey, P. (1986) *The Search For Government Efficiency*. Philadelphia: Temple University Press.

Doyal, L. and Gough, I. (1991) *A Theory of Human Need*. Basingstoke: Macmillan.

Dror, Y. (1976) Strategies for administrative reform, in A. Leemans (ed.) *The Management of Change in Government*. The Hague: Martinus Nijhoff.

Dunleavy, P. (1991) *Bureaucracy, Democracy and Public Choice*. Hemel Hempstead: Harvester Wheatsheaf.

Echols, F., McPherson, A. and Willms, J.D. (1990) Parental choice in Scotland, *Journal of Education Policy*, 5(2): 207–22.

Edelman, M. (1964) *The Symbolic Uses of Politics*. Urbana: University of Illinois Press.

Edwards, P., Ezzamel, M., McLean, C. and Robson, K. (1999) *New Public-Sector Reform and Institutional Choice: The Local Management of Schools Initiative*. London: The Chartered Institute of Management Accountants.

Edwards, T., Whitty, G. and Power, S. (1999) Moving back from comprehensive secondary education, in J. Demaine (ed.) *Education Policy and Contemporary Politics*. London: Macmillan.

Edwards, T., Fitz, J. and Whitty, G. (1989) *The State and Private Education: An Evaluation of the Assisted Places Scheme*. Lewes: Falmer Press.

Enthoven, A. (1999) *In Pursuit of an Improving National Health Service*. London: Nuffield Trust.

Exworthy, M. and Powell, M. (2000) Variations on a theme: New Labour, health inequalities and policy failure, in A. Hann (ed.) *Analysing Health Policy*. Aldershot: Ashgate.

Exworthy, M., Powell, M. and Mohan, J. (1999) The NHS: quasi-market, quasi-hierarchy and quasi-network? *Public Money and Management*, 19(4): 15–22.

Farrell, C.M. (2000) Citizen participation in governance, *Public Money and Management*, 20(1): 31–7.

Farrell, C.M. and Jones, J. (2000) Evaluating stakeholder participation in public services – parents and schools, *Policy and Politics*, 28(2): 251–62.

Farrell, C.M. and Law, J. (1994) *Educational Accountability in Wales*. York, YPS and Joseph Rowntree Foundation.

Farrell, C.M and Law, J. (1999a) The accountability of school governing bodies, *Educational Management and Administration*, 27(1): 5–15.

Farrell, C.M and Law, J. (1999b) Changing forms of accountability in education: a case study of LEAs in Wales, *Public Administration*, 77(2): 293–310.

Farrell, C.M. and Morris, J. (2001) *Teachers' Perceptions of Performance Related Pay*. Cardiff: Morfa Press.

Ferlie, E. and Shortell, S. (2001) Improving the quality of health care in the United Kingdom and the United States: a framework for change, *Milbank Quarterly*, 79(2): 281–315.

Fitzgibbon, C. (1996) *Monitoring Education: Indicators, Quality and Effectiveness*. London: Cassell.

Ford, J. and Wilcox, S. (1994) *Affordable Housing, Low Incomes and the Flexible Labour Market*. London: National Federation of Housing Associations.

Forrest, K. (1996) Catchment 22, *Education*, March: 8.

Forrest, R. and Murie, A. (1991) *Selling the Welfare State. The Privatisation of Council Housing*. London: Routledge.

Fountain, J. (2001) Paradoxes of public sector customer service, *Governance*, 14: 55–73.

Franklin, B. and Clapham, D. (1997) The social construction of housing management, *Housing Studies*, 12: 7–26.

Fraser, D. (1984) *The Evolution of The British Welfare State*. London: Macmillan.

Gewirtz, S., Ball, S. and Bowe, R. (1995) *Markets, Choice and Equity in Education*. Buckingham: Open University Press.

Gillborn, D. and Youdell, D. (2000) *Rationing Education: Policy, Practice, Reform and Equity*. Buckingham: Open University Press.

Glatter, R. and Woods, P. (1994) The impact of competition and choice on parents and schools, in W. Bartlett, C. Propper, D. Wilson and J. Le Grand (eds) *Quasi-markets in the Welfare State*. Bristol: SAUS Publications.

Glennerster, H. and Turner, T. (1993) *Estate Based Housing Management: An Evaluation*. London: HMSO.

Glennerster, H., Matsaganis, M., Owens, P. and Hancock, S. (1993) GP fundholding, in R. Robinson and J. Le Grand (eds) *Evaluating the NHS Reforms*. London/Newbury: King's Fund Institute, Policy Journals.

Glennerster, H., Matsaganis, M., Owens, P. and Hancock, S. (1994) *Implementing GP Fundholding*. Buckingham: Open University Press.

Glover, D., Bennett, N., Crawford, M. and Levačić, R. (1997) Strategic and resource management in primary schools: evidence from Ofsted inspection reports, *School Organisation*, 17(3): 357–74.

Goddard, M. and Smith, P. (1998) *Equity of Access to Health Care*. York: Centre for Health Economics, University of York.

Goddard, M., Mannion, R. and Smith, P.C. (1999) Assessing the performance of NHS Hospital Trusts: the role of 'hard' and 'soft' information, *Health Policy*, 48: 119–34.

Goddard, M., Mannion, R. and Smith, P.C. (2000) Enhancing performance in health care, *Health Economics*, 9: 95–107.

Goodsell, C. (1994) *The Case for Bureaucracy*. Chatham, NJ: Chatham House.

Goodwin, N. (1998) GP Fundholding, in J. Le Grand, N. Mays and J. Mulligan (eds) *Learning from the NHS Internal Market*. London: King's Fund.

Gorard, S. and Fitz, J. (2000) Markets and stratification: a view from England and Wales, *Educational Policy*, 14(3): 405–28.

Gray, A. and Jenkins, B. (1993) Markets, managers and the public service: the changing of a culture, in P. Taylor-Gooby and R. Lawson (eds) *Markets and Managers*. Buckingham: Open University Press.

Gray, J. and Wilcox, B. (1995) *Good School, Bad School*. Buckingham: Open University Press.

Greenwood, R. and Hinings, C. (1976) Contingency theory and public bureaucracies, *Policy and Politics*, 5: 159–80.

Griffith, B. (2000) Competition and containment in health care, *International Journal of Health Services*, 30(2): 257–84.

Griffiths, M., Smith, R.S.G., Stirling, T. and Trott, T. (1996) *Local Lettings Policies*. York: Joseph Rowntree Foundation.

Guardian, The (2001) 'Great Wales', 2 October.

Hall, R. (1996) *Organizations: Structures, Processes and Outcomes*. Englewood Cliffs, NJ: Prentice Hall.

Halpin, D., Fitz, J. and Power, S. (1991) Local education authorities and the grant-maintained schools policy, *Educational Management and Administration*, 19(4): 233–42.

Ham, C. (1999a) *Health Policy in Britain*, 4th edn. Basingstoke: Macmillan.

Ham, C. (1999b) The third way in health care reform: does the Emperor have any clothes? *Journal of Health Services Research and Policy*, 4(3): 168–73.

Ham, C. and Woolley, M. (1996) *How Does the NHS Measure Up?* Birmingham: National Association of Health Authorities and Trusts.

Harrison, M., with Davis, C. (2001) *Housing, Social Policy and Difference. Disability, Ethnicity, Gender and Housing.* Bristol: Policy Press.

Harrison, A. and Dixon, J. (2000) *The NHS: Facing the Future.* London: King's Fund.

Harrison, S., Hunter, D. and Pollitt, C. (1990) *The Dynamics of British Health Policy.* London: Routledge.

Her Majesty's Inspectorate (1989) *The Use Made by LEAs of Public Examination Results.* London: Department of Education and Science.

Hill, M. (2000) *Understanding Social Policy.* Oxford: Blackwells.

Hirschman, A. (1970) *Exit, Voice and Loyalty.* Cambridge, MA: Harvard University Press.

Hoffman, W. (1977) The democratic response of urban governments: an empirical test with simple spatial models, *Policy and Politics*, 4: 51–74.

Hogwood, B. and Gunn, L. (1984) *Policy Analysis for the Real World.* Oxford: Oxford University Press.

Holliday, I. (1995) *The NHS Transformed.* Manchester: Baseline Books.

Housing Corporation (1979) *Annual Report 1978–79.* London: Housing Corporation.

Housing Corporation (1981) *Annual Report 1980–81.* London: Housing Corporation.

Housing Corporation (1997) *Registered Social Landlords in 1996: Performance Indicators.* London: Housing Corporation.

Housing Corporation (1998a) *Tenant Participation. A Consultation Paper.* London: Housing Corporation.

Housing Corporation (1998b) *Benchmarking Housing Performance. A Guide for RSLs.* London: Housing Corporation.

Housing Corporation (2001) *Annual Review.* London: Housing Corporation.

Housing for Wales (1996) *Annual Report 1995–96.* Cardiff: Housing for Wales.

Howlett, P. (1991) The implications of dissolving the Inner London Education Authority, *Public Money and Management*, 11(1): 19–25.

Hughes, M., Wikeley, F. and Nash, T. (1994) *Parents and Their Children's Schools.* Oxford: Blackwell.

Hull, C. (1997) Keys to the door, *Inside Housing*, 17 October: 27.

Hutton, J. and Smith, P. (2000) Non-experimental quantitative methods, in H. Davies, S. Nutley and P. Smith (eds) *What Works?* Bristol: Policy Press.

Iliffe, S. and Munro, J. (2000) New Labour and Britain's National Health Service: an overview of current reforms, *International Journal of Health Services*, 30(2): 309–34.

Ingraham, P. (1997) Play it again Sam; it's still not right: finding the right notes in administrative reform, *Public Administration Review*, 57: 325–31.

Jackson, A. and Kleinman, M., with Whitehead, C. and Whitehouse, L. (1992) *A Normative Study of Local Authority Housing Management Costs.* London: HMSO.

Jackson, P. (1982) *The Political Economy of Bureaucracy.* London: Phillip Allan.

Judge, K. and Solomon, M. (1993) Public opinion and the National Health Service: patterns and perspectives in consumer satisfaction, *Journal of Social Policy*, 22(3): 299–327.

Karn, V. and Sheridan, L. (1994) *New Homes in the 1990s: A Study of Design, Space and Amenity in Housing Association and Private Sector Production.* Manchester/York: University of Manchester Press/Joseph Rowntree Foundation.

Kemp, P.A. (1995) Researching housing management performance, *Urban Studies,* 32: 779–90.

Kenyon, T. (1995) Conservative education policy: its educational contradictions, *Government and Opposition,* 30(2): 198–220.

Kickert, W. (ed.) (1997) *Public Management and Administrative Reform in Western Europe.* Cheltenham: Edward Elgar.

Klein, R. (1998) Why Britain is reorganising its National Health Service – yet again, *Health Affairs,* 17(4): 111–25.

Klein, R. (2001) *The New Politics of the NHS,* 4th edn. Harlow: Longman.

Klein, R., Day, P. and Redmayne, S. (1996) *Managing Scarcity.* Buckingham: Open University Press.

Lane, J.E. (ed.) (1997) *Public Sector Reform.* London: Sage.

Le Grand, J. (1982) *The Strategy of Equality.* London: George Allen & Unwin.

Le Grand, J. (1993) Evaluating the NHS reforms, in R. Robinson and J. Le Grand (eds) *Evaluating the NHS Reforms,* pp. 243–60. London: King's Fund.

Le Grand, J. (1997) Knights, knaves or pawns? Human behaviour and social policy, *Journal of Social Policy,* 26(2): 149–69.

Le Grand, J. (1999) Competition, cooperation, or control? Tales from the British National Health Service, *Health Affairs,* 18(3): 27–39.

Le Grand, J. (2002) Further tales from the British National Health Service, *Health Affairs,* 21(3): 116–28.

Le Grand, J. and Bartlett, W. (1993) *Quasi-markets and Social Policy.* Basingstoke: Macmillan.

Le Grand, J., Mays, N. and Mulligan, J.-A. (eds) (1998) *Learning from the NHS Internal Market.* London: King's Fund.

Leemans, A. (ed.) (1976) *The Management of Change in Government.* The Hague: Martinus Nijhoff.

Levačić, R. (1993) Local Management of Schools as an organisational form: theory and application, *Journal of Education Policy,* 8(2): 123–41.

Levačić, R. (1994) Evaluating the performance of quasi-markets in education, in W. Bartlett, C. Propper, D. Wilson and J. Le Grand (eds) *Quasi-markets in the Welfare State.* Bristol: SAUS Publications.

Levačić, R. (1995) *Local Management of Schools: Analysis and Practice.* Buckingham: Open University Press.

Levačić, R. (1998) Local Management of Schools in England: results after six years, *Journal of Education Policy,* 13(3): 331–50.

Levačić, R. and Glover, D. (1997) Value for money as a school improvement strategy: evidence from Ofsted secondary school inspections, *School Improvement and School Effectiveness,* 8(2): 231–53.

Levačić, R. and Glover, D. (1998) The relationship between efficient resource management and school effectiveness: evidence from Ofsted secondary school reports, *School Effectiveness and School Improvement,* 9(1): 95–122.

Lipsky, M. (1980) *Street Level Bureaucracy.* New York: Russell Sage Foundation.

Lowe, R. (1993) *The Welfare State in Britain since 1945.* Basingstoke: Macmillan.

Lowndes, V., Pratchett, L. and Stoker, G. (2000) Trends in public participation: Part I – Local government perspectives, *Public Administration*, 79(1): 205–27.

Lupton, C., Peckham, S. and Taylor, P. (1998) *Managing Public Involvement in Healthcare Purchasing*. Buckingham: Open University Press.

MacBeath, J. and Mortimore, P. (2000) *Improving School Effectiveness*. Buckingham: Open University Press.

Maclennan, D., Clapham, D., Kemp, P.A. *et al.* (1989) *The Nature and Effectiveness of Housing Management in England*. London: HMSO.

Malpass, P. and Murie, A. (1990) *Housing Policy and Practice*. Basingstoke, Macmillan.

Malpass, P., Warburton, M., Bramley, G. and Smart, G. (1993) *Housing Policy in Action. The New Financial Regime for Council Housing*. Bristol: SAUS Publications.

Mannion, R. and Goddard, M. (2001) Impact of published clinical outcomes data: case study in NHS hospital trusts, *British Medical Journal*, 323: 260–3.

Marsh, D. and Rhodes, R. (eds) (1992) *Implementing Thatcherite Policies*. Buckingham: Open University Press.

Mays, N. and Dixon, J. (1998) Purchaser plurality in UK healthcare, in W. Bartlett, J. Roberts and S. Le Grand (eds) *A Revolution in Social Policy*, Bristol: Policy Press.

Mays, N., Mulligan, J.-A. and Goodwin, N. (2000) The British quasi-market in health care: a balance sheet of the evidence, *Journal of Health Services Research and Policy*, 5(1): 49–58.

Mays, N., Wyke, S., Malbon, G. and Goodwin, N. (2001) *The Purchasing of Health Care by Primary Care Organizations*. Buckingham: Open University Press.

Mayston, D. and Jesson, D. (1991) Educational performance assessment: a new framework of analysis, *Policy and Politics*, 19(2): 99–108.

McKean, R. (1965) The unseen hand in government, *American Economic Review*, 55: 496–506.

McMaster, R. and Sawkins, J. (1996) The contract state, trust distortion and efficiency, *Review of Social Economy*, 54: 145–67.

McVicar, M. (1996) Education, in D. Farnham and S. Horton, *Managing the New Public Services*. London: Macmillan.

Milleti, D., Gillespie, D. and Eitzen, D. (1980) The multidimensionality of organizational size, *Sociology and Social Research*, 65: 401–16.

Mueller, D.C. (1989) *Public Choice II*. Cambridge: Cambridge University Press.

Mulligan, J.-A. (1998) Health authority purchasing, in J. Le Grand, N. Mays and J.-A. Mulligan (eds) *Learning from the NHS Internal Market*. London: King's Fund.

Mulligan, J.-A. (2000) What do the public think? in J. Appleby and A. Harrison (eds) *Health Care UK, Winter 2000*. London: King's Fund.

Mullins, D. (1997) From regulatory capture to regulated competition: an interest group analysis of the regulation of housing associations in England, *Housing Studies*, 12: 301–20.

Mullins, D. (1998) Flocking to join mega-mergers, *Housing Today*, 77: 13.

Mullins, D., Niner, P. and Riseborough, M. (1993) Large-scale voluntary transfers, in P. Malpass and R. Means (eds) *Implementing Housing Policy*, pp. 169–84. Buckingham: Open University Press.

Mullins, D., Reid, B. and Walker, R.M. (2001) Modernization and change in social housing: the case for an organizational perspective, *Public Administration*, 79: 599–623.

National Assembly for Wales (1998) *Local Voices – Modernising Local Government in Wales*. Cardiff: National Assembly for Wales.

National Assembly for Wales (2001a) *Housing Association Performance Indicators*. Cardiff: National Assembly for Wales.

National Assembly for Wales (2001b) *Should the National Assembly Publish Secondary Schools' Performance Information?* Consultation paper, 2 April. Cardiff: National Assembly for Wales.

National Audit Office (2001) *Inappropriate Adjustments to NHS Waiting Lists*. London: NAO.

National Commission on Education (1993) *Learning to Succeed: A Radical Look at Education Today and a Strategy for the Future*. London: Heinemann.

National Federation of Housing Associations (1987) *Standards for Housing Management*. London: NFHA.

New, B. (1999) *A Good Enough Service*. London: King's Fund.

Newman, J. (2001) *Modernising Governance*. London: Sage.

Niskanen, W. (1968) The peculiar economics of bureaucracy, *American Economic Review*, 58: 293–305.

Niskanen, W. (1971) *Bureaucracy and Representative Government*. Chicago: Aldine-Atherton.

Noden, P. (2000) Rediscovering the impact of marketisation: dimensions of social segregation in England's secondary schools, 1994–99, *British Journal of Sociology of Education*, 21(3): 371–90.

Noden, P., West, A., David, M. and Edge, A. (1998) Choices and destinations at transfer to secondary school, *Journal of Education Policy*, 13(2): 221–36.

North, N. (1993) Empowerment in welfare markets, *Health and Social Care*, 2(1): 129–37.

Norton, A. (1994) *International Handbook of Local and Regional Government* Aldershot: Edward Elgar.

Ofsted (2000) *LEA Support for School Improvement*. London: Ofsted.

Olsen, J. and Peters, B. (eds) (1998) *Lessons from Experience*. Oslo: Scandinavian University Press.

OECD (Organisation for Economic Co-operation and Development) (1995) *Internal Markets in the Making*. Paris: OECD.

OHE (Office of Health Economics) (1999) *Compendium of Health Statistics*, 10th edn. London: OHE.

Øvretveit, J. (1998) *Evaluating Health Interventions*. Buckingham: Open University Press.

Ozga, J. (2000) Education: New Labour, new teachers, in J. Clarke, S. Gewirtz and E. McLaughlin (eds) *New Managerialism, New Welfare*. London: Sage.

Page, D. (1993) *Building Communities*. York: Joseph Rowntree Foundation.

Paton, C. (1998) *Competition and Planning in the NHS*. Cheltenham: Stanley Thornes.

Paton, C. (1999) New Labour's health policy, in M. Powell (ed.) *New Labour, New Welfare State?* Bristol: Policy Press.

Paton, C. (2002) Health policy, in M. Powell (ed.) *Evaluating New Labour's Welfare Reforms*. Bristol: Policy Press.

Pawson, H. (2001) The only way is up? *Inside Housing*, 7 September: 14–15.

Pawson, R. and Tilley, N. (1997) *Realistic Evaluation*. London: Sage.

Petchey, R. (1995) General practitioner fundholding: weighing the evidence, *Lancet*, 346: 1139–42.

Peters, B. and Savoie, D. (eds) (1998) *Taking Stock: Assessing Public Sector Reforms*. Montreal: McGill-Queen's University Press.

Pettigrew, A., Ferlie, E. and McKee, L. (1992) *Shaping Strategic Change*. London: Sage.

Pollitt, C. (1984) *Manipulating the Machine*. London: Allen & Unwin.

Pollitt, C. (1995) Justification by works or faith?, *Evaluation*, 1: 133–54.

Pollitt, C. and Bouckaert, G. (2000) *Public Management Reform*. Oxford: Oxford University Press.

Pollitt, C., Birchall, J. and Putnam, K. (1998) *Decentralising Public Service Management*. London: Macmillan.

Powell, M. (1995) The strategy of equality revisited, *Journal of Social Policy*, 24(2): 163–85.

Powell, M. (1996) Granny's footsteps, fractures and the principles of the NHS, *Critical Social Policy*, 16(2): 27–44.

Powell, M. (1997) *Evaluating the National Health Service*. Buckingham: Open University Press.

Powell, M. (1998a) In what sense a National Health Service? *Public Policy and Administration*, 13(3): 56–69.

Powell, M. (1998b) Policy evaluation in the past, present and future of the NHS, in R. Skelton and V. Williamson (eds) *Fifty Years of the National Health Service*. Brighton: Health and Social Policy Research Centre, University of Brighton.

Powell, M. (1999) New Labour and the third way in the British NHS, *International Journal of Health Services*, 29(2): 353–70.

Powell, M. (2000) Analysing the 'new' British National Health Service, *International Journal of Health Planning and Management*, 15: 89–101.

Powell, M. and Boyne, G. (2001) The spatial strategy of equality and the spatial division of welfare, *Social Policy and Administration*, 35(2): 181–94.

Power, A. (1987) *Property before People: The Management of Twentieth-century Council Housing*. London: Allen & Unwin.

Power, S. (1992) Researching the impact of education policy: difficulties and discontinuities, *Journal of Education Policy*, 7(5): 493–500.

Power, S. and G. Whitty (1999) New Labour's education policy: first, second or third way? *Journal of Education Policy*, 14(5): 535–46.

Price Waterhouse (1992) *Empirical Study into the Costs of Local Authority Housing Management*. London: HMSO.

Price Waterhouse (1995) *Tenants in Control: An Evaluation of Tenant-led Housing Management Organisations*. London: HMSO.

Public Housing News (1996/97) CCT contracts: LA winners and losers, *Public Housing News*, 31, Winter: 8–9.

Ranade, W. (ed.) (1998) *Markets and Health Care*. Harlow: Longman.

Ranson, S. (1990) *The Politics of Re-organising Schools*. London: Unwin Hyman.

Reay, D. and Ball, S. (1997) Spoilt for choice: the working-classes and educational markets, *Oxford Review of Education*, 23(1): 89–101.

Reekie, D. (1979) *Industry, Prices, and Markets*. Oxford: Phillip Allen.

Reeves, C. and Bednar, D. (1994) Defining quality: alternatives and implications, *Academy of Management Review*, 19: 419–45.

Rhodes, R. (1994) The hollowing out of the state: the changing nature of the public service in Britain, *Political Quarterly*, 55: 138–51.

Richmond, J. (1992) The concept of the small secondary school, *Education Studies*, 18(3): 267–75.

Riley, K. (1993) The abolition of the ILEA: some implications for the restructuring of local government, *Public Money and Management*, 13(2): 57–60.

Robinson, R. (1996) The impact of the NHS reforms 1991–1995: a review of research evidence, *Journal of Public Health Medicine*, 18(3): 337–42.

Robinson, R. and Le Grand, J. (eds) (1993) *Evaluating the NHS Reforms*. London: King's Fund.

Rossi, P. and Freeman, R. (1996) *Evaluation*. London: Sage.

Russell, S., Simkins, T. and Fidler, B. (1997) Overview, in B. Fidler, S. Russell and T. Simkins (eds) *Choices for Self-Managing Schools: Autonomy and Accountability*. London: Paul Chapman.

Saltman, R. and Figueras, J. (eds) (1997) *European Health Care Reform*. Copenhagen: WHO Regional Office for Europe.

Satsangi, M. and Clapham, D. (1990) *Management Performance in Housing Co-operatives*. London: HMSO.

Satsangi, M. and Kearns, A. (1992) The use and interpretation of tenant satisfaction surveys in British social housing. *Environment and Planning C: Government and Policy*, 10: 317–31.

Scarpaci, J. (ed.) (1989) *Health Services Privatization in Industrial Societies*. New Brunswick, NJ: Rutgers University Press.

Scott, C. (2001) *Public and Private Roles in Health Care Systems*. Buckingham: Open University Press.

Scott, S., Clapham, D., Clark, A., Goodlad, R. and Paikey, H. (1994a) *Training and Tenant Management*. London: HMSO.

Scott, S., Clarke, A., Parkey, H. and Williams, M. (1994b) *Learning to Manage: A Good Practice Guide to Training for Tenant Management Organisations*. London. HMSO.

Self, P. (1993) *The Politics of Public Choice*. Basingstoke: Macmillan.

Shackley, P. and Ryan, M. (1994) What is the role of the consumer in health care? *Journal of Social Policy*, 23: 517–41.

Shah, C. (2000) *Strategies for Success. Effective Risk and Business Management*. London: Housing Corporation.

Shaw, M., Dorling, D., Gordon, D. and Davey-Smith, G. (1999) *The Widening Gap: Health Inequalities and Policy in Britain*. Bristol: Policy Press.

Shepherd, W. (1990) *The Economics of Industrial Organisation*. Englewood Cliffs, NJ: Prentice Hall.

Simkins, T. (1994) Efficiency, effectiveness and the local management of schools, *Journal of Education Policy*, 9(1): 15–31.

Smith, P. (ed.) (2000) *Reforming Markets in Health Care*. Buckingham: Open University Press.

Smith, R.S.G. (2000) Allocating social housing: trends, prospects and proposals, in S. Wilcox (ed.) *Housing Finance Review 2000/01*. York: Joseph Rowntree Foundation, Chartered Institute of Housing and the Council of Mortgage Lenders.

Smith, R.S.G. and Walker, R.M. (1994) The role of performance indicators in housing management: a critique, *Environment and Planning A*, 26: 609–21.

Soderland, N. and van der Merwe, R. (1999) *Hospital Benchmarking Analysis and the Derivation of Cost Indices*. Centre for Health Economics Discussion Paper 174. York: University of York.

Sommerville, P. (1998) Empowerment through residence, *Housing Studies*, 13: 233–58.

Stillman, A. (1990) Legislating for choice, in M. Flude and M. Hammer (eds) *The Education Reform Act 1988*. London: Falmer Press.

Strand, S. (1997) Key performance indicators for primary school improvement, *Educational Management and Administration*, 25(2): 145–53.

Stretton, H. and Orchard, L. (1994) *Public Goods, Public Enterprise, Public Choice*. London: Macmillan.

Symon, P. and Walker, R.M. (1995) A consumer perspective on performance indicators: the report to tenants regime in England and Wales, *Environment and Planning C: Government and Policy*, 13: 195–216.

Taylor, C. (2001) Hierarchies and 'local' markets: the geography of the 'lived' marketplace in secondary education provision, *Journal of Education Policy*, 16(3): 197–214.

Taylor, C., Gorard, S. and Fitz, J. (2000) Size matters: does school choice lead to 'spirals of decline?' Working paper 36. Cardiff: School of Social Sciences.

Taylor, M. (1995) *Unleashing the Potential: Bringing Residents to the Centre of Regeneration*. York: Joseph Rowntree Foundation.

Taylor-Gooby, P. and Lawson, R. (eds) (1993) *Markets and Managers*. Buckingham: Open University Press.

Tiebout, C. (1956) A pure theory of local expenditure, *Journal of Political Economy*, 64: 416–24.

Timmins, N. (1996) *The Five Giants*. London: Fontana.

Tomkins, C. (1987) *Achieving Economy, Efficiency and Effectiveness in the Public Sector*. London: Kogan Page.

Townsend, P., Davidson, N. and Whitehead, M. (eds) (1992) *Inequalities in Health*. Harmondsworth: Penguin.

Tullock, G. (1965) *The Politics of Bureaucracy*. Washington, DC: Public Affairs Press.

Tymms, P. (1995) Influencing educational practice through performance indicators, *School Effectiveness and School Improvement*, 6(2): 123–45.

Udehn, L. (1996) *The Limits of Public Choice*. London: Routledge.

Walford, G. (1988) The Scottish assisted places scheme: a comparative study of the origins, nature and practice of the APSs in Scotland, England and Wales, *Journal of Education Policy*, 3(2): 137–53.

Walford, G. (1994) *Choice and Equity in Education*. London: Cassell.

Walker, R.M. (1994) Putting performance measurement into context: classifying social housing organisations, *Policy and Politics*, 22: 191–202.

Walker, R.M. (1998a) New public management and housing associations: from comfort to competition, *Policy and Politics*, 26: 71–87.

Walker, R.M. (1998b) Social housing management, in M. Laffin (ed.) *Beyond Bureaucracy? New Approaches to Public Management*. Aldershot: Ashgate.

Walker, R.M. (2000) The changing nature of social housing management: the impacts of externalisation and managerialisation, *Housing Studies*, 15: 281–99.

Walker, R.M. (2001) How to abolish public housing: implications and lessons from public management reform, *Housing Studies*, 16: 674–96.

Walker, B. and Marsh, A. (1998) Pricing public housing services: mirroring the market?, *Housing Studies*, 13: 549–66.

Walker, R.M. and Smith, R.S.G. (1999) Regulatory and organisational responses to restructuring housing association finance in England and Wales, *Urban Studies*, 36: 737–54.

Walker, R.M. and Williams, P. (1995) Implementing local government reorganisation in the housing service: the case of Wales, *Local Government Studies*, 21: 483–508.

Walsh, K. (1991) Quality and public services, *Public Administration*, 69: 503–14.

Walsh, K. (1995) *Public Services and Market Mechanisms*. Basingstoke: Macmillan.

Ward, C. (1974) *Tenants Take Over*. London: Architectural Press.

Welsh Office (1992) *A Charter for Tenants in Wales*. Cardiff: Welsh Office.

West, A., Noden, P., Edge, A. and David, M. (1998) Parental involvement in education in and out of school, *British Educational Research Journal*, 24(2): 461–84.

West, A. and Pennell, H. (2000) Publishing school examination results in England: incentives and consequences, *Educational Studies*, 26(4): 423–36.

West, P. (1997) *Understanding the National Health Service Reforms*. Buckingham: Open University Press.

Westoby, A. (1989) Parental choice and voice under the 1988 Education Reform Act, in R. Glatter (ed.) *Educational Institutions and Their Environments: Managing the Boundaries*. Milton Keynes: Open University Press.

Whitehead, M. (1993) Is it fair? Evaluating the equity implications of the NHS reforms, in R. Robinson and J. Le Grand (eds) *Evaluating the NHS Reforms*, pp. 208–41. London: King's Fund.

Whitty, G. (1996) Creating quasi-markets in education: a review of recent research on parental choice and school autonomy in three countries, *Review of Research in Education*, 22: 3–47.

Whitty, G., Edwards, T. and Gewirtz, S. (1993) *Specialisation and Choice in Urban Education: The City Technology Experiment*. London: Routledge.

Wilcox, S. (ed.) (1992) *Housing Finance Review 1991/92*. York: Joseph Rowntree Foundation.

Wilcox, S. (ed.) (1997) *Housing Finance Review 1997/98*. York: Joseph Rowntree Foundation.

Wilcox, S. (ed.) (2000) *Housing Finance Review 2000/01*. York: Joseph Rowntree Foundation, Chartered Institute of Housing and the Council of Mortgage Lenders.

Wilding, P. (1982) *Professional Power and Social Welfare*. London: Routledge & Kegan Paul.

Wilson, G. (1993) Users and providers: different perspectives on community care services, *Journal of Social Policy*, 22: 507–26.

Wolf, C. (1988) *Markets or Governments: Choosing between Imperfect Alternatives*. Cambridge, MA: MIT Press.

Woods, P. (1992) Empowerment through choice? Towards an understanding of parental choice and school responsiveness, *Educational Management and Administration*, 20(4): 204–11.

Woods, P. and Bagley, C. (1996) Market elements in a public service: an analytical model for studying educational policy, *Journal of Education Policy*, 11(6): 641–53.

Woods, P., Bagley, C. and Glatter, R. (1998) *School Choice and Competition: Markets in the Public Interest*. London: Routledge.

World Health Organization (1993) *Evaluation of Recent Changes in the Financing of Health Services*. Geneva: WHO.

World Health Organization (2000) *The World Health Report 2000. Health Systems: Improving Performance*. Geneva: WHO.

Wright, V. (1997) The paradoxes of administrative reform, in W.J.M. Kickert (ed.) *Public Management and Administrative Reform in Western Europe*. Cheltenham: Edward Elgar.

Yates, J. (1995) *Private Eye, Heart and Hip*. Edinburgh: Churchill Livingston.

Zifack, S. (1994) *New Managerialism: Administrative Reform in Whitehall and Canberra*. Buckingham: Open University Press.

Index

STRATEGIC MANAGEMENT FOR THE PUBLIC SERVICES

Paul Joyce

This is an accessible introduction to the theory and practice of strategic management in the public sector. It is written for new and experienced managers, undergraduate and postgraduate students of the public services. *Strategic Management for the Public Services*:

- provides an understanding of the theory of strategic management;
- introduces ideas which guide the effective practice of strategic management in the public services (and which do not copy blindly private sector habits);
- gives conceptual tools and material (in the form of worksheets) which can be used to carry out analysis and planning;
- explores key issues for public sector managers including governance, involving the public, transformational strategies, managing crisis, and interorganizational strategic planning;
- draws on research from various countries;
- examines how strategic management can be applied and developed to help improve the public services.

Contents

Introducing strategic management in the public services – Mission statements, performance and situational analysis – Strategic decisions and evaluation – Systems and implementation – Strategic leadership – Co-ordination and cooperation – Strategy and crisis – Public-friendly strategic management – Transformational strategic management – Appendix: Worksheets for comprehensive strategic planning – Bibliography – Index.

224pp   0 335 20047 8 (Paperback)   0 335 20048 6 (Hardback)

ETHICAL MANAGEMENT FOR THE PUBLIC SERVICES

Alan Lawton

This is an accessible introduction to the role of ethics in public services management. It is written for new and experienced managers, undergraduate and postgraduate students of the public services. *Ethical Management for the Public Services*:

- deals with key issues for public services managers;
- integrates theory and practice throughout;
- uses vignettes, case studies and original research from various countries to illustrate the issues;
- helps managers identify ethical dilemmas;
- provides ethical frameworks to support managers in their practical decisions;
- explores ethical relationships between managers and a range of stakeholders including politicians, citizens and clients;
- locates ethics at different levels: the individual, the organizational, and the societal.

Contents

192pp   0 335 19919 4 (Paperback)   0 335 19920 8 (Hardback)

FINANCIAL MANAGEMENT FOR THE PUBLIC SERVICES

John Wilson (ed.)

Written for new and existing managers, undergraduates and postgraduate students of the public services, the essential textbook explores the meaning and significance of financial management for the public services. It combines both theoretical arguments and practical applications, and:

- examines the economics of public services;
- considers the extent to which the management of public services has actually changed in practice;
- explains the meaning and applicability of financial management tools including those relating to budgets and capital investment;
- presents original work on the issue of audit expectations;
- presents case studies on the problems which can arise when traditional concerns on probity and stewardship are neglected;
- considers the benefits and problems of measuring performance in the public services;
- includes specific chapters on financial management in health services and local government.

Contents

Part one Public service environment – Economics of public service provision – The new management of public services – Part two Understanding finance – Budgeting and budgetary control – Costing and pricing in the public sector – Capital investment appraisal – Part three Applied accountability – Audit quality – The mismanagement of financial resources – Performance measurement – Part four Key sectors – Local government financial management – National Health Service financial management – Part five Towards the future – Financial management: an overview – Index.

304pp   0 335 19845 7 (Paperback)   0 335 19846 5 (Hardback)